EVERY KNEE SHOULD BOW

Biblical Rationales for Universal Salvation in Early Christian Thought

Steven R. Harmon

University Press of America,® Inc.
Dallas · Lanham · Boulder · New York · Oxford

Library of Congress Control Number: 2003111859
ISBN 0-7618-2719-6 (paperback : alk. ppr.)

To My Parents:

Gerald Travis Harmon
Royce Jenne Harmon

Contents

Preface

Every Knee Should Bow: Biblical Rationales for Universal Salvation in Early Christian Thought has its origins as a Ph.D. dissertation submitted to the faculty of Southwestern Baptist Theological Seminary, Fort Worth, Texas, in December 1997 under the title "*Apokatastasis* and Exegesis: A Comparative Analysis of the Use of Scripture in the Eschatological Universalism of Clement of Alexandria, Origen, and Gregory of Nyssa." This book is a revision of that earlier work.

Many mentors and colleagues made substantial contributions to the research and writing of both the original dissertation and its transformation into a published monograph. In particular, I wish to express my gratitude to Dr. James Leo Garrett, Jr., my dissertation supervisor, whose passion for critical retrieval of the theological tradition of the church catholic as an endeavor of vital importance to systematic theological reflection continues to influence my own teaching and research; Dr. Wm. David Kirkpatrick, my advisor during the coursework phase of doctoral studies, who initially encouraged my shift in intended doctoral specialization from New Testament studies to patristic theology during my M.Div. systematic theology courses; and Dr. Brian E. Daley, S.J., of the University of Notre Dame and Dr. David L. Balás, O.Cist., of the University of Dallas, who both offered helpful criticism of my work in its early stages. By their encouragement of faculty research and writing, Dr. M. Dwaine Greene, Provost and Vice President for Academic Affairs at Campbell University, and Dr. Michael G. Cogdill,

Dean of the Campbell University Divinity School, have fostered an institutional environment conducive to the publication of this book.

Special thanks are due to the Deutscher Akademischer Austausch Dienst for the award of a generous Short-Term Research Grant for Ph.D. Candidates and Recent Ph.D.s, which enabled me to spend five weeks doing research on Gregory of Nyssa at the Forschungsstelle Gregor von Nyssa an der Westfälischen Wilhelms-Universität in Münster during the summer of 1997. Thanks are also due to Dr. Friedhelm Mann, Wissenschaftliche Mitarbeiter at the Forschungsstelle, who graciously assisted me in numerous ways during my stay in Münster. A Lilly Theological Research Expense Grant awarded by the Association of Theological Schools in the United States and Canada for my current work on a translation of Gregory of Nyssa's *Oratio catechetica magna* and associated article-length studies during 2002-2003 made possible a fresh inquiry into some of the aspects of Gregory's thought treated in chapter 4 of the present book.

In this book I have quoted Greek and Latin texts only when doing so might contribute to a better understanding of those texts. Sufficient bibliographic information has been supplied in notes and bibliography for readers who wish to consult the primary texts more extensively in their original languages. Unless otherwise noted, all English translations of patristic texts that appear in this volume are my own.

Words cannot communicate adequately the depth of my gratitude to Kheresa Wedding Harmon, my wife and best friend, for her contributions to the publication of this book. She patiently endured my countless utterances of "I'll be done as soon as I finish this sentence/paragraph/note," and her companionship has enriched my thinking and sustained my spirits in ways that have greatly enhanced my research and writing.

I gratefully dedicate this work to my parents, Gerald Travis and Royce Jenne Harmon, who fostered my love of learning and desire for God (and the connection between the two) as a child and gave me much support, encouragement, and love during—and before and since—my graduate studies.

Steven R. Harmon
Buies Creek, North Carolina
The Nativity of St. John the Baptist 2003

Abbreviations

Old Testament

Gen	Genesis	Nah	Nahum
Exod	Exodus	Hab	Habakkuk
Lev	Leviticus	Zeph	Zephaniah
Num	Numbers	Hag	Haggai
Deut	Deuteronomy	Zech	Zechariah
Josh	Joshua	Mal	Malachi
Judg	Judges	Ps(s)	Psalm(s)
1-2 Sam	1-2 Samuel	Job	Job
1-2 Kgs	1-2 Kings	Prov	Proverbs
Isa	Isaiah	Ruth	Ruth
Jer	Jeremiah	Cant	Song of Solomon
Ezek	Ezekiel	Eccl	Ecclesiastes
Hos	Hosea	Lam	Lamentations
Joel	Joel	Esth	Esther
Amos	Amos	Dan	Daniel
Obad	Obadiah	Ezra	Ezra
Jonah	Jonah	Neh	Nehemiah
Mic	Micah	1-2 Chr	1-2 Chronicles

Deuterocanonical Books

Add Esth	Additions to Esther	1-4 Macc	1-4 Maccabees
Bar	Baruch	Pr Azar	Prayer of Azariah
Bel	Bel and the Dragon	Pr Man	Prayer of Manasseh
1-2 Esdr	1-2 Esdras	Sir	Sirach
4 Ezra	Fourth Ezra	Sus	Susanna
Jdt	Judith	Tob	Tobit
Ep Jer	Epistles of Jeremiah	Wis	Wisdom of Solomon

New Testament

Matt	Matthew	Acts	Acts
Mark	Mark	Rom	Romans
Luke	Luke	1-2 Cor	1-2 Corinthians
John	John	Gal	Galatians

Eph	Ephesians		Heb	Hebrews
Phil	Philippians		Jas	James
Col	Colossians		1-2 Pet	1-2 Peter
1-2 Thess	1-2 Thessalonians		1-3 John	1-3 John
1-2 Tim	1-2 Timothy		Jude	Jude
Tit	Titus		Rev	Revelation
Phlm	Philemon			

Patristic Literature

Clement of Alexandria (Clem.)

ecl.	*Eclogae propheticae*
exc. Thdot.	*Excerpta e Theodoto*
hyp.	*Hypotyposes*
paed.	*Paedagogus*
prot.	*Protrepticus*
q.d.s.	*Quis dives salvetur*
str.	*Stromata*

Origen (Or.)

Cant.	*Libri in Canticum canticorum*
Cels.	*Contra Celsum*
comm. in Mt.	*Commentarii in Matthaeum*
comm. in Rom.	*Commentarii in Epistulam ad Romanos*
comm. ser. in Mt.	*Commentariorum series in Matthaeum*
dial.	*Diputatio cum Heracleida*
ep. ad caros	*Epistula ad quosdam caros suos Alexandriam*
Eph. cat.	*Commentarii in Ephesios (fragmenta e catenis)*
fr. in Pr.	*Fragmenta in Proverbia*
hom. in 1 Reg.	*Homiliae in 1 Regnorum*
hom. in Ex.	*In Exodum homiliae*
hom. in Ez.	*In Ezechielem homiliae*
hom. in Gen.	*In Genesim homiliae*
hom. in Jer.	*Homiliae in Ieremiam*
hom. in Jos.	*In Iesu Nave homiliae*
hom. in Jud.	*In librum Iudicum homiliae*
hom. in Lc.	*In Lucam homiliae*
hom. in Lev.	*In Leviticum homiliae*
hom. in Num.	*In Numeros homiliae*
Jo.	*Commentarii in Iohannem*
mart.	*Exhortatio in Martyrium*
or.	*De oratione*
princ.	*De principiis*

Gregory of Nyssa (Gr. Nyss.)

anim. et res.	*Dialogus de anima et resurrectione*
Apoll.	*Antirrheticus adversus Apollinarium*
Ar. et Sab.	*Adversus Arium et Sabellium de patre et filio*
ascens.	*In ascensionem Christi*
bapt. diff.	*De iis qui baptismum differunt*
beat.	*Orationes viii de beatitudinibus*
benef.	*De beneficentia*
ep.	*Epistulae*
Eun.	*Contra Eunomium libri*
Flacill.	*Oratio funebris in Flacillam imperatricem*
hex.	*Apologia in Hexaemeron*
hom. in 1 Cor. 15:28	*In illud: Tunc et ipse filius*
hom. in cant.	*In Canticum canticorum homiliae xv*
hom. in Eccl.	*In Ecclesiasten homiliae viii*
hom. opif.	*De opificio hominis*
infant.	*De infantibus praemature abreptis*
Melet.	*Oratio funebris in Meletium episcopum*
mort.	*De mortuis non esse dolendum*
nativ.	*Oratio in diem natalem Christi*
or. catech.	*Oratio catechetica magna*
or. dom.	*De oratio dominica orationes v*
ordin.	*In suam ordinationem*
pasch.	*In sanctam pascha*
pent.	*In sanctam pentecosten*
perf.	*De perfectione christiana ad Olympium monachum*
Ps. 6	*In sextum psalmum*
Pss. titt.	*In inscriptiones psalmorum*
Pulch.	*Oratio consolatoria in Pulcheriam*
python.	*De pythonissa ad Theodosium episcopum*
Quat.	*In illud: Quatenus uni ex his fecistis mihi fecistis*
ref. conf. Eun.	*Refutatio confessionis Eunomii*
sanct. sal. pasch.	*In sanctum et salutare pascha*
Steph. 1, 2	*Encomia in s. Stephanum protomartyrem i, ii*
tres dii	*Ad Ablabium quod non sint tres dei*
trid.	*De tridui inter mortem et resurrectionem domini nostri Iesu Christi spatio.*
v. Gr. Thaum.	*De vita Gregorii Thaumaturgi*
v. Mos.	*De vita Moysis*
virg.	*De virginitate*

Other Patristic Literature

Bas. *moral.*	Basil of Caesarea *Moralia*
Bas. *reg. br.*	Basil of Caesarea *Regulae brevius tractatae*
Didym. *comm. in Zach.*	Didymus the Blind *Commentarii in Zacharium*
Didym. *ep. cath.*	Didymus the Blind *In epistulas catholicas brevis enarratio*
Didym. *frag. in Pss.*	Didymus the Blind *Fragmenta in psalmos*
Didym. *man.*	Didymus the Blind *Contra Manichaeos*
Didym. *Trin.*	Didymus the Blind *De Trinitate*
Evagr. Pont. *ep.*	Evagrius of Pontus *Epistulae lxii*
Evagr. Pont. *Keph. gnost.*	Evagrius of Pontus *Kephalaia gnostica*
Gr. Naz. *or.*	Gregory of Nazianzus *Orationes*
Jer. *com. in Is.*	Jerome *Commentarii in Esaiam*
Jer. *ep.*	Jerome *Epistulae*
Just. *ep. ad Men.*	Justinian *Epistula ad Menam*
Phot. *bibl. cod.*	Photius *Bibliothecae codices*
Ps.-Barn. *Barn.*	Pseudo-Barnabas *Epistula Barnabae*

Journals, Series, and Reference Works

AAWG.PH	Abhandlungen der Akademie der Wissenschaften in Göttingen: Philologisch-Historische Klasse, 3d ser.
ACO	*Acta Conciliorum Oecumenicorum*, ed. Edward Schwartz
ACW	Ancient Christian Writers
AILEHS	Archbishop Iakovos Library of Ecclesiastical and Historical Sources
AKG	Arbeiten zur Kirchengeschichte
ANF	Ante-Nicene Fathers, ed. Alexander Roberts and James Donaldson
ASNU	Acta Seminarii Neotestamentici Upsaliensis
AThR	*Anglican Theological Review*
Aug	*Augustinianum*
AUSS	*Andrews University Seminary Studies*
BAGD	*A Greek-English Lexicon of the New Testament and Other Early Christian Literature*, 5th ed., ed. Walter Bauer
BEHE.E	Bibliotheque de l'École des hautes études: Sciences historiques et philologiques
BETL	Bibliotheca ephemeridum theologicarum lovaniensium
BHT	Beiträge zur historischen Theologie
Bib	*Biblica*
BibPatr	*Biblia Patristica: Index des citations et allusions bibliques dans la littérature patristique*, Centre d'Analyse et de Documentation Patristiques
BKAW	Bibliothek der klassischen Altertumswissenschaft
BKV	Bibliothek der Kirchenväter

BTH	Bibliothèque de Théologie Historique
BZAW	Beihefte zur Zeitschrift für die alttestamentliche Wissenschaft
CCSL	Corpus Christianorum: Series Latina
CCWJCW	Cambridge Commentaries on Writings of the Jewish and Christian World
CD	Karl Barth, *Church Dogmatics*, trans. and ed. G. W. Bromiley
CdR	Classici delle Religioni
CH	*Church History*
CJAn	Christianity and Judaism in Antiquity
ClassRev	*Classical Review*
COCG	Collecion Oro de Cultura General
CPG	Maurice Geerard, *Clavis Patrum Graecorum*
CPT	Cambridge Patristic Texts
CRINT	Compendia Rerum Iudaicarum ad Novum Testamentum
CTePa	Collana di Testi Patristici
CWS	Classics of Western Spirituality
DOP	*Dumbarton Oaks Papers*
EAJT	*East Asia Journal of Theology*
EAug	Études Augustiniennes
EL	*Ephemerides Liturgicae*
ERE	*Encyclopaedia of Religion and Ethics*, 2d ed., ed. James Hastings
EvT	*Evangelische Theologie*
FC	Fathers of the Church
FKGG	Forschungen zur Kirchen- und Geistesgeschichte
FontChr	Fontes Christiani
GCS	Die griechischen christlichen Schriftsteller der ersten drei Jahrhunderte
GNO	Gregorii Nysseni Opera, ed. Werner Jaeger *et al.*
GOTR	*Greek Orthodox Theological Review*
Greg	*Gregorianum*
GRLH	Garland Reference Library of the Humanities
HTh	Histoire de la Thèologie
HTR	*Harvard Theological Review*
ITS	Innsbrucker theologische Studien
JAC	*Jahrbuch für Antike und Christentum*
JECS	*Journal of Early Christian Studies*
JQR	*Jewish Quarterly Review*
JTS	*Journal of Theological Studies*
LCC	Library of Christian Classics
LCL	Loeb Classical Library
LSJ	*Greek-English Lexicon*, ed. Henry George Liddell and Robert Scott, rev. Henry Stuart Jones and Roderick McKenzie
MFC	Message of the Fathers of the Church

MLS	Marian Library Studies
NovTSup	Supplements to Novum Testamentum
NPNF[2]	Nicene and Post-Nicene Fathers, 2d ser., ed. Philip Schaff and Henry Wace
NTA	Neutestamentliche Abhandlungen
OCA	Orientalia Christiana Analecta
OCD	*The Oxford Classical Dictionary*, 2d ed., ed. N. G. L. Hammond and H. H. Scullard
OECS	Oxford Early Christian Studies
OTM	Oxford Theological Monographs
PatSorb	Patristica Sorbonensia
PG	*Patrologiae Cursus Completus: Series Graecae*, ed. Jacques Paul Migne
PGL	*A Patristic Greek Lexicon*, ed. G. W. H. Lampe
PMS	Patristic Monograph Series
PO	Patrologia Orientalis
PatSor	Patristica Sorbonensia
PTS	Patristische Texte und Studien
QVC	Quaderni di "Vetera Christianorum"
REByz	*Revue des Études Byzantines*
REG	*Revue des Études Grecques*
RelS	*Religious Studies*
RelSRev	*Religious Studies Review*
ROC	*Revue de l'Orient Chrétien*
RSR	*Recherches de Science Religieuse*
SBEC	Studies in the Bible and Early Christianity
SBLDS	Society of Biblical Literature Dissertation Series
SC	Sources Chrétiennes
ScrTh	*Scripta Theologica*
SD	Studies and Documents
SecCent	*The Second Century*
SGPS	Structure and Growth of Philosophic Systems from Plato to Spinoza
SPM	Studia Patristica Mediolanensia
STL	*Studia Theologica Ludensia*
StMon	*Studia Monastica*
StrThS	Straßburger theologische Studien
StudAnselm	Studia Anselmiana
StudPat	*Studia Patristica*
SVC	Supplements to Vigiliae Christianae
SVTQ	*St. Vladimir's Theological Quarterly*
TDNT	*Theological Dictionary of the New Testament*, ed. Gerhard Kittel, trans. Geoffrey W. Bromiley
ThGl	*Theologie und Glaube*
ThTo	*Theology Today*
TLG	Thesaurus Linguae Graecae

TLZ	*Theologische Literaturzeitung*
TS	*Theological Studies*
TU	Texte und Untersuchungen zur Geschichte der altchristlichen Literatur
TZ	*Theologische Zeitschrift*
ULD	Universitas Lovaniensis Dissertationes
UUC	*Unitarian Universalist Christian*
VC	*Vigiliae Christianae*
ZKG	*Zeitschrift für Kirchengeschichte*
ZNW	*Zeitschrift für die neutestamentliche Wissenschaft*
ZWT	*Zeitschrift für wissenschaftliche Theologie*

Other Abbreviations

ET	English translation
frg(s).	fragment(s)
LXX	Septuagint
MS(S)	Manuscript(s)
MT	Masoretic Text
praef.	preface

Chapter 1

"They Employ These Testimonies": *Apokatastasis* and Exegesis

Histories of Christian thought and manuals of patrology routinely identify the concept of a universal "restoration" (*apokatastasis*[1]) as a distinctive feature of the eschatology of Origen (ca. 185-ca. 251 C.E.) and his fourth-century admirer Gregory of Nyssa (331/340-ca. 395 C.E.). Anticipated by the eschatology of Clement of Alexandria (ca. 160-215 C.E.),[2] Origen affirmed hope in an ultimate restoration of all rational creatures to their original, pre-fall state of union with God.[3] On the basis of this hope Origen viewed punishment after death as limited in duration and redemptive in nature.[4]

Gregory of Nyssa appropriated Origen's perspectives on the *apokatastasis* and eternal punishment.[5] Yet unlike Origen, Gregory held neither to a preexistence of unembodied souls nor to a fall from the contemplation of God as the cause of the present corporeal existence of souls.[6] Gregory's rejection of Origen's protology resulted in a much stronger emphasis on the resurrection of the body in the *apokatastasis*.[7]

Although Origen and Gregory of Nyssa are usually recognized as the two principal patristic exponents of a universal *apokatastasis*, other early Christian writers expressed some measure of hope for universal salvation and accordingly an end to the torments of hell. In addition to

Clement of Alexandria, Gregory of Nyssa's fellow Cappadocian Gregory of Nazianzus (ca. 329-390 C.E.) cautiously advocated these views,[8] and in Egypt Didymus the Blind (313-398 C.E.)[9] and Evagrius of Pontus (345-399 C.E.)[10] were proponents of Origenist eschatologies. In the West, Ambrose (ca. 339-397 C.E.) hinted at Origenist sympathies in his eschatological reflections, as did Jerome (ca. 347-419/20 C.E.) prior to his conversion from Origenism in 394.[11]

These patristic universalists maintained their hope for "a wideness in God's mercy"[12] primarily because they believed this hope was the most coherent reading of the biblical story. Although Hellenistic thought might also have suggested an eschatology in which the end corresponds to the beginning, the eschatologies of these ancient Christian theologians were shaped mainly by the Hebrew story of creation, fall, redemption, and consummation, read through the lenses of the church's experience of God's saving work in the person of Jesus Christ.

The New Testament telling of this story suggests two possible conclusions to the part played by human beings. On the one hand, there are passages that seem to require a "double outcome of judgment":[13] Matthew 5:29-30, Matt 8:12, Matt 10:28/Luke 12:5, Matt 18:8-9/Mark 9:42-48, Matt 25:31-46, Luke 16:19-31, 2 Thess 1:7-9, Rev 20:14-15, and Rev 21:8 suggest that the finally impenitent will experience death as everlasting retribution, while believers will experience the heavenly reward of everlasting life. On the other hand, there are passages that, read literally, could conceivably function as prooftexts for the notion of an ultimately universal salvation: John 12:32, Acts 3:21, Rom 5:18-21, Rom 11:25-26a, Rom 11:32, 1 Cor 3:12-15, 1 Cor 15:22-28, 2 Cor 5:19, Eph 1:10, Phil 2:9-11, Col 1:20, 1 Tim 2:4, Tit 2:11, 2 Pet 3:9, and 1 John 2:2 either contain language with universalistic overtones such as "all" or "whole" with reference to the objects of God's saving work or else declare the universality of God's salvific intentions.

In a commentary on Isaiah, the post-Origenist Jerome noted that the proponents of a universal restoration following an end to the torments of hell "employ these testimonies"—Romans 11:25-26a and other similar texts.[14] The present book explores the manner in which the biblical testimonies adduced in patristic rationales for universal salvation functioned as hermeneutical keys to a coherent understanding of biblical eschatology. Clement of Alexandria, Origen, and Gregory of Nyssa are the focal figures for this inquiry. Although Didymus the Blind and Evagrius of Pontus certainly maintained an Origenist perspective on the *apokatastasis*, they are representatives of a more doctrinaire, scholastic Origenism. As the goal is to determine the role of biblical exegesis in the genesis of the theological positions later reflected in scholastic Origenism, we will limit ourselves to Clement of Alexandria as a forerunner of Origen's thought, Origen himself, and Gregory of Nyssa as a figure who drank deeply at the well of Origenist eschatology but who predated the scholastic solidifying of the Origenist tradition. Traces of a universal eschatological hope also appeared in Ambrose and the early Jerome, but the paucity of relevant material in their corpora does not allow us to explore sufficiently the place of the Bible in this asepct of their thought. Clement, Origen, and Gregory, on the other hand, articulated their universalism explicitly enough and often enough to make feasible a full-scale analysis and comparison of the relationship between *apokatastasis* and exegesis in their theologies. Although the works of Clement and Origen survived in fragmentary fashion, enough material has been preserved to insure the probability that ideas expressed in multiple works are representative of their eschatological thought.

Excursus: The Alexandrian Exegetical Tradition

Most theological students are introduced to Origen as the principal shaper of the Alexandrian exegetical tradition with the theory of multiple senses of Scripture expressed in book 4 of *De principiis*. As is commonly observed, Origen identified three senses in Scripture: the literal, the moral, and the spiritual, analogous to a trichotomous anthropology.[15] On occasion, the addition of an eschatological sense, the ἀναγωγή, yields four senses.[16] Often, however, Origen distinguished only between a literal sense and a spiritual sense. August Zöllig suggested that for all practical purposes the non-literal senses in the threefold and fourfold divisions are subsumed in the spiritual sense.[17]

While the examination of Origen's biblical interpretation has produced a burgeoning literature in recent decades,[18] the contributions of Clement of Alexandria and Gregory of Nyssa to the Alexandrian exegetical tradition have commanded less attention. A brief treatment of the hermeneutical theory of Gregory and Clement is therefore warranted before commencing our inquiry into the place of exegesis in their eschatologies.

Clement of Alexandria

Clement, steeped in the exegesis of Philo of Alexandria (ca. 20 B.C.E.-ca. 50 C.E.),[19] followed Philo's location of the meaning of Scripture in both literal and non-literal readings of the text.[20] These senses of Scripture, however, had different audiences. Clement distinguished between two kinds of Christians: "believers" (πιστοί), who "have only tasted the Scriptures," and "gnostics" (γνωστικοί),[21] who "because they have advanced further are accurate interpreters of the truth." He compared the relationship between the two to that between an ordinary layperson and a skilled craftsman.[22] The literal sense made a rudimentary understanding of Scripture accessible to all, but a deeper understanding was available to the more advanced Christian Gnostic, as demonstrated by an episode Clement recounted from the *Shepherd of Hermas*:

> Did not also the power that appeared to Hermas in the Vision in the form of the Church give in transcription the book she wished to be proclaimed to the elect? This he transcribed "to the letter," it says, without discovering how to complete the syllables. It showed then that Scripture is clear to all when understood according to the bare reading, and that this is the faith which has the rank of the elementary principles, on which account the reading "to the letter" is spoken allegorically; but we understand the enlightened explication of the Scriptures, when faith is now advanced, to be like reading according to the syllables.[23]

Clement's emphasis on the superiority of the "enlightened (γνωστικὴν) explication of the Scriptures" was rooted in his theory of biblical symbolism, which he developed in extended sections of books 5 and 6 of the *Stromata*. Divine truth by necessity is concealed from those unable to comprehend it; Clement found examples of this "method of concealment (τῆς ἐπικρύψεως τὸν τρόπον)" in the writings of the ancient Egyptians and Greeks as well as in the Scriptures of the Hebrews.[24] Clement identified four reasons for this concealment, which John Ferguson summarized: "The first is *ethical*: the object is to conceal the truth from those who might profane it; the second is *didactic*: veiled truths need interpreters, they need training, and the result is to ensure that the underlying truths are not lost; the third is *psychological*: indirect statements make more impression than direct ones; the fourth relates to *complexity*: symbolic interpretations allow more than one layer of meaning."[25] Clement appealed to Jesus and the apostles as authority for his understanding of biblical truth as concealed in symbols, for "both the Lord himself, in clarifying the Scriptures for them, and his disciples (γνώριμοι) who similarly proclaimed the word after his life, made use of parables."[26] Indeed, "the character of the Scriptures is parabolic (παραβολικὸς γὰρ ὁ χαρακτὴρ ὑπάρχει τῶν γραφ-ῶν)."[27] Paul,[28] Barnabas,[29] John,[30] and Peter[31] wrote or spoke of the mysteries of God as being hidden from the masses but revealed to some as "instruction for the perfect (τελείων μάθησις)."[32] For Clement, this hidden knowledge of the true meaning of the Scriptures was mediated by unwritten traditions,[33] which Jesus committed to his apostles[34] and which constituted the "ecclesiastical rule (κανὼν ἐκκλησιαστικὸς)" by which Scripture was to be interpreted.[35] As an example of such "enlightened exposition (σαφήνειαν γνωστικὴν)" Clement offered an extended allegorical interpretation of the Decalogue.[36]

Clement most closely approached an explicit theory of multiple senses of Scripture (beyond the previously noted basic distinction between literal and deeper, non-literal meanings) in a pair of passages in book 1 of the *Stromata*:

> The Mosaic philosophy therefore is divided into four parts: into both the historic and that which is properly called legislative, which are characteristic features of an ethical approach; third, into the ceremonial, which is actually part of reflection on the natural order; and fourth, above all, the theological classification, the full initiation,[37] which Plato says belongs to the truly great mysteries, and Aristotle calls this classification "metaphysics."[38]

> We must also understand the meaning of the Law in a fourfold manner: [as disclosing some type],[39] or as displaying a sign, or as establishing a commandment for right living, or as pronouncing a prophecy. Now I know well that both to discern and to speak such things belongs to mature people; for indeed as regards its sense all Scripture is not "a unified Myconos," as the proverb goes. Those who seek the coherence of the divine teaching must approach it in a more dialectical manner as much as possible.[40]

Instead of distinguishing between four senses of Scripture, the first passage seems to distinguish between four literary genres in which the "Mosaic philosophy" is expressed,[41] which may be classified under three categories corresponding to the three traditional divisions of Greek philosophy: ethics (history and legislation), physics (ceremonial or sacrificial instructions), and metaphysics (theology).[42] As there are multiple genres of Scripture, so there are multiple ways in which Scrip-

ture may be understood: typological, symbolic, ethical, and prophetic.
While Charles Bigg has taken the second passage to be a reiteration of
the four divisions mentioned in the first passage,[43] the place of the passages in the larger rhetorical structure of 1.28 suggests otherwise. It is
true that the link between "τετραχῇ" and "τετραχῶς" establishes a
parallel relationship between the two enumerations, but the two passages are part of a larger μὲν . . . δὲ construction: on the one hand
("μὲν"), "the Mosaic philosophy is divided into four parts"
(1.28.176.1-2); on the other hand ("δὲ"), "we must *also* (καὶ) understand the meaning of the Law in a fourfold manner" (1.28.179.3-4).[44]
One should not press the parallel between four genres and four senses
for a direct correlation between a given genre and a given sense,[45] nor
should one fix the number of ways in which Clement could understand
Scripture at four.[46] Clement found in Scripture a plain meaning available to all and a multi-faceted deeper meaning available to the enlightened interpreter.

The discernment of deeper meanings in Scripture was for Clement
controlled by at least four guiding criteria that in theory excluded arbitrary and self-serving interpretations. Any interpretation must be consistent first with the context and intention of the passage in question,
second with the character of God, and third with other passages of
Scripture dealing with similar matters:

> Even if those who pursue heresies also dare to make use of the pro-
> phetic Scriptures, to begin with (they make use of them) not in all
> points, then neither in full nor as the kernel and larger structure of
> the prophecy dictate; but rather picking out ambiguous sayings they
> transfer (them) to their own opinions, plucking off a few scattered
> utterances, not contemplating what is meant by them but rather
> abusing the plain letter itself. . . . But the truth is discovered not in
> changing the meanings . . . , but rather in examining what perfectly
> belongs to and is proper for the Lord and the Almighty God and in
> establishing each thing that is demonstrated according to the Scrip-
> tures in turn from their similar passages of Scripture.[47]

Fourth, all interpretation must be faithful to the apostolic tradition:

> They are lazy who, though they have it in their power to provide
> the proper proofs for the divine Scriptures from the Scriptures
> themselves, pick out only what assists their own pleasures; and they
> covet glory who willingly evade through the imposition of other
> things the things handed down by the blessed apostles and teachers

which are attached to the inspired words, resisting divine tradition with human teachings in order to establish heresy.[48]

Clement's own exegetical practice did not always meet these criteria, especially the criterion of consistency with context and intention. When read against the background of the capriciousness of the heretical Gnostic exegesis to which Clement was opposed,[49] however, Clement may be seen as having exercised relative restraint in the quest for the deeper meaning of Scripture.[50]

Gregory of Nyssa

Gregory followed Origen in his distinction between two basic senses of Scripture: the literal (λέξις) and the allegorical (ἀλληγορία).[51] Contemporary controversy over ἀλληγορία[52] led to the frequent substitution of θεωρία, "insight,"[53] and the occasional use of other equivalents: ὑπόνοια, "underlying meaning" (Platonic terminology); τροπολογία, "figurative interpretation"; ἀναγωγή, "elevation"; αἴνιγμα, "riddle"; and μυστήριον, "mystery."[54] Gregory did maintain that there were texts for which a literal reading was the preferred interpretation.[55] Certain indicators, however, called for the rejection of the literal sense. If a literal interpretation of a text is doctrinally improper, physically or logically impossible, unuseful, or immoral, the meaning of the text must be sought elsewhere.[56]

The apostle Paul was both precedent and pattern for Gregory in seeking the θεωρίαν of Scripture.[57] The Law, which included the historical narratives of the Old Testament ("τὰ ἱστορικὰ διηγήματα") is "πνευματικὸν" (Rom 7:14).[58] In using the two children of Abraham to speak of the two covenants, Paul called the "θεωρίαν" concerning them "ἀλληγορίαν" (Gal 4:24).[59] Historical events recounted in the Old Testament happened "τυπικῶς" (1 Cor 10:11).[60] Paul could cite Dt 25:4, which literally had to do with the just treatment of beasts of burden, and then say that it was written not about oxen but "especially for our sake" (1 Cor 9:9-10).[61] The movement from the "fleshly things (τῶν σωματικῶν)" of the text to "spiritual things (τὰ νοητά)" was a "turning to the Lord" and a "lifting of the veil" (2 Cor 3:16).[62] Many biblical narratives, interpreted literally, provided patterns for living that were unworthy of emulation; Paul therefore maintained that "the letter kills, but the spirit gives life" (2 Cor 3:6).[63]

This tension between the literal and spiritual senses of many texts suggests that Gregory employed a theological method in which Scripture functioned not as the sole determinant of dogma but rather as part of a complex of sources of dogmatic authority. Scripture was preeminent for Gregory.[64] The authority of Scripture alone, however, did not in Gregory's opinion guarantee orthodoxy, for heretics such as Eunomius also appealed to biblical authority.[65] The role of exegesis in Gregory's theology was therefore relative to a parallel source of authority: the tradition of the church. "Theological impropriety" in the literal sense of the text required the interpreter to seek its meaning beyond the λέξις;[66] the existence of such impropriety was discerned by means of tradition.[67] Reason and experience also informed Gregory's theological exegesis, for when the literal sense of a text presented logical impossibilities or failed to be useful, he believed that it must be rejected in favor of the spiritual sense.[68]

Gregory's theological system as a pre-understanding influenced his exegesis, and his exegesis in turn undergirded his theological system in a hermeneutical circle. A prominent example of this pattern is the connection between Gregory's concept of ἐπέκτασις, the never-ending "stretching out" of the human soul for God, and his exegesis.[69] Ἐπέκτασις provided Gregory with the key for understanding the spiritual significance of the structure of biblical passages, narratives, and even whole books. In the exegetical treatise *In inscriptiones psalmorum*, Gregory discerned in the arrangement of the Psalter in five books five progressive steps in the ascent of humanity from sin to beatitude.[70] In the *Orationes de beatitudinibus* he found in the sequence of the Beatitudes of Jesus "a ladder by which the Divine Word conducts us gradually up to the heights of perfection."[71] The work *De vita Moysis* exemplified both Gregory's hermeneutical theory and its relationship to ἐπέκτασις: the first half of the treatise set forth the ἱστορία of the life of Moses; the second half found in the θεωρία of these narratives an account of the mystical ascent of the human soul to God.[72] As a key component of Gregory's hermeneutical pre-understanding, ἐπέκτασις led him to an eschatological interpretation of the biblical text.

Notes

[1]Ἀποκατάστασις in classical Greek literature was a technical astronomical term referring to the periodic return of the stars to the same place in the heavens as in the previous year (LSJ, s.v. "Ἀποκατάστασις"). It appears in the New Testament only in Acts 3:21, where it refers to the Messianic restitution of the created order (BAGD, s.v. "Ἀποκατάστασις"; Albrecht Oepke, "Ἀποκαθίστημι, ἀποκατάστασις," in *TDNT*, 1:391). In Origen and subsequent Origenism, ἀποκατάστασις is the universal restoration of all rational

souls or created beings to their pre-fall position (ibid., 1:392-93; *PGL*, s.v. "᾽Αποκατάστασις").

On the use of ἀποκατάστασις in the New Testament and the early Alexandrians, see also André Méhat, "Apocatastase: Origène, Clément d'Alexandrie, Act 3:21," *VC* 10 (1956): 196-214.

[2]E.g., Clem. *str.* 1.27.173.5; ibid., 4.24.154.1-2; ibid., 5.1.9.4; ibid., 5.14.91.2; ibid., 6.12.99.2; ibid., 7.2.12.2-3.13.1; ibid., 7.6.34.4; ibid., 7.10.56.5; ibid., 7.10.57.1; ibid., 7.12.78.3; ibid., 7.16.102.

[3]E.g., Or. *princ.* 1.6.3; ibid., 2.3; ibid., 3.5.6-6.6; idem, *Jo.* 1.16.91; ibid., 1.264; ibid., 2.62; ibid., 6.302-3; ibid., 13.391-92; ibid., 87-88; ibid., 28.152-55; idem, *hom. in Jos.* 8.5; idem, *comm. in Rom.* 8.9; idem, *hom. in Jer.* 14.18.

[4]E.g., Or. *princ.* 2.11.3-7; ibid., 3.6.9; idem, *Jo.* 13.138; ibid., 28.63-66; idem, *hom. in Jos.* 8.5; ibid., 14.2; idem, *or.* 27.15; ibid., 29.15; idem, *comm. in Mt.* 15.31; idem, *comm. ser. in Mt.* 16; ibid., 20; ibid., 51; idem, *hom. in Ez.* 1.3, 13; ibid., 5.1; idem, *hom. in Jer.* 1.3; ibid., 2.3; ibid., 19.15; ibid., 20.3, 8; idem, *hom. in Ex.* 6.4; idem, *hom. in Num.* 25.6; idem, *fr. in Pr.* (PG 17:615-16); idem, *hom. in Lc.* 24; idem, *mart.* 36; idem, *Cant.* 3. References in parentheses preceded by "PG" indicate volume and column numbers in Jacques Paul Migne, ed., *Patrologiae Cursus Completus: Series Graecae* (Paris: n.p., 1857-66). Whenever the edition from which a reference is taken provides insufficient subdivision of chapters and paragraphs, references to the edition are given in parentheses to facilitate location of the reference.

[5]On the *apokatastasis*, see Gr. Nyss. *anim. et res.* (PG 46:69, 71-72, 148, 153, 156-57); idem, *or. catech.* 26; idem, *v. Mos.* 2.82; idem, *hom. in cant.* 15 (GNO 6:468-69); idem, *hom. opif.* 17.2; idem, *hom. in Eccl.* 1.9; idem, *Pulch.* (GNO 9:472); idem, *or. dom.* 4; idem, *beat.* 8; idem, *mort.* (GNO 9:51). On the nature and duration of eternal punishment, see idem, *anim. et res.* (PG 46:97-101, 152, 157); idem, *virg.* 12; idem, *or. catech.* 8; ibid., 35; idem, *infant.* (PG 46:168); idem, *mort.* (GNO 9:54). References in parentheses preceded by "GNO" indicate volume and page numbers in Werner Jaeger, ed., *Gregorii Nysseni Opera* (Leiden: E. J. Brill, 1921-).

[6]Gr. Nyss. *anim. et res.* (PG 46:113, 125); idem, *hom. opif.* 28.4.

[7]Gr. Nyss. *anim. et res.* (PG 46:28-29, 48, 76-80, 85, 108-9, 128-32); idem, *hom. opif.* 27.5.2.

[8]Gr. Naz. *or.* 3.7; ibid., 30.6; ibid., 39.19; ibid., 40.36.

[9]Didym. *comm. in Zach.* 1.264; ibid., 3.307-8; idem, *ep. cath.* (PG 39:1759, 1770); idem, *frag. in Pss.* (PG 39:1340); idem, *Man.* 2 (PG 39:1088); idem, *Trin.* 2.6.4; ibid., 2.6.12..

[10]Evagr. Pont. *Keph. gnost.* 2.84; ibid., 3.18; ibid., 5.20; ibid., 6.27; idem, *ep.* 59.

[11]Brian E. Daley, *The Hope of the Early Church: A Handbook of Patristic Eschatology* (Cambridge: Cambridge University Press, 1991), 98-99, 103-4. On Jerome's perspective prior to 394, see Elizabeth A. Clark, "The Place of Jerome's Commentary on Ephesians in the Origenist Controversy: The Apokatastasis and Ascetic Ideals," *VC* 41, no. 2 (June 1987): 154-71.

[12]Phrase from *There's a Wideness in God's Mercy*, hymn text by Frederick W. Faber.

[13]This is the label applied to the traditional understanding of the last judgment by Jürgen Moltmann in *The Coming of God: Christian Eschatology*, trans. Margaret Kohl (Minneapolis: Fortress Press, 1996), 235-55. In these pages Moltmann considers the biblical evidence for a double outcome of judgment on the one hand and universalism on the other before arguing that both perspectives may ultimately be two aspects of the same hope.

[14]Jer. *com. in Is.* 18.66.24: *"Porro qui uolunt supplicia aliquando finiri, et licet post multa tempora, tamen terminum habere tormenta, his utuntur testimoniis: Cum intrauerit plenitudo genitum, tunc omnis Israel saluus fiet."*

[15]Richard P. C. Hanson, *Allegory and Event: A Study of the Sources and Significance of Origen's Interpretation of Scripture* (Richmond: John Knox Press, 1959), 235.

[16]Denis Farkasfalvy, "Interpretation of the Bible," in *Encyclopedia of Early Christianity*, ed. Everett Ferguson, GRLH, vol. 846 (New York: Garland Publishing, 1990), 468.

[17]August Zöllig, *Die Inspirationslehre des Origenes*, StrThS, vol. 5, no. 1 (Freiburg: Herder, 1902), 101-2.

[18]E.g., Henri de Lubac, *Histoire et Esprit: L'intelligence de l'Écriture d'après Origène* (Aubier: Éditions Montaigne, 1950); Karen Jo Torjesen, "'Body,' 'Soul,' and 'Spirit' in Origen's Theory of Exegesis," *AThR* 67, no. 1 (January 1985): 17-30; idem, *Hermeneutical Procedure and Theological Method in Origen's Exegesis*, PTS, vol. 28 (Berlin: Walter de Gruyter, 1986).

[19]Annewies van den Hoek, *Clement of Alexandria and His Use of Philo in the Stromateis: An Early Christian Reshaping of a Jewish Model*, SVC, vol. 3 (Leiden: E. J. Brill, 1988), 220-24, identified in Clement 125 instances of certain or probable dependence on Philo. Of these, 61 (49 percent) involved interpretations of biblical texts borrowed from Philo, of which 35 (28 percent) were allegorical and 26 (21 percent) were non-allegorical. Fifty-nine (47 percent) of the 125 certain or probable borrowings involved philosophical or theological concepts, but 31 of these were linked with biblical materials, bringing the total number of borrowings from Philo involving use of the Bible to 92 (74 percent). Philo therefore influenced Clement not only in his general approach to biblical interpretation but also in specific points of exegesis. For discussion of these specific exegetical appropriations, see ibid., 23-208 passim. David T. Runia, *Philo in Early Christian Literature: A Survey*, CRINT, Section 3, Jewish Traditions in Early Christian Literature, vol. 3 (Assen: Van Gorcum, 1993; Minneapolis: Fortress Press, 1993), 155, pointed to a Philonic hermeneutical influence more basic to Clement's thought than a focus on direct borrowings of exegetical patterns and conclusions might suggest: "It cannot be emphasized enough that in all probability Clement, because he had a pagan philosophical training before he became a Christian, will have read Plato before he gained acquaintance with Philo. Most likely he did not come across Philo until he reached Alexandria and joined his last teacher Pantaenus. This means that Philo did not teach Clement Platonism, but rather *how to connect his Platonism to biblical thought*, and specifically to biblical exegesis, above all through the use of allegory" (emphasis is that of Runia).

[20]Claude Mondésert, *Clément d'Alexandrie: Introduction à l'étude de sa pensée religieuse à partir de l'Écriture*, Théologie, no. 2 (Paris: Aubier, 1944), 154-55. That Clement was concerned about the accurate interpretation of the literal sense of the text is evident in his polemic against the heretics who "color the bare letter (ψιλῇ ἀποχρώμενοι τῇ λέξει)" in *Str.* 7.96.

[21]Clement distinguished these possessors of true Christian γνῶσις from the heretical Valentinian Gnostics; see John Ferguson, "The Achievement of Clement of Alexandria," *RelS* 12, no. 1 (March 1976): 78-79.

[22]Clem. *str.* 7.16.95.

[23]Clem. *str.* 6.15.131.2-3. The passage to which Clement referred is *Herm. Vis.* 2.1. Clement seems to have regarded the *Shepherd of Hermas* as inspired and authoritative, but it is unclear whether he accorded to it the same degree of authority as the writings which came to comprise the New Testament canon; see J. Ruwet, "Clément d'Alexandrie: Canon des Écritures et Apocryphes," *Bib* 29, no. 4 (1948): 394-95, and James A. Brooks, "Clement of Alexandria as a Witness to the Development of the New Testament Canon," *SecCent* 9, no. 1 (Spring 1992): 46-47.

[24]Clem. *str.* 5.4-8 (quoted material is from 5.4.19.3).

[25]John Ferguson, *Clement of Alexandria: Stromateis, Books One to Three*, FC, vol. 85 (Washington, D.C.: The Catholic University of America Press, 1991), 18-19. See Clem. *str.* 5.9.56.3-57.2 and 6.15.126.1-3.

[26]Clem. *str.* 6.15.127.5. Clement also appealed to Jesus' use of parables to veil truth in *str.* 5.12.80.6-9 and 6.15.126.2-127.1.

[27]Clem. *str.* 6.15.126.3.

[28]Clem. *str.* 5.10.60.1-62.4, quoting Eph 3:3-5, Col 1:9-11, 1:25-27, 2:2-3, 4:2-4, and Heb 5:12-14, 6:1 (the latter of which Clement attributed to Paul; see Brooks, "Clement of Alexandria," 43); 5.10.64.5-6, quoting Rom 15:29 and 16:25-26; 5.10.65.4-66.2, quoting 1 Cor 2:6-7 and 3:1-3; and 5.12.80.1-6, quoting 1 Cor 2:6-7 and Col 2:2-3.

[29]Clem. *str.* 5.10.63.1-6, quoting *Epistula Barnabae* 6.5,8-10. Clement attributed this pseudonymous epistle to the apostle Barnabas and according to Eus. *h.e.* 6.14.1 commented upon it in the lost *Hypotyposes*, possibly indicating that he considered it authoritative Scripture. See Ruwet, "Clément d'Alexandrie," 391-92, and Brooks, "Clement of Alexandria," 44, 46-47.

[30]Clem. *str.* 5.12.81.3, quoting John 1:18.

[31]Clem. *str.* 6.15.128.1, quoting *Kerygma Petri* frg. 9.10. Clement's extant works contain ten references to the *Kerygma*, which Clement treated as authentic oracles of Peter. The six fragments of the *Kerygma* preserved by Clement are the principal witnesses to this lost document. See Ruwet, "Clément d'Alexandrie," 403-3, and Brooks, "Clement of Alexandria," 46-47.

[32]Clem. *str.* 5.10.60.2. The "τελείων" were for Clement the more advanced Christian believers, as evidenced by his subsequent clarification of Col 1:28: " . . . οὐδὲ μὴν πάντα τὸν πιστεύοντα τέλειον ἐν Χριστῷ . . . ." (ibid., 5.10.61.3).

[33]Clem. *str.* 5.10.62.2: "ἦν γάρ τινα ἀγράφως παραδιδόμενα."

[34]Clem. *str.* 6.15.131.5: "Now after the Savior taught the apostles, the unwritten tradition of what is written has now been handed over also to us, inscribed in new hearts according to the renewal of the book (the Old Testament?) by the power of God."

[35]Clem. *str.* 6.15.124.3-125.4. The "κανὼν ἐκκλησιαστικὸς" along with equivalent terminology (κανὼν τῆς ἐκκλησίας, κανὼν τοῦ εὐαγγελίου, εὐαγγελικὸς κανὼν, κανὼν τῆς ἀληθείας) probably referred to the developing *regula fidei*. On the nature of the *regula fidei* in Clement, see William R. Farmer, "Galatians and the Second-Century Development of the *Regula Fidei*," *SecCent* 4, no. 3 (Fall 1984): 152-56.

[36]Clem. *str.* 6.16.133.1-148.6. Van den Hoek, *Clement of Alexandria*, 201-5, has demonstrated Clement's dependence on Philo *Legum allegoriarum libri i-iii* 1.1-21 in this passage, *contra* Armand Delatte, *Études sur la littérature pythagoricienne*, BEHE.E, no. 217 (Paris: E. Champion, 1915), 231-47, who minimized the influence of Philo.

[37]In classical literature ἐποπτεία referred to the highest level of initiation into the Eleusinian mysteries; see LSJ, s.v. "Ἐποπτεία, ἡ."

[38]Clem. *str.* 1.28.176.1-2.

[39]Only three ways of understanding the Law follow "τετραχῶς" in Codex Laurentianus (11th century; the sole manuscript witness for the *Stromata*; hereinafter L), leading Stählin (following the Latin translation of Gentian Hervet [Paris: n.p., 1566]) to print the conjectural emendation "τριχῶς" in the text of his first edition (1906) of books 1-6 of the *Stromata*. An excerpt from *str.* 1.28 in a scholion on Psalm 76:21, however, has "ὡς τύπον τινὰ δηλοῦσαν" after "βούλησιν," supplying the missing first way of understanding the Law for a total of four. Stählin's second (1939) and subsequent editions retained "τετραχῶς" from L and printed the reading from the scholion in the apparatus. Stählin was persuaded by Erik Peterson, "Mitteilung, zur Textkritik des Clemens Alex. und Euagrios," *TLZ* 56, no. 3 (January 1931): 69-70, who had called attention to the importance of this scholion for rectifying the lacuna in L at 1.28.179.3. W. den Boer, "Hermeneutic Problems in Early Christian Literature," *VC* 1, no. 2 (April 1947): 159-61, on the other hand, viewed "ὡς τύπον τινὰ δηλοῦσαν" in the scholion as a later interpolation of an anachronistic distinction between typology and allegory in the service of the Alexandrian school in its controversy with the Antiochian school.

[40]Clem. *str.* 1.28.179.3-4. "Μία Μύκονος" appears in classical literature as a proverb meaning "it's all one" or "it's all alike," alluding to the island Myconus, the inhabitants of which were said to be all bald (LSJ, s.v. "Μύκονος, ἡ").

[41]Maxime Hermaniuk, *La Parabole Évangélique: enquête exégètique et critique*, Universitas Lovaniensis Dissertationes, ser. 2, vol. 38 (Paris: Desclée de Brouwer, 1947), 427: "genre historique," "genre juridique," "genre liturgique," "genre théologique." Harry Austryn Wolfson, *The Philosophy of the Church Fathers*, 2d rev. ed., SGPS, no. 3 (Cambridge: Harvard University Press, 1964), 1:53, held that "Clement's fourfold division of the Pentateuch is based upon a division of the Pentateuch found in Philo." The Philonic texts

Wolfson cited, however, are not convincing. The alleged fourfold division is found not in a single enumeration but rather is extrapolated from widely separated texts in book 2 of *De vita Mosis* (2.8.46, 2.13.66, 2.15.71ff., 2.23.109, 2.35.187ff.) which deal not with divisions of the Mosaic Law (apart from 2.8.46, which divides the writings of Moses into only two categories, one historical and another concerning commands and prohibitions) but rather with different aspects of the life of Moses. Philo's announced intention at the beginning of book 2 was to demonstrate the excellence of Moses as king, lawgiver, high priest, and prophet, with special attention to the last three (Philo *De vita Mosis* 2.1.1-3).

[42]Charles Bigg, *The Christian Platonists of Alexandria* (Oxford: n.p., 1886; reprint, New York: AMS Press, 1970), 57, n. 2 (page citations are to the reprint edition). Bigg noted that "[t]he identification of Sacrificial Typology with Physics is very arbitrary" (ibid.).

[43]Ibid. Bigg accepted the reading "τετραχῶς" in L at 1.28.179.3, but explained the presence of only three items in the enumeration by suggesting that Clement omitted the literal sense. Bigg did not have access to the then-unpublished scholion on Psalm 76:21.

[44]*Contra* André Méhat, "Clément d'Alexandrie et les sens de l'Écriture (Ier *Stromate*, 176,1 et 179,3)," in *Epektasis: Mélanges patristiques offers au Cardinal Jean Daniélou*, ed. Jacques Fontaine and Charles Kannengiesser (Paris: Éditions Beauchesne, 1972), 356-57, who interpreted "μὲν" in 1.28.76.1 as an indicator of a change of subject and "δὲ" in 1.28.179.3 as logically connected "non à ce qui la précède, mais à ce qui suit" (ibid., 356).

[45]Wolfson, *Philosophy of the Church Fathers*, 1:55, n. 113, rejected the reading "τετραχῶς" in L at 1.28.179.3 along with the missing sense in the scholion and opted for the emended reading "τριχῶς," but rightly granted that "if the scholia [*sic*] is followed, then the four senses in this second part of the passage are unrelated to the fourfold division in the first part . . . ." Henri de Lubac, *Exégèse médiévale: Le quartre sens de l'Écriture*, vol. 1, pt. 1, Théologie, no. 41 (Lyons: Aubier, 1959), 173-74, cautiously proposed a correlation by modifying the order of senses in the second passage ("Histoire = Types," "Prescriptions légales = Préceptes moraux," "Liturgie = Signes," "Théologie = Prophétie"), but admitted that this was a "pure hypothèse."

[46]Mondésert, *Clément d'Alexandrie*, 151-62, classified "les divers sens possibles de l'Écriture" in Clement under five categories (beyond "la division fondamentale des deux sens," "littéral" and "figuré"), some with subdivisions: (1) "[u]n sens *historique*"; (2) "[u]n sens *doctrinal*," which included "moral, religieux, théologique" senses; (3) "[u]n sens *prophétique*," which encompassed both prophecy proper and typology; (4) "[u]n sens *philosophique*," which included a "sens cosmique" and a "sens psychologique"; and (5) "un sens *mystique*" (emphasis is that of Mondésert). None of these senses is mutually exclusive, for as Robert M. Grant (with David Tracy), *A Short History of the Interpretation of the Bible*, 2d rev. ed. (Philadelphia: Fortress Press, 1984), 56, noted, "Clement is quite capable of taking a text in two or three ways at the same time. But any of them can be found in any text of scripture."

[47]Clem. *str.* 7.16.96.

[48]Clem. *str.* 7.16.103.

[49]On Gnostic biblical exegesis, see, e.g., Orval S. Wintermute, "A Study of Gnostic Exegesis of the Old Testament," in *The Use of the Old Testament in the New and Other Essays: Studies in Honor of William F. Stinespring*, ed. J. M. Efrid (Durham, N.C.: Duke University Press, 1972), 241-70; Elaine H. Pagels, *The Johannine Gospel in Gnostic Exegesis* (New York: Abingdon Press, 1973); idem, *The Gnostic Paul: Gnostic Exegesis of the Pauline Letters* (Philadelphia: Fortress Press, 1975); Robert McL. Wilson, "The Gnostics and the Old Testament," in *Proceedings of the International Colloquium on Gnosticism*, ed. G. Widengren (Stockholm: Almqvist & Wiskell, 1977), 164-68; Jacqueline Williams, *Biblical Interpretation in the Gnostic Gospel of Truth from Nag Hammadi*, SBLDS, no. 79 (Atlanta: Scholars Press, 1988); and Louis Painchaud, "The Use of Scripture in Gnostic Literature," *JECS* 4, no. 2 (Summer 1996): 129-46.

[50]For examples of Clement's exegetical practice, see Hanson, *Allegory and Event*, 118-20; Bertrand de Margerie, *Introduction à l'histoire de l'exégèse*, vol. 1 (Paris: Éditions du Cerf, 1980), 103-8; and Manlio Simonetti, *Biblical Interpretation in the Early Church: An Historical Introduction to Patristic Exegesis*, trans. John A. Hughes, ed. Anders Bergquist and Markus Bockmuehl (Edinburgh: T. & T. Clark, 1994), 38.

[51]On the influence of Origen's concept of allegory on Gregory as demonstrated in the prologue to *In Canticum canticorum homiliae*, see Ronald E. Heine, "Gregory of Nyssa's Apology for Allegory," *VC* 38, no. 4 (December 1984): 360-64. For a comparison of the allegorical approaches of Origen and Gregory in their exegesis of the Song of Songs, see Franz Dünzl, "Die Canticum-Exegese des Gregor von Nyssa und des Origenes im Vergleich," *JAC* 36 (1993): 94-109.

[52]Heine, "Apology for Allegory," 306-11, identified the opponents of Gregory's interpretation mentioned in the prologue to the commentary on the Song of Songs as the Antiochene school of interpretation in general and Diodore of Tarsus and/or his followers in particular. The prologue to the *In Canticum canticorum homiliae* (GNO 6:3-13) is a concise, forthright statement of Gregory's hermeneutical theory. Joseph W. Trigg, *Biblical Interpretation*, MFC, vol. 9 (Wilmington, Del.: Michael Glazier, 1988), 144-50, has provided an English translation of the prologue with an introduction to the hermeneutical theory set forth therein.

[53]Θεωρία was Gregory's customary term for allegorical or spiritual exegesis (Heine, "Apology for Allegory," 368). The Antiochenes, however, employed θεωρία as a technical term for a "spiritual sense" of Scripture that is consistent with the literal sense and must be distinguished from allegory. Joining Gregory in the equation of θεωρία with ἀλληγορία were, *inter alios*, Didymus the Blind, Hesychius of Jerusalem, and Cyril of Alexandria. On the patristic usage of θεωρία as an exegetical term, see *PGL*, s.v. "Θεωρία" D.2.

[54]Trigg, *Biblical Interpretation*, 144-45. Gregory explicitly equated some of these terms in the prologue to the commentary on the Song of Songs: "ὧν

τὴν διὰ τῆς ἀναγωγῆς θεωρίαν εἴτε τροπολογίαν εἴτε τι ἄλλο τις ὀνομάζειν ἐθέλοι, οὐδὲν περὶ τοῦ ὀνόματος διοισόμεθα, μόνον εἰ τῶν ἐπωφελῶν ἔχοιτο νοημάτων" (Gr. Nyss. *hom. in Cant.* proem. [GNO 6:5.6-9]).

[55]While not the only exemplars of literal interpretation in Gregory, the two treatises on the Genesis creation narratives (*De opificio hominis* and *Apologia in hexaemeron*, both written to complete his elder brother Basil's work on the Hexaemeron or six days of creation) emphasized the literal sense almost exclusively. Simonetti, *Biblical Interpretation*, 65-66, seemed to attribute this to an early phase in Gregory's hermeneutical development, but it is more probable that Gregory was careful to maintain fidelity to Basil's exegesis: "Since Basil, *Hexaem.* 9, 80, explicitly states that he was interested in the literal sense only and not allegory . . . , Gregory is anxious to follow in his footsteps throughout the two works that supplement his brother's treatise. Thus towards the end he asserts with a certain satisfaction that he never distorted the literal sense of the Bible into figurative allegory (εἰς τροπικὴν ἀλληγορίαν)" (Johannes Quasten, *Patrology* [Utrecht: Spectrum, 1950; reprint, Westminster, Md.: Christian Classics, 1990], 3:264).

[56]Monique Alexandre, "La théorie de l'exégèse dans le *De hominis opificio* et l'*In Hexaemeron*," in *Écriture et culture philosophique dans la pensée de Grégoire de Nysse: Actes du Colloque de Chevetogne*, ed. Marguerite Harl (Leiden: E. J. Brill, 1971), 104. Alexandre labels these disqualifiers of the literal sense "inconvenance théologique, impossibilité matérielle et logique, inutilité, immoralité de la lettre."

[57]Gregory followed Origen in making a case for allegorical exegesis by appealing to Pauline precedents. Origen had cited eight Pauline texts: Rom 7:14; 1 Cor 2:10; 2:12,16; 9:9-10; 10:11; 2 Cor 3:6; 3:15-16; Gal 4:24 (see, e.g., Or. *princ.* 4.2.1-9; idem, *In Iesu Nave homiliae* 9.8). In *hom. in Cant.* proem. (GNO 6:5.9-7.4), Gregory utilized six of these eight texts in a similar manner. On Gregory's dependence on Origen for the appeal to Pauline authority in defense of allegory, see Heine, "Apology for Allegory," 360-64.

[58]Gr. Nyss. *hom. in Cant.* proem. (GNO 6:5.9-18).

[59]Ibid. (GNO 6:5.19-6.3).

[60]Ibid. (GNO 6:6.3-5). While Paul seems to have used τυπικῶς in the sense of "as an example," for Gregory the adverb meant "symbolically" or "figuratively." See BAGD, s.v. "Τυπικῶς"; *PGL*, s.v. "Τυπικῶς."

[61]Gr. Nyss. *hom. in Cant.* proem. (GNO 6:6.6-8).

[62]Ibid. (GNO 6:6.10-12).

[63]Ibid. (GNO 6:7.1-4).

[64]"The Holy Scriptures" are "the rule and measure of every tenet (κανόνι παντὸς δόγματος καὶ νόμῳ)" (Gregory of Nyssa *Dialogus de anima et resurrectione* [NPNF[2] 5:439; PG 46:49C]). They constitute the standard by which the conclusions of human reason must be judged: "And to those who are expert only in the technical methods of proof (τὰς τεχνικὰς ἐφόδους . . . τῶν ἀποδείξεων) a mere demonstration suffices to convince; but as for ourselves, we were agreed that there is something more trustworthy (πιστότερον) than any of these artificial conclusions, namely, that which the teachings of Holy

Scripture point to: and so I deem that it is necessary to inquire, in addition to what has been said, whether this inspired teaching (ἡ θεόπνευστος διδασκαλία) harmonizes (συμφέρεται) with it all" (ibid. [NPNF² 5:442; PG 46:64]).

[65]Jaroslav Pelikan, *Christianity and Classical Culture: The Metamorphosis of Natural Theology in the Christian Encounter with Hellenism* (New Haven: Yale University Press, 1993), 227-28.

[66]Alexandre, "Théorie de l'exégèse," 104.

[67]Mariette Canévet, *Grégoire de Nysse et l'herméneutique biblique: Études des rapports entre le langage et la connaissance de Dieu* (Paris: Études Augustiniennes, 1983), 235-87, identified five aspects of tradition in its fourth-century form which influenced Gregory's exegetical conclusions: the rejection of an opposition between the Old and New Testaments, the two natures of Christ, the mediatorial role of Christ, the virginal birth, and the Trinity.

[68]Alexandre, "Théorie de l'exégèse," 104. It must be noted, however, that Gregory claimed to subordinate reason to Scripture: "our reason," he said, is "under the guidance of Scripture (ἡμῖν ὁ λόγος διὰ τῆς ἁγίας γραφῆς ὁδηγούμενος)" (Gr. Nyss. *Eunom.* 1.315 [NPNF² 5:65; GNO 1:120.17-18]). Reason was also subservient to tradition for Gregory: "But if our rather feeble powers of reason (ἀτονώτερος . . . ὁ ἡμέτερος λόγος) prove unequal to the problem, we must guard the traditions we have received from the Fathers (τὴν μὲν παράδοσιν ἣν παρὰ τῶν πατέρων διεδεξάμεθα φυλάξομεν), as ever sure and immovable, and seek from the Lord a means of defending our faith" (Gregory of Nyssa *Ad Ablabium quod non sint tres dei* [Cyril C. Richardson, trans., "An Answer to Ablabius: That We Should Not Think of Saying There Are Three Gods," in Edward Rochie Hardy, ed., *Christology of the Later Fathers*, LCC (Philadelphia: Westminster Press, 1954), 257; GNO 3,1:39.1-4]).

[69]Canévet, *Herméneutique biblique*, 253-54. Cavénet also demonstrated the influence of other elements of Gregory's own theological system on his exegesis: the "ladder of being," the incomprehensibility of God, the permanence of good, and the radical exclusiveness of light and darkness (ibid., 249-53, 254-65).

[70]Simonetti, *Biblical Interpretation*, 65; Quasten, *Patrology*, 3:265; Gregory of Nyssa *In inscriptiones psalmorum* (GNO 5:24-175). This conclusion about the structure of the Psalter has recently been discussed in detail in Ronald E. Heine, *Gregory of Nyssa's Treatise on the Inscriptions of the Psalms: Introduction, Translation, and Notes*, OECS (Oxford: Clarendon Press, 1995), 50-79 (section entitled "The Structure of the Psalter and the Stages of the Spiritual Life").

[71]Quasten, *Patrology*, 3:268; Gregory of Nyssa *Orationes viii de beatitudinibus* (PG 44:1193-1301; Hilda C. Graef, trans., *St. Gregory of Nyssa: The Lord's Prayer, The Beatitudes*, ACW, no. 18 [Westminster, Md.: Newman Press, 1954], 85-175).

[72]Simonetti, *Biblical Interpretation*, 66-67; Quasten, *Patrology*, 3:265; Gregory of Nyssa *De vita Moysis* (GNO 7:1-145; Abraham J. Malherbe and

Everett Ferguson, trans., *Gregory of Nyssa: The Life of Moses*, CWS [New York: Paulist Press, 1978], 29-137).

Chapter 2

"He Indeed Saves All": Clement of Alexandria

Although it is not certain that Clement was Origen's teacher in the catechetical school of Alexandria, Clement anticipated the thought of Origen in many respects. As this was the case especially in the area of individual eschatology, an examination of the relationship between Clement's concept of *apokatastasis* and biblical exegesis is the proper starting point for investigating the topic in Origen and those influenced by him.

I. *Apokatastasis* in the Thought of Clement of Alexandria

A. The Universal Restoration

Clement was "the first Christian writer to suggest, with great caution, the . . . prospect of universal salvation for all intelligent creatures."[1] Clement suggested this most explicitly in two passages. A section in book 7 of the *Stromata* has been cited frequently in the secondary literature as a key expression of Clement's concept of *apokatastasis*:

Therefore he both made and showed all things to be conducive to virtue, but not to the extent of hindering a person's free choice, so that even to those who can see only dimly, the God who is unique, one, and almighty might be shown to be good, forever saving through his Son, and on the other hand in all ways absolutely guilt-less of evil; for by the Lord of the universe all things are arranged both in general and in particular toward the end of the salvation of the universe. Therefore it is the work of the righteousness of salva-tion always to advance each one for the better as much as possible; for even the less significant things are managed toward the end of the salvation and continuance of the more significant things in ac-cordance with their own accustomed places. For example, every-thing that is virtuous changes to better dwellings, having as the cause of change the free choice of knowledge with which the soul is well furnished in its own power; but necessary chastisements through the goodness of the great overseeing judge compel those who have become more hardened to repent, either through attend-ing angels or through various preliminary judgments or through the final, complete judgment.[2]

"The salvation of the universe (τὴν τοῦ ὅλου σωτηρίαν)" is thus neces-sary for theodicy,[3] does not violate human free will,[4] and comes about through free human response to divine discipline either in the present life ("through various preliminary judgments") or in the age to come ("through the final, complete judgment").[5]

A rarely noted passage in a lost commentary on 1 John provides a much more explicit expression of this idea.[6] In a fragment of the lost *Hypotyposes* preserved in Latin by Cassiodorus (ca. 485-ca. 580), Clement commented on 1 John 2:2:

"But not only," he says, "for our sins is the Lord the propitiator"— that is, for the faithful—"but also for the whole world." Therefore he indeed saves all: but some, converting them through punish-ments; and others, who follow willingly, voluntarily, and with dig-nity of honor, "that every knee may should bow to him of things in heaven, things on earth, and things under the earth"—that is, an-gels, people, and souls which before his advent have departed from this temporary life.[7]

This is Clement's most direct affirmation of the salvation of all rational creatures, both humans and angels, some of whom will be saved only through redemptive punishment after death.

Elsewhere Clement emphasized the universality of God's salvific intention[8] and offer of salvation,[9] but without mention of an ultimately universal outcome. Clement used ἀποκατάστασις/ἀποκαθίστημι with reference to the end result of the divinization of the "true Gnostic," but in doing so did not explicitly specify whether some might ultimately fail to attain to this final *apokatastasis*:

> Now this comes about whenever anyone clings to the Lord through faith, knowledge, and love and ascends with him to the place where the God and guardian of our faith and love is, from whom ultimately knowledge is given over to those who are fitted and approved for this, because more preparation and training is necessary both for the hearing of the things that are said and for moderation of life and for advancing with care beyond the "righteousness which is according to the law." This leads to the end which is endless and perfect, after we have been taught the way of life we will have according to God with the gods, after we are delivered from all chastisement and punishment which "for" saving "discipline we endure" as a consequence of sins; after which deliverance reward and honors are assigned to those who have been perfected, who have ceased purification and who have ceased all other worship, even if it be holy and among holy ones. Then after they have become "pure in heart" with reference to nearness to the Lord, restoration to everlasting contemplation awaits. And they are given the name "gods" who will be enthroned with the other gods who have been stationed under the Savior. Knowledge is therefore quick for purification and suitable for the acceptable change to the better state. For this reason it also easily transfers a person to that divine and holy state which is kin to the soul and by a certain light of its own carries that one through the mystic stages of progress, until it restores that one to the chief place of rest, after teaching "the pure in heart" to behold "God" "face to face" with knowledge and by direct apprehension. For here is the perfection of the enlightened soul: after going beyond all purifications and acts of worship, to be "with the Lord," where he is, being in direct submission.[10]

André Méhat contended that Clement uniformly employed ἀποκατάστασις and ἀποκαθίστημι not to refer to a restoration to a primitive state as did Origen but rather with the sense of fulfillment or realization, comparable to the connotation of "χρόνων ἀποκαταστάσεως πάντων" in Acts 3:21,[11] but the idea of restoration is not so easily excluded from the usages in this passage. Although Méhat correctly cautioned against appeal to passages in book 8 of the *Stromata* and the *Excerpta e Theodoto* in which Clement quoted, summarized, or responded to Valentinian texts and rightly noted instances in which ἀποκατάστασις cannot conceivably be translated "rétablissement,"[12] he failed to treat the use of ἀποκατάστασις/ἀποκαθίστημι in *Stromata* 7.10.56 and a significant number of other passages in which the meaning is more ambiguous.[13] In addition, he seems to have assumed wrongly that a concept of the restoration of an original state is necessarily connected to a doctrine of the preexistence of souls and accordingly concludes that the exclusion of "restoration" as Clement's intended meaning also excludes the possibility that Clement had a Platonic position on the origin of the soul.[14] Despite these reservations about Méhat's conclusions,[15] one must be careful not to read into Clement's language the conceptual accretions found in its later use by Origen, subsequent Origenists, and anti-Origenist writers.[16]

B. The Nature and Duration of Punishment after Death

In *Quis dives salvetur*, Clement warned that the "penalty (τὸ ἐπιτίμιον)" for neglecting the needy friends of God through the misguided attempt to avoid giving to the undeserving is "fiery eternal punishment (κόλασις ἔμπυρος αἰώνιος)."[17] Although this expression by itself may certainly be understood as a reference to unending torment, Clement's treatment of punishment after death elsewhere demands a different interpretation of the nature of "κόλασις ἔμπυρος" and the duration of "αἰώνιος." "Punishments after death (Τάς . . . μετὰ θάνατον κολάσεις)" and "punishment[18] by fire (τὴν διὰ πυρὸς τιμωρίαν)," concepts in Greek philosophy which along with Tartarus Clement believed were derived from ancient Hebrew thought,[19] are "chastening tortures for corrective discipline (εἰς τὴν παίδευσιν σωφρονίζοντα . . . κολαστήρια)."[20] Punishment after death is thus primarily educational ("εἰς τὴν παίδευσιν") and redemptive[21] rather than retributive in nature and purpose.

This view of punishment is linked to the goodness of God: "necessary chastisements through the goodness of the great overseeing judge compel those who have become more hardened to repent, either through attending angels or through various preliminary judgments or through the final, complete judgment."[22] Numerous biblical texts suggested to Clement that "the aim of mercy and reproof is the salvation of the one being reproved."[23] Other passages treat pedagogical punishment as an expression of divine goodness, but these seem to refer to punishment in the present life rather than punishment after death.[24] Whether it occurred in the present life or in the life to come, to Clement divine punishment could never be retributive in motive, for that would be contrary to the character of God:

But as children are punished by their teacher or their father, so we are punished by Providence. Now God does not exact vengeance (for vengeance is retribution for evil), but rather he punishes for the good, both public and private, of those who are being punished.[25]

In addition to the educational theme, Clement emphasized two other motifs in his treatments of eschatological punishment: the medicinal nature of punishment and the accomplishment of punishment by the φρόνιμον πῦρ, the "wise" or "discerning fire." Medical imagery abounds in Clement's explanation of the nature and purpose of punishment as the "healing of the passions (ἴασις . . . τῶν παθῶν),"[26] which he compared to lancing, cauterizing, or amputation performed by a physician for the cure of a diseased part or limb[27] and the removal of diseased tissue by a surgeon's knife.[28] Related to the image of a physician who chooses different cures for the unique needs of each patient[29] is the portrayal of the fiery punishment that sanctifies human souls as "discerning (τὸ φρόνιμον)" rather than "all-devouring and unsophisticated (τὸ παμφάγον καὶ βάναυσον)."[30] Although the contexts in which Clement employed these images either relate such punishment to discipline in the present life or do not specify whether the punishment takes place before or after death, along with the educational motif they point to a consistency in the divine motive for punishment: God punishes not for retribution but rather for the redemption of the one undergoing punishment.

Clement's concept of the salvific purpose of punishment leads to the logical conclusion that the corrective tortures of hell must ultimately come to an end. The goodness of the God who created all things with the "salvation of the whole" in mind will eventually persuade all people to repent freely "through the complete, final judgment."[31]

II. *Apokatastasis* and Exegesis

A. The Use of Scripture in the Articulation of Apokatastasis

1. The Universal Restoration. In *str.* 7.2.12.1-5, the most commonly cited passage suggesting that all will ultimately be saved, Clement cited no biblical texts (apart from a possible echo of Eph 4:19 in 7.2.12.5, which will be treated below in conjunction with the use of Scripture in Clement's understanding of the nature and duration of punishment after death). He directly appealed to Scripture in support of a universal salvation, however, in his comments on 1 John 2:2 in the lost *Hypotyposes* partially preserved by Cassiodorus.[32] Because the Lord is the propitiator for the sins of the whole world ("*pro toto mundo*"), "therefore indeed he saves all (*proinde universos quidem salvat*)." The ultimately universal success of God's saving work is also foreseen in Phil 2:10: some of the "all" who are saved will be converted only through punishments, after which "every knee should bow." Clement interpreted "things in heaven" as angels, "things on earth" as people, and "things under the earth" as the souls of those who died before the first advent of Christ. Significantly, Clement's most explicit expression of his hope for a universal *apokatastasis* occurs in the context of direct commentary on a biblical text and incorporates yet another biblical text. Evidently 1 John 2:2 and Phil 2:10 are the first biblical texts in the documented history of Christian biblical exegesis to be interpreted as teaching universal salvation.

First John 2:2 and Phil 2:10 are the only passages of Scripture that Clement employed in direct support of the ultimate salvation of all rational creatures. Appeals to Scripture are more frequent in the development of two related ideas: the universality of God's offer of salvation and *apokatastasis* as the end result of the divinization of those who are saved.

(a) The Universality of the Offer of Salvation. In *prot.* 9.82.1-88.3, Clement employs an extensive montage of biblical quotations and allusions in order to convince his pagan readers that God intends to save them and invites all to respond to this offer of salvation. Clement could cite "countless Scriptures"[33] to that effect, the fulfillment of which is guaranteed by the promise of Matt 5:18 that "not even one letter-stroke will pass away without being accomplished."[34] A series of quotations illustrates the divine voice that calls all to repent and accept the salvation God offers.[35] As evidence for the assertion that "nothing other than this is his only work—to save humanity,"[36] Clement referred to other texts that suggested that God offers salvation to all people. Jesus himself extended this offer by declaring that "the kingdom of heaven is near" (Matt 4:17), as did Paul in writing "the Lord is near . . . take care that you are not caught empty-handed."[37] Three quotations in sequence from Psalm 33 (LXX) express the invitation God gives to all people: "Taste and see that God is good"; "Come, O children, . . . listen to me, I will teach you the fear of the Lord"; "Who is the person who delights in life, who loves to see good days?"[38] Clement concluded this line of argumentation with echoes of biblical language which underscore the universality of the invitation and an allusion to John 1:9: "Then listen,

'you who are far off'; listen, 'you who are near': the word has not been hidden from anyone; light is common, it shines upon all people."[39]

Nothing in this biblical argument, which Clement developed in terms of an essentially literal understanding of the quotations and allusions, offers direct support for the idea that all rational creatures will ultimately be saved. Clement used these texts to establish the universality of God's offer of salvation; one must look elsewhere in Clement for a biblical rationale for the eventual universal acceptance of this offer.

(b) Apokatastasis as the Outcome of Divinization. In *str.* 7.10.56.1-57.1, Clement made use of biblical expressions in describing the "restoration to everlasting contemplation (τῇ θεωρίᾳ τῇ ἀϊδίῳ ἀποκατά-στασις)" that awaits believers at the end of their ascent to God. En route to this restoration, believers will surpass "the righteousness which is according to the law," an echo of the language and concepts of Matt 5:20 and Rom 10:5.[40] They will arrive at "the end which is endless and perfect" only after undergoing corrective, salvific punishment, which in the words of Heb 12:7 "for discipline we endure."[41] Those who have been thus corrected have become "pure in heart" (Matt 5:8), will see God "face to face" (1 Cor 13:12), and will be "with the Lord" (1 Thess 4:17).[42]

Is the "restoration to everlasting contemplation" an allusion to Acts 3:21? The apparatuses of Stählin and Hort and Mayor did not list it as such, and the compilers of the first volume of *Biblia Patristica* did not find a reference to Acts 3:21 in this passage of the *Stromata*.[43] There are no verbal parallels apart from the presence of the word ἀπο-κατάστασις,[44] and as Hort and Mayor suggested, its usage here reflects a Stoic rather than biblical background.[45]

As in the case of the texts Clement used to establish the universality of God's offer of salvation, none of the passages quoted or alluded to in the description of the state of those who attain to the final restoration was employed in an argument for the final restoration of all people. One could argue that the quotation of Heb 12:7 in a reference to punishment that is corrective and salvific in nature should be interpreted as applicable to all people in light of Clement's general understanding of punishment as consistently redemptive. In context, however, it is "anyone" who "clings to the Lord through faith and through knowledge and through love,"[46] presumably in his or her earthly existence, who must undergo the discipline referenced by Heb 12:7 before experiencing the restored state. Although this does not preclude the possibility that

Clement believed others who did not "cling to the Lord" during their earthly existence would be restored through redemptive punishment after death, neither this passage nor the biblical texts embedded therein advance such a position.

2. The Nature and Duration of Punishment after Death. Five aspects of Clement's understanding of eschatological punishment need to be probed for a relationship to biblical texts: (a) the conclusion that punishment after death is redemptive in nature and limited in duration; (b) the portrayal of punishment as pedagogical; (c) the portrayal of punishment as medicinal; (d) the portrayal of punishment as discerning; and (e) redemptive punishment as consistent with the character of God.

(a) Punishment as Redemptive and Limited. In *str.* 7.2.12.5, Clement expressed his belief that hardened sinners who are not brought to repentance "through various preliminary judgments" will ultimately be compelled to repent "through the final, complete judgment," so that punishment is redemptive in nature and limited in its duration. Editors of book 7 of the *Stromata* have found in the reference to "those who have become more hardened (τοὺς ἐπὶ πλέον ἀπηλγηκότας)" an allusion to Eph 4:19: "they [the Gentiles] have become hardened (οἵτινες ἀπηλγηκότες) . . . ."[47] Although the verbal parallel could be attributed to coincidence in lexical choice rather than intentional allusion, the probability that Clement consciously alluded to Eph 4:19 is strengthened by four factors. First, the substantive participles from ἀπαλγέω are identical in tense, voice, gender, and number and differ only in case. Second, ἀπαλγέω in any tense appears nowhere in the LXX and in Eph 4:19 is a New Testament *hapax legomenon*.[48] Third, apart from Eph 4:19, ἀπαλγέω in any tense occurs only fourteen times in Greek literature from the eighth century B.C.E. to Clement, and apart from one instance in Philo it appears exclusively in secular literature.[49] Fourth, of Clement's other three uses of ἀπαλγέω, one occurrence is in a verbatim quotation of Eph 4:19,[50] and another is a probable allusion to that text.[51] Only one other second-century ecclesiastical writer employed ἀπαλγέω: in the Greek remains of Origen's corpus there are six instances of ἀπαλγέω, four of which appear in verbatim quotations of Eph 4:19.[52] It is therefore highly probable that Clement incorporated an allusion to Eph 4:19 into his argument for the ultimately redemptive achievement of punishment after death.

What role did Eph 4:19 play in this argument? In the context of Eph 4:17-24, the "ἀπηλγηκότες" of v. 19 are contrasted with those who have committed themselves to Christ. It is possible that Clement indirectly referenced the language of Eph 4:19 in a subtle expression of a hope that even those who do not become Christians during their earthly existence will be brought to repentance after death "through the final, complete judgment."

Clement also expressed this as a biblical hope in describing the Christian Gnostic as one who "pities those who are disciplined after death and through punishment confess involuntarily."[53] This appears to be a previously unrecognized allusion to Phil 2:10-11. Although neither *Biblia Patristica* nor the apparatuses of the critical editions nor the footnotes of the translations note an allusion to Phil 2:10-11 in this passage,[54] there is nonetheless a verbal and conceptual intertextuality present. In Philippians, "every tongue will confess (ἐξομολογήσηται)," including "those under the earth (καταχθονίων)"; in the *Stromata*, there are some who after death will "confess unwillingly (ἀκουσίως ἐξο-μολογουμένους)." Clement has implicitly interpreted καταχθονίων as a reference to those dead who must undergo purgative punishment before they too can confess, "Jesus Christ is Lord."[55]

(b) Pedagogical Punishment. Clement's understanding of the pedagogical nature of punishment is rooted in his image of Christ as *Pedagogue*, a theme that not only provided the title for the second volume in his trilogy[56] but also appeared elsewhere in his writings. Clement found this idea explicitly stated in Hos 5:2: "Indeed the Word says of himself most clearly through Hosea, 'I am your Teacher.'"[57] Clement could also adduce biblical texts that portrayed punishment as an instrument of divine pedagogy, several of which appear in an extended passage in book 1 of the *Paedagogus*. According to Scripture, "lashes and correction are always of wisdom" (Sir 22:6).[58] Jesus' teaching about the pruning of the branches (John 15:1-8) shows "allegorically" his "manifold and most beneficial healing."[59] Moses had said, "Be of good courage, for God has come near to test you, so that his fear might be in you, that you might not sin" (Exod 20:20).[60] The fear of God instilled by the prospect of punishment was for Clement an important aspect of its pedagogical function according to the Scriptures: "Indeed fear itself is beneficial and is found to be for the good of people, for 'the spirit fearing the Lord will live; for the hope is in the one who saves them'" (Sir 34:13).[61] Through Moses God gave words of warning about impending punishment (Deut 32:23-25), showing that God threatens punishment not out of anger but rather "evokes fear that we might not sin."[62] As "the Scripture" teaches, "the fear of the Lord

drives away sins, but the one who is without fear cannot be justified" (Sir 1:21-22).[63]

An implicit biblical argument for the pedagogical nature of punishment is found in *str.* 5.1.9.4, in which Clement approvingly noted Heraclitus's (alleged) derivation of the concept of "the purification by fire of those who have lived evil lives" from the "Barbarian philosophy," that is, from Hebrew thought as contained in the Hebrew Scriptures.[64] Elsewhere there are more explicit references to biblical texts in passages dealing with pedagogical punishment, but these do not function as direct exegetical arguments for it. In *str.* 5.14.90.4-91.2, Clement alleged that Plato also depended on the Hebrew concept of *Gehenna* in his portrayal of Tartarus as a place of "chastening tortures for corrective discipline (εἰς τὴν παίδευσιν σωφρονίζοντα . . . κο-λαστήρια)"[65] and found in his description in *Respublica* 10 of the "fiery men" who execute such punishment a connection with Ps 103:4 (LXX): "who makes his angels spirits and his ministers flaming fire."[66] A more incidental use of Scripture appears in *str.* 7.16.102.3, where Clement paraphrased Ps 57:5-6 (LXX) with reference to heretics who stand in need of divine discipline, who like "deaf serpents . . . do not give ear to the song."[67]

(c) Medicinal Punishment. It has been suggested that Clement's use of medical imagery in depicting punishment as redemptive was derived from Plato, either directly or via Philo.[68] Clement employed such imagery with reference to divine punishment in *paed.* 1.1.1.4, 1.1.3.1, 1.8.64.4, and *exc. Thdot.* 45.1 without quoting or alluding to a single biblical text. In *paed.* 1.9.83.2-3, however, he clearly made use of Luke 5:31 in developing this idea:

> Now as those who are healthy do not need a physician, because they are strong, but those who are sick are in need of his skill, so also we, who are sick in life as regards shameful lusts and blameworthy failures in self-control and inflamations caused by other passions, need the Savior. He dispenses not only soothing medicines, but also astringent ones; for instance, the bitter roots[69] of fear halt the spread of sins. Fear, therefore, though bitter, is also salutary. It is then reasonable that we who are sick need a Savior . . . .[70]

Here Clement has conjoined the Platonic/Philonic concept of punishment as painful cure administered by a skilled physician with the biblical image of Jesus as physician of the soul. It is likely that this image underlies the other texts in which Clement portrayed punishment as medicinal, for by implication it is God or Christ who administers the salutary punishment. The Christological reformulation of Platonic/Philonic medical imagery in light of Luke 5:31 is clearly present in *prot.* 1.8.2-3, in which the "ἰατρὸς ἀγαθὸς" who chooses the painful remedy appropriate to the disease of each patient is "ὁ σωτὴρ."[71]

(d) Discerning Punishment. Scripture plays some role in all three passages in which Clement used the expression φρόνιμον πῦρ with reference to the agent of divine punishment. In *paed.* 3.8.44, the punishment of the Sodomites in Genesis 19 functions as a salvific paradigm in that it warns people to avoid the sin that led to so terrible a punishment. Clement interpreted the "πῦρ" by which the Sodomites were said to be punished in Gen 19:24 as "ὀλίγον τι τοῦ φρονίμου πυρός."[72] Although not an explicit reference to punishment, *str.* 7.6.34.4 interprets the fire by which the sacrifices required by the Mosaic law were consumed in a non-literal manner consistent with the category of σημεῖον in Clement's list of the multiple ways in which the multiple genres of the Law may be understood:[73] the fire does not sanctify the flesh of the sacrificial animals, but the souls of sinners. Clement further interpreted the true significance of the sacrificial fire via echoes of other biblical texts: it is a "φρόνιμον πῦρ," in the opinion of Hort and Mayor an allusion to 1 Cor 3:13;[74] it "pierces through the soul," a close verbal echo of Heb 4:12;[75] this soul "walks through the fire," a slightly adapted quotation from Isa 43:2.[76] The latter intertextual relationship implicitly defines the nature of the φρόνιμον πῦρ in terms of the unquoted remainder of Isa 43:2: those who walk through the fire will be neither burned nor consumed. In *ecl.* 25.1-4, the image of the φρόνιμον πῦρ interprets the words of John the Baptizer about the "baptism by fire" by which Jesus will burn the chaff without burning the wheat (Matt 3:11-12; Luke 3:16-17). According to Clement, this understanding of punishment by a "discerning fire" is found "among the prophets."[77] Since the expression is nowhere to be found in the Old Testament, K. Reinhardt proposed that Clement referred instead to Heraclitus, whom Clement elsewhere designated a "prophet," and W. C. van Unnik suggested that through a "slip of memory" Clement simply mistook philosophical language for biblical phraseology.[78] A better explanation is that Clement understood the overall message of the Old Testament prophets concerning the nature of divine punishment in terms of punishment which discerns that which is evil and that which is good, destroying the former while preserving the latter.

(e) Punishment and the Character of God. There are no biblical quotations or allusions in five of the passages in which Clement viewed the redemptive nature of punishment as a corollary of the goodness of God.[79] In response to objections to the goodness of God on account of God's execution of punishment, Clement did appeal to a number of biblical texts that suggested punishment as an expression of God's goodness. In *paed.* 1.8.62.3-63.1, Clement utilized Wis 11:23-12:2 in arguing that God is not only good and loving but punishes precisely because God is good and loving:

> "There is nothing which the Lord hates." For surely he does not hate something yet wish what he hates to exist, nor does he wish something not to exist yet become the cause for the existence of what he does not wish to exist, nor does he wish what exists not to exist. If then the Word hates something, he does not wish it to exist; but there is nothing for which God does not provide the cause of its existence. Nothing then is hated either by God or by the Word. . . . But if he does not hate any of the things he has made, it follows that he loves them. It is then reasonable that he will love humanity much more than the others, as humanity is the noblest of the things created by him and is the living thing that loves God. Therefore God loves humanity; therefore the Word loves humanity.[80]

Although Stählin and *Biblia Patristica* rightly identified the first sentence, "there is nothing which the Lord hates," as an allusion to Wis 11:24, they failed to note the conceptual background provided by its surrounding context in Wis 11:23-12:2 not only for the argument in *paed.* 1.8.62.3-63.1 but also for the whole subsequent argument for punishment as an expression of God's love and goodness:

> But you show mercy to all, for you are able to do all things, and you overlook people's sins that they may repent. For you love all things that exist and have loathing for none of the things you have made; for after making something you would not hate it. How would anything have continued to exist, if you had not willed it, or how would that which is not called forth by you be preserved? You spare all things, because they are yours, O Lord, lover of souls; for your immortal spirit is in all things. Therefore you reprove little by little those who trespass and warn them, reminding them of the things in which they sin, that being delivered from evil they may believe in you, O Lord.[81]

It seems clear that Clement drew consciously from Wis 11:24b-25 in the development of the argument in *paed.* 1.8.62-63. Although he never cited or alluded to Wis 12:2 in the remainder of this section of the *Pae-dagogus* that concludes in 1.8.74.4, the consistency of Wis 12:2 with Clement's argument, coupled with the use of preceding verses in Wisdom 11 at the beginning of the argument, suggests the possibility that Wis 12:2 has influenced Clement's understanding of the connection between divine punishment and the character of God.

Later in the section Clement set forth a more explicit biblical argument for the goodness of the God who punishes with a series of references to the Gospels, Sirach, and Paul's letter to the Romans. Clement affirmed divine punishment as inflicted for the good of those who are punished, but he could not agree that God "wishes to exact vengeance" because of Paul's teaching in Rom 12:17 and Jesus' teaching in Luke 6:28: "Vengeance is a returning of evil sent forth in the interest of the one exacting vengeance, but the one who teaches us to pray for those who mistreat us would never desire to exact vengeance."[82] Sir 16:11-12 shows that God intends both mercy and punishment for salvation:

> In this connection Wisdom also explicitly says, "Mercy and wrath are with him"; for he alone is Lord of both. "He is Lord of propitiations and of pouring out wrath. As extensive as is his mercy, so also is his reproof"; for the goal of mercy and reproof is the salvation of the one who is reproved.[83]

Clement appealed to a pastiche of quotations from Jesus, the divine *logos* himself, for evidence of God's goodness: "He is kind to those who are ungrateful and evil" (Luke 6:35); "Be merciful, just as your Father is merciful" (Luke 6:36); "No one is good except my Father in heaven" (Mark 10:18/Luke 18:19); "My Father makes his sun to shine upon all" and "My Father sends rain upon the just and the unjust" (Matt 5:45).[84] Finally, Paul's juxtaposition of the divine virtues of justice and goodness in Rom 7:12 meant for Clement that in Rom 3:21, 22, 26 God is good in the exercise of justice:

> Therefore Paul also says, "But now apart from the Law the justice of God has been manifested," and again, that you may understand God more and more, "the righteousness of God through faith in Jesus Christ, unto all who believe; for there is no distinction," and after a few lines he adds, bearing witness to the truth, "in the forbearance of God, for the demonstration that he is just and the justifier of the one who has faith in Jesus." And that he knows that justice is good comes to light where he says, "so that the Law is

holy, and the commandment holy and just and good," assigning to both words the same force.[85]

B. Apokatastasis and the Interpretation of Other Selected Biblical Texts

1. Universalistic Texts. Of the biblical texts with universalistic language or overtones, Clement neither cited nor alluded to John 12:32, Rom 5:18-21, Col 1:20, or 2 Pet 3:9. The following texts are referenced at least once by Clement and provide some indication of the relationship between his eschatology and his reading of the biblical text.

(a) Acts 3:21. *Biblia Patristica* lists a reference to Acts 3:21 in *exc. Thdot.* 22.3,[86] but this seems to be material Clement has quoted from Theodotus or an unnamed Valentinian source.[87] The only point of contact with Acts 3:21 is the presence of "ἀποκατασταθέντες," but this is a participle from ἀποκαθίστημι rather than a form of the noun ἀποκατάστασις. In any case, the mere presence of the word is a dubious criterion for establishing an allusion to Acts 3:21.[88]

(b) Romans 11:25-26a. The compilers of *Biblia Patristica* listed two references to Rom 11:25-26 in Clement's works.[89] Both references, however, appear in a portion of the *Excerpta ad Theodoto* attributed to Theodotus rather than Clement.[90] It is therefore apparent that Jerome did not have Clement in mind in his reference to those who appealed to this text as support for an end to the torments of hell.[91]

(c) Romans 11:32. Clement alluded to Rom 11:32 once, in *str.* 7.2.11.2. Although "συνέκλεισεν τὴν ἀπιστίαν" echoes "συνέκλεισεν γὰρ ὁ θεὸς τοὺς πάντας εἰς ἀπείθειαν," Clement did not make use of the remainder of the verse, "ἵνα τοὺς πάντας ἐλεήσῃ (that he might have mercy on all)," which could conceivably have supported an argument for the ultimate restoration of all people.

(d) 1 Corinthians 3:12-15. Clement referred to 1 Cor 3:12-15 in two passages. In *str.* 5.4.26.3-5, he incorporated language from vv. 12 and 13 into a polemic against the heretical Gnostics, whose teachings are the "stubble and wood and hay" which will be tried by fire. *Str.* 6.17.152.1 includes a reference only to the "gold, silver, precious stones" which are to be built on the foundation of Christ (v. 12a). Stählin, Henri Crouzel, and *Biblia Patristica* suggested an allusion to 1 Cor 3:13 in *q.d.s.* 25.6, but the reference to a "burning . . . which works trial (πύρωσις ἡ . . . δοκιμασίαν κατεργάζεται)" is probably a conceptual

parallel rather than an intentional allusion.[92] In addition to these two passages, Hort and Mayor identified "τὸ φρόνιμον . . . τὸ πῦρ" in *str.* 7.6.34 as an allusion to 1 Cor 3:13, but this seems to be a conceptual similarity rather than an intentional intertextual relationship.[93] In none of these cases did Clement use the text in support of his remedial understanding of the nature of punishment.[94]

(e) 1 Corinthians 15:22-28. In *str.* 1.24.159.6, Clement prefaced a quotation of Phil 2:10-11 with a reference to the subjection of all things to the authority of Christ ("πάντα γὰρ παρέδωκεν ὁ θεὸς καὶ πάντα ὑπέταξεν Χριστῷ τῷ βασιλεῖ ἡμῶν"), echoing the language of 1 Cor 15:28 ("ὅταν δὲ ὑποταγῇ αὐτῷ τὰ πάντα"). It is improbable that Clement intended this allusion to suggest an eschatological universalism, since the preceding sentence, to which the allusion is connected logically with an inferential "γὰρ," limits "πάντα" to "those who have faith in him and through him."[95]

(f) 2 Corinthians 5:19. A brief verbal echo of a phrase from 2 Cor 5:19 appears in *q.d.s.* 39.5 ("μὴ λογίσασθαι παραπτώματα"; cf. 2 Cor 5:19, "μὴ λογιζόμενος αὐτοῖς τὰ παραπτώματα αὐτῶν"), but without any reference to the first part of the verse, "God was in Christ reconciling the world to himself."

(g) Ephesians 1:10. *Paed.* 2.2.29.1 contains a reference to the "συμπλήρωσιν τοῦ χρόνου," possibly an allusion to "τοῦ πληρώματος τῶν καιρῶν" in Eph 1:10, but there is no reference to the remainder of the verse: "to sum up all things in Christ, things in heaven and things on earth."

(h) Philippians 2:9-11. Clement made use of some portion of Phil 2:9-11 in five passages, not counting a reference in material quoted from unnamed Valentinian sources in *exc. Thdot.* 43.4. Apart from the use of Phil 2:10 in the *Hypotyposes* in direct support of eschatological universalism, the remaining four references play no role in a biblical rationale for a universal *apokatastasis*. *Paed.* 2.8.74.1 refers only to "τῷ ὑπὲρ πᾶν ὄνομα ἐπηρμένῳ" (cf. Phil 2:9). *Str.* 1.24.159.6 combines an allusion to 1 Cor 15:28 with a quotation from Phil 2:10-11, but the limitation of the extent of "πᾶν" and "πᾶσα" by "τοὺς εἰς αὐτὸν καὶ δι' αὐτοῦ πιστεύοντας" in *str.* 1.24.159.5 suggests that Clement did not use Phil 2:10-11 in support of a concept of universal restoration in this passage. In *str.* 5.6.34.7, "ὑπὲρ πᾶν ὄνομα ἐξαναχωρῶν" merely

echoes Phil 2:9, as does "ὄνομα ὑπεράνω πάσης ἀρχῆς καὶ ἐξουσίας" in *str.* 5.6.38.6.[96]

(i) 1 Timothy 2:4. Clement quoted a phrase from 1 Tim 2:4 in a series of quotations which highlighted the universality of the divine offer of salvation, but without any suggestion that all would in fact accept the offer and come "to the knowledge of the truth."[97]

(j) Titus 2:11. Clement quoted Titus 2:11-13 in the opening chapter of the *Protrepticus* as an expression of the invitation God extends to Clement's pagan readers, but there is no suggestion of an eventual universal acceptance of that invitation.[98]

(k) 1 John 2:2. In addition to the explicitly universalistic interpretation of 1 John 2:2 in connection with Phil 2:10 in the *Hypotyposes*,[99] Clement quoted 1 John 2:2-6 in *paed.* 3.12.98.2 as evidence of the good purposes of Christ the Teacher for his pupils. There is no implication here that Christ's propitiation for the sins of "the whole world" was efficacious for all rational creatures as in the *Hypotyposes*.

2. Texts Suggesting Eternal Punishment. Clement did not refer to Rev 21:8 anywhere in his extant writings, but he does interact with other texts that have traditionally supported the understanding of punishment as eternal torment of the wicked.

(a) Matthew 5:29-30. In *paed.* 3.11.70.1, Clement dealt only with the exhortation to pluck out the offending member without reference to the warning about being cast "εἰς γέενναν." After quoting Matt 5:29a in *q.d.s.* 24.2, he alluded to "γέενναν" in v. 29b with a contrast between "βασιλεία θεοῦ" and "τὸ πῦρ," the latter of which may be avoided in the life to come if the offending member is destroyed in this life. Clement did not elaborate on the nature or duration of this eschatological fire.

(b) Matthew 8:12. Clement viewed the prospect of the "outer darkness" of Matt 8:12 as a means by which "the Lord calls humanity to salvation"[100] in *paed.* 1.9.91.1, but here the salvific value of eschatological punishment lies in its ability to warn one away from sin during one's earthly life rather than in cleansing one from sin after death. *Str.* 3.18.109.2 cites Matt 8:12 with reference to the destiny of the sexually licentious, but without further comment.

(c) Matthew 10:28/Luke 12:5. Clement quoted or alluded to Matt 10:28 and/or the parallel text in Luke 12:5 on four (or possibly five) occasions, but these passages shed no light on Clement's understanding of the nature of "ἀπολέσαι ἐν γεέννῃ" (Matt 10:28) or "ἐμβαλεῖν εἰς τὴν γέενναν" (Luke 12:5). Portions of Matt 10:28 and Luke 12:5 appear in *ecl.* 26.1 and 26.4, but these passages lack any reference to γέενναν/γεέννῃ. In *exc. Thdot.* 14.3 and 51.3 Clement cited Matt 10:28 as evidence for his concept of the corporeality of the soul but offered no explanation of the phrases in question. Although Stählin and *Biblia Patristica* noted *str.* 2.2.4.3 as an allusion to Matt 10:28, the verbal parallels actually appear in a citation of Prov 3:7.[101]

(d) Matthew 18:8-9/Mark 9:42-48. Of the four references to Matt 18:8-9 and Mark 9:42-48 attributed to Clement in *Biblia Patristica*, two (*paed.* 3.11.70.1 and *q.d.s.* 24.2) are better identified as references to Matt 5:29.[102] *Str.* 3.18.107.2 quotes from Matt 18:6-7/Mark 9:42 without mention of the references to eternal fire and Gehenna in Matt 18:8-9 and Mark 9:43, 47-48. Although *paed.* 3.12.83.4 mentions actions that ultimately lead "εἰς πῦρ," the parallel to "εἰς τὸ πῦρ τὸ αἰώνιον" in Matt 18:8 is probably coincidental rather than intentional, and Clement does not elaborate here on the nature of this "fire."

(e) Matthew 25:31-46. In five passages Clement quoted or alluded to Matt 25:33 with reference to those who will be invited to join Christ at his right hand, but with no commentary on the significance of the division of the sheep from the goats.[103] *Q.d.s.* 30.1-6 quotes Matt 25:34-40 and 41-45 in explanation of the relationship between love of God and love of neighbor in the love commands of Matt 22:34-40 and parallels but makes no reference to eschatological reward or punishment. In *paed.* 3.12.93.4-5 Clement cited Matt 25:34-40 and alluded to v. 46 with reference to those who will enjoy eternal life but made no mention of an alternative eternal destiny. Other passages make ethical[104] or theological[105] applications of the text without addressing the nature of the "eternal fire" and "eternal punishment" in vv. 41 and 46. On three occasions, however, Clement did interact with those verses. In *prot.* 9.83.2, Clement's pagan audience is graciously invited to salvation but prefers instead the fate of v. 41. Clement alluded to vv. 35-46 in *q.d.s.* 13.4-6, mentioning the obligation of the rich to give food, drink, clothing, and shelter to those who need these things and the penalty for failing to do this as "fire" and "the outer darkness."[106] Similarly, in *q.d.s.*

33.3 the penalty for neglecting people whom God loves is the "punishment of eternal fire (κόλασις ἔμπυρος αἰώνιος)," an allusion to v. 46. Although these passages attest to Clement's belief in eschatological punishment, they neither define the nature of that punishment nor address the question of the duration of αἰώνιος.

(f) Luke 16:19-31. Clement mentioned the parable of Lazarus and the rich man four times. Two of these references have little relevance for the nature of eschatological punishment: in *str.* 4.6.30.4, the parable demonstrates the "image (εἰκόνα)" of rich and poor, and in *exc. Thdot.* 14.4 the fact that the characters in the parable have "bodily members (τῶν σωματικῶν μελῶν)" provides proof of the corporeal nature of the soul. Two passages in the *Paedagogus* have somewhat more relevance for the question under investigation. After introducing Lazarus and the rich man by quoting vv. 19-20, Clement contrasted the reward of Lazarus with the fate of the rich man, who "was punished in Hades, partaking of fire."[107] Clement did not specify the duration or purpose of this punishment.[108] The other passage existentializes the consequences suffered by the rich man: an unjust and arrogant rich man like the one who despised Lazarus "is miserable and lives wretchedly and will not live."[109] "[Z]ήσεται" probably does not refer to the cessation of existence, as Clement nowhere hints at belief in conditional immortality or the annihilation of the wicked, but rather to the failure truly to live.[110] Clement's interpretation of Luke 16:19-31 does not explicitly reflect his concept of punishment after death as redemptive in nature and limited in duration, but neither does it preclude such an understanding.

(g) 2 Thessalonians 1:7-9. *Biblia Patristica* does not identify a reference to any portion of 2 Thess 1:7-9 in the works of Clement.[111] It is nevertheless possible that the image of angels who accompany the Lord Jesus in executing vengeance "in flaming fire" provided part of the conceptual background for Clement's linking of Plato's concept of corrective punishment and the "fiery men" who execute such punishment in *Respublica* 10 with the angels of Ps 103:4 (LXX) in *str.* 5.14.90.6.

(h) Revelation 20:14-15. Stählin and *Biblia Patristica* suggested an allusion to Rev 20:14-15 in *str.* 3.18.109.2,[112] probably on account of the verbal parallel between "γεγραμμένος" in Rev 20:15 and "ἐγγράφους" in *str.* 3.18.109.2 and the conceptual similarity at the point of the exclusion of the wicked from the kingdom. The tenuousness of this

connection probably excludes a conscious allusion, and in any case Clement offered no interpretation of this text.

III. Conclusions

The concept of a universal restoration of all rational creatures accomplished through eschatological punishment that is redemptive in nature and limited in duration is rarely articulated explicitly in Clement, and only once is it directly substantiated with biblical texts (1 John 2:2 and Phil 2:10). Although the paucity of appeals to the biblical materials might suggest a source other than Scripture (such as Middle Platonic philosophical presuppositions) as the primary motivation for Clement's thought in this area,[113] three considerations qualify such a conclusion. First, the concept of a universal *apokatastasis* and its corollary of remedial punishment do not appear to have been clearly formulated doctrines in the theology of Clement in comparison with their expression in the thought of Origen, Gregory of Nyssa, and later Origenists. The passages which hint at eschatological universalism (some of which do so more strongly than others) are too few and too brief to allow conclusive determination of the relative roles of Scripture and other sources of religious authority in Clement's formulation of these concepts. Second, of the two clearest statements of Clement's belief in the eventual salvation of all people and remedial punishment as an instrument by which this is accomplished, one not only makes use of Scripture but also sets forth these ideas as the meaning of the biblical text. Clement therefore found his concept of *apokatastasis* in the Scriptures. Whether he moved from the Scriptures to the concept or from the concept to the Scriptures cannot easily be ascertained. Third, although Clement cited only two texts that could be classified as prooftexts for universal salvation and remedial punishment, he utilized Scripture more extensively in connection with auxiliary ideas and motifs. The relationship between biblical exegesis and concepts consistent with *apokatastasis* in Clement's thought suggests that Clement himself may have related *apokatastasis* to Scripture more comprehensively than a narrow focus on unambiguous expressions of the concept might indicate.

Clement's use of Scripture in his rationale for a universal salvation falls into three categories. First, there are texts that Clement directly related to the concept of *apokatastasis*. Clement offered only 1 John 2:2 and Phil 2:10 in direct support of the idea of a universal restoration, and no texts in direct support of punishment conceived as redemptive in nature and limited in duration. Second, there are texts that Clement used in connection with concepts that are auxiliary to universal restoration and remedial punishment. This category includes texts which Clement linked with the universality of God's offer of salvation (Deut 9:19; Pss 33:9, 12-13; 109:3[LXX]; Matt 3:3, 17; 4:17; 18:3; 25:41; Luke 2:49; John 3:5; 15:26; Rom 8:29; Eph 4:17-19; 5:14; Phil 4:5; Col 1:15, 18; 1 Tim 1:14; 2:4; 4:8, 10; 2 Tim 3:7, 13-17; Heb 1:6; 3:7-8, 10-11; 12:5, 21-23; 1 John 1:9), the results of restoration (Matt 5:8; 1 Cor 13:12; 1 Thess 4:17), the redemptive outcome of punishment (Phil 2:10-11; Eph 4:19, if its quotation is taken in context as an implicit expression of hope that the "hardened" who have rejected Christ during their earthly existence will ultimately be brought to repentance), the pedagogical nature of punishment (Exod 20:20; Deut 32:23-25; Ps 103:4 [LXX]; Hos 5:2; Sir 1:21-22; 22:6; 34:13; John 15:1-8), the depiction of punishment as medicinal (Luke 5:31), the accomplishment of punishment by a "discerning fire" (Gen 19; Isa 43:12; Matt 3:11-12; Luke 3:16-17; 1 Cor 3:13; Heb 4:12), and punishment as an expression of God's goodness (Sir 16:11-12; Wis 11:23-12:2; Matt 5:45; Mark 10:18; Luke 6:28, 36; 18:19; Rom 7:12; 12:17). Third, some texts cited in connection with these areas of Clement's thought have only an incidental relationship to them; these are utilized to express or illustrate some tangent in Clement's argument. Under this category may be classified Matt 5:18, Matt 5:20, and Rom 10:5, which appear in the course of Clement's case for the universality of God's invitation to humanity, and Ps 57:5-6 (LXX), which expresses the obstinacy of those who do not respond to this invitation.

Clement's concept of *apokatastasis* does not appear to have had a significant impact on his interpretation of the other texts selected as test cases. Although Clement did make direct use of 1 John 2:2 and Phil 2:10 in support of eschatological universalism, it is surprising that he did not similarly use a number of other texts which could conceivably receive a universalistic interpretation. Clement did not cite John 12:32, Acts 3:21, Rom 5:18-21, Col 1:20, or 2 Pet 3:9 at all. He failed to make use of universalistic portions of Rom 11:32, 2 Cor 5:19, or Eph 1:10, and he used 1 Cor 15:28, 1 Tim 2:4, and Titus 2:11-13 in such a way that the possibility of a universalistic interpretation of these texts is precluded or ignored. Clement's failure to appeal to such biblical texts in support of universal salvation when they could have strengthened his case suggests that he did not make a sustained argument for such a concept. On the other hand, while Clement did not interact with texts suggesting the traditional view of eternal punishment in such a way as to reveal his own understanding of the nature of punishment, his failure to interpret them explicitly as references to punishment understood as the unending torment of the damned is consistent with his view of punishment as remedial rather than retributive.

For an early Christian writer renowned as the first major practitioner of allegorical exegesis, Clement interpreted the texts under consideration in a surprisingly literal manner. His most explicit affirmation of eschatological universalism is tied to a rather literal interpretation of 1 John 2:2 and Phil 2:10: the Lord is the propitiator for the sins of "the whole world," with the result that "every knee should bow." Although an occasional passage exhibits some similarity to the non-literal levels of meaning in Scripture identified by Clement (e.g., his allegorical ["ἀλληγορῶν"] understanding of John 15:1-8 in *paed.* 1.8.66.4 and his non-literal understanding of the true significance of the ancient Hebrew sacrifices in *str.* 7.6.34.4), his appeals to Scripture in support of a universal *apokatastasis* reflects a basic fidelity to the literal senses (λέξις) of the biblical text.

Notes

[1]Daley, *Hope of the Early Church*, 47.

[2]Clem. *str.* 7.2.12.1-5.

[3]See W. E. G. Floyd, *Clement of Alexandria's Treatment of the Problem of Evil* (Oxford: Oxford University Press, 1971).

[4]But cf. Clem. *str.* 7.12.78.3, where those who are disciplined after death "confess involuntarily through punishment (διὰ τῆς κολάσεως ἀκουσίως ἐξομολογουμένους)."

[5]Cf. the emphases in this passage with the summary of Clement's concept of *apokatastasis* in John R. Sachs, "Apocatastasis in Patristic Theology," *TS* 54 (1993): 620: "In summary, then, there are four principles basic to Clement's approach: (1) the absolute supremacy and goodness of divine providence; (2) the fact that God's plan of salvation is not directed merely toward individuals but to the whole of humanity; (3) the power of God to persuade human freedom; and (4) the pedagogical, purifying nature of divine punishment."

[6]In the secondary literature, this passage is noted only by G. Anrich, "Clemens und Origenes als Begründer der Lehre vom Fegfeuer," in *Theologische Abhandlungen: Eine Festgabe für Heinrich Julius Holtzmann* (Tübingen and Leipzig: J. C. B. Mohr, 1902), 101, n. 1. Anrich's mention of the text had primary reference to Clement's role as precursor to the later doctrine of purgatory; treatments of Clement's eschatological universalism have cited *str.* 7.2.12.1-5 rather than the text from the *Hypotyposes* as the *locus classicus* for the concept.

[7]Clem. *hyp.* (fragment in Otto Stählin, ed., *Clemens Alexandrinus*, vol. 3, *Stromata Buch VII und VIII, Excerpta ex Theodoto, Eclogae Propheticae, Quis Dives Salvetur, Fragmente*, GCS, no. 17, pt. 2 [Leipzig: Hinrichs'sche Buchhandlung, 1909], 211).

[8]Clem. *prot.* 9.87.3: "For nothing other than this is his only work—to save humanity (οὐδὲν γὰρ ἀλλ' ἢ τοῦτο ἔργον μόνον ἐστὶν αὐτῷ σώζεσθαι τὸν ἄνθρωπον)."

[9]Ibid., 9.82.1-88.3 (passim).

[10]Clem. *str.* 7.10.56.1-57.2.

[11]Méhat, "'Apocatastase'," 203-10, 214: "Plutôt que l'idée de retour à un état primitif, il impliquait chez les écrivains ecclésiastiques, en *Act.* 3,21, chez Irénée probablement, chez Clément d'Alexandrie certainement, l'idée d'une libération, d'un réglement définitif ou d'une réalisation des prophéties. La langue usuelle ou même populaire, plus que l'astrologie ou la philosophie, en commandait l'usage. C'est Origène qui, le premier, du moins à l'intérieur de la grande Eglise et de la tradition alexandrine, l'a lié à la doctrine de la restauration à l'état primitif" (quoted material from p. 214).

[12]Ibid., 204-7.

[13]Cf. the eleven passages treated by Méhat with the references in Otto Stählin, *Clemens Alexandrinus*, vol. 4, *Register*, GCS, vol. 39 (Leipzig: Hinrichs'sche Buchhandlung, 1936), s.v. "ἀποκατάστασις" (16 occurrences); ibid., s.v. "ἀποκαθίστημι" (13 occurrences). A keyword search of Clement's corpus in TLG confirms the accuracy of Stählin's concordance for these two entries. See Ignacio Escriban-Alberca, "Zum zyklischen Zeitbegriff der alexandrinischen und kappadokischen Theologie," in *StudPat*, ed. F. L. Cross, vol. 11, pt. 2, TU, ed. O. von Gebhardt and A. von Harnack, no. 108 (Berlin: Akademie-Verlag, 1972), 45, who convincingly argued for the translation "Wiederherstellung" for at least one of these occurrences (Clement of Alexandria *ecl.* 56.6).

[14]Méhat maintained that his analysis of the passages in Clement "achevent d'écarter l'idée d'une préexistence des âmes chez Clément" (Méhat, "'Apocatastase,'" 207). Although it is true that first of the anathemas against Origen linked the Origenist concept of an ultimately universal *apokatastasis* to the preexistence of souls (*Canones xv contra Origenem* 1: "Εἴ τις τὴν μυθώδη προύπαρξιν τῶν ψυχῶν καὶ τὴν ταύτηι ἑπομένην τερατώδη ἀποκατάστασιν πρεσβύει, ἀνάθεμα ἔστω" [*ACO*, bk. 4, *Concilium Universale Constantinopolitanum sub Iustiniano Habitum*, ed. Johannes Straub, vol. 1 (Berolini: Walter de Gruyter, 1971), 248]), Gregory of Nyssa rejected Origen's protology while retaining a similar concept of the outcome of the *apokatastasis* (Gr. Nyss. *hom. opif.* 28.4; idem, *anim. et res.* [PG 46:113B1-D2, 125A1-C2]). Unfortunately Clement's intended work "περὶ ψυχῆς" (mentioned in *str.* 3.3.13.3 and 5.13.88.4), if in fact ever written, is no longer extant, but his discussions of the soul in his existing works do not suggest a belief in its preexistence.

[15]Cf. the reservations of Paolo Siniscalco, "'Ἀποκατάστασις e ἀποκαθίστημι nella tradizione della Grande Chiesa fino ad Ireneo," in Frank Leslie Cross, ed., *StudPat*, vol. 3, TU, vol. 78 (Berlin: Akademie-Verlag, 1961), 395,

who questioned whether the idea of a restoration to a primitive state can be so uniformly excluded from the pre-Origenian use of ἀποκατάστασις and ἀπο- καθίστημι, especially in the case of Irenaeus: "In realtà, come creadiamo di avere mostrato, non sempre l'idea di una restaurazione, di un ritorno ad uno stato primitivo è esclusa dai significati di ἀποκαθίστημι e di ἀποκατάστασις; al contrario essa è sovente espressa dai termini; mentre è vero, d'altronde, che in alcuni casi tale idea cede il passo ad altre, a quelle appunto di cui parla il Méhat."

[16]Cf. Sachs, "Apocatastasis in Patristic Theology," 619: "[Clement] uses the term in a variety of contexts but in general it seems to refer to the end or final perfection of a process of growth in the spiritual life, rather than in the narrower sense of a *universal* restoration that the term acquired especially after Origen."

[17]Clem. *q.d.s.* 33.3.

[18]Although τιμωρία has as its basic meaning retribution or vengeance (see LSJ, s.v. "τιμωρία, ή"), it can also refer to punishment in general (see *PGL*, s.v. "τιμωρία, ή," A.). To render it "penal retribution" in this instance (as did William Wilson in ANF 2:465) imparts to the word a meaning that Clement's concept of punishment will not sustain.

[19]Clement often employed βάρβαρος with reference to the Hebrew people, language, or thought vis-à-vis things Hellenistic. The dependence of Greek philosophy on Hebrew thought was a common (though mistaken) *topos* in second-century Christian literature; cf., e.g., Justin Martyr *Apologia* 59.

[20]Clem. *str.* 5.14.90.4-91.2; see also 5.1.9.4.

[21]Clem. *hyp.* (frg. in Stählin, *Clemens Alexandrinus*, 3:211): "Therefore he indeed saves all: but some, converting them through punishments (*Proinde universos quidem salvat, sed alios per supplicia convertens*)."

[22]Ibid., 7.2.12.5.

[23]Clem. *paed.* 1.8.72.1: "ἐλέους γὰρ καὶ ἐλέγχου σκοπὸς ἡ τῶν ἐλεγ- χομένων σωτηρία." Clement drew this conclusion from a number of biblical texts (which will be treated below) in an extensive response to "some who say that the Lord is not good on account of the rod and threats and fear (τινες οὐκ ἀγαθὸν εἶναι φάμενοι τὸν κύριον διὰ τὴν ῥάβδον καὶ τὴν ἀπειλὴν καὶ τὸν φόβον)" (ibid., 1.8.62.1-74.4; quoted material is from 1.8.62.1).

[24]*Contra* Daley, *Hope of the Early Church*, 46, and Sachs, "Apocatastasis in Patristic Theology," 618-19, who cite Clem. *str.* 1.27.173.5, 6.12.99.2, and 7.16.102.5 with reference to punishment after death. In each instance, however, the context demands that punishment be understood as the corrective discipline by which God steers the erring Christian toward perfection during his or her earthly existence. In another passage cited by Daley and Sachs (Clem. *str.* 4.24.154.1-2), it is unclear whether the purgation of post-baptismal sins occurs before death, after death, or both: "One must know, then, that those who fall into sin after baptism are those who are chastised; for the things which were done previously were forgiven, but the things which come after are purified" (ibid., 4.24.154.3). It should be noted that Sachs acknowledged dependence on

Daley for some of the references to texts in Clement (Sachs, "Apocatastasis in Patristic Theology," 618, n. 2).

[25]Clem. *str.* 7.16.102.5.

[26]Clem. *paed.* 1.1.3.1; cf. ibid., 1.1.1.4; 1.8.64.4; idem, *exc. Thdot.* 45.1.

[27]Clem. *prot.* 1.8.2.

[28]Clem. *paed.* 1.8.64.4. Hanson, *Allegory and Event,* 229-30, pointed out that Clement was preceded by Philo in this use of medical imagery and concluded that they both derived it from Plato. On the Platonic precedents for Clement's use of medical imagery, see Mondésert, *Clément d'Alexandrie,* 166, n. 3.

[29]Clem. *prot.* 1.8.2.

[30]Clem. *str.* 7.6.34.4; cf. idem, *paed.* 3.8.44.2; idem, *ecl.* 25.4. Clement's contrast of "φρόνιμον" and "βάναυσον" reflects the use of βάναυσος as an epithet for "the class of handicraftsmen or artisans" (LSJ, s.v. "βάναυσος, [α], ον"), hence the translation "unsophisticated" for "βάναυσον." W. C. van Unnik, "The 'Wise Fire' in a Gnostic Eschatological Vision," in *Kyriakon: Festschrift Johannes Quasten,* ed. Patrick Granfield and Josef A. Jungmann (Münster: Verlag Aschendorff, 1970), 277-88, examined the expression "wise fire" (and conceptual parallels) in the Gnostic *Pistis Sophia,* Clement of Alexandria, Origen, Minucius Felix, Tertullian, and Jerome. Van Unnik identified Stoic doctrine as the background for the expression and found that for Clement "the fire from heaven burns away the sins of Sodom (a); purifies the sinners in offering (b); distinguishes between good and evil, the former it saves, the latter it destroys (c); it heals from paganism by destruction (d); it works already on earth and has also its place in eschatology" (ibid., 285).

[31]Clem. *str.* 7.2.12.1-5.

[32]Clem. *hyp.* (frg. in Stählin, *Clemens Alexandrinus,* 3:211).

[33]"Countless" is a better rendering of μύριος in this context than Wilson's translation "ten thousand" in ANF 2:195.

[34]Clem. *prot.* 9.82.1; cf. Matt 5:18. The quotation is a paraphrase with close verbal parallels. On the characteristics of the New Testament text used by Clement, see Michael Mees, *Die Zitate aus dem Neuen Testament bei Clemens von Alexandrien,* QVC, no. 2 (Rome: Istituto di Letteratura Cristiana Antica, 1970), 217, who concluded that "Der Clemenstext ist der frühägyptischen Gruppe zuzuzählen."

[35]Clem. *prot.* 9.82.1-87.2, with citations of Heb 12:5, Heb 12:21, Matt 18:3, John 3:5, Matt 25:41, Eph 4:17-19, Eph 5:14, Ps 109:3 (LXX), Heb 3:7-8, Heb 3:11, 1 Tim 2:4, 1 Tim 4:8, 1 Tim 4:10, 2 Tim 3:14-15, and 2 Tim 3:16-17, and possible allusions to Deut 9:19, Luke 2:49, Matt 3:17 (or parallels), Heb 12:22-23, Rom 8:29, Col 1:15, 18, Heb 1:6, Heb 3:7, 13, John 1:9, 1 Tim 1:14, Heb 3:10-11, Matt 3:3 (or parallels), and John 15:26.

[36]Clem. *prot.* 9.87.3, which Clement linked to the following sentence with γοῦν. Although Wilson (ANF 2:196) translated γοῦν "therefore," according to J. D. Denniston, *The Greek Particles,* 2d ed. (Oxford: Clarendon Press, 1954), 451, "the commonest use of γοῦν is to introduce a statement which is, *pro tanto,* evidence for a preceding statement."

[37]Clem. *prot.* 9.87.4. The source of this quotation is elusive. As Theodor Zahn, *Geschichte des neutestamentlichen Kanons* (Erlangen: Andreas Deichert, 1888), 1:174, n. 1, observed, "Von einem apokryphen Paulusbrief an die Macedonier ist nichts bekannt." The apparatus of Stählin suggests Phil 4:5 plus an agraphon as the source of this citation, but the first part of the quotation, "ὁ κύριος ἤγγικεν," is not a verbatim quotation of Phil 4:5 ("ὁ κύριος ἐγγύς"). Zahn, *Geschichte des neutestamentlichen Kanons*, 1:174, n. 1, suggested that the quotation may be a conceptual composite drawn from Phil 4:5, 1 Thess 2:19, 3:13, and 5:23.

[38]Clem. *prot.* 9.87.4-88.1, quoting Ps 33:9, 12, 13 (LXX). A significant textual problem appears in the quotation from Ps 33:9 (LXX): Parisinus Graecus 451 (P) and the original hand of Mutinensis III D 7 (M*) have the *nomen sacrum* χ̄σ̄ where the second hand of Mutinensis III D 7 (M²) reads χρηστός. The edition of Potter reproduced in Migne (PG 8:200B3-4) adopted the reading of P and M*, printed "Χριστὸς" in the text, and punctuated the sentence before the quotation in such a manner that "γεύσασθε καὶ ἴδετε ὅτι Χριστὸς ὁ θεός" became a Pauline agraphon rather than a quotation from Ps 33:9 (LXX). Stählin adopted the reading of M² ("χρηστὸς") and placed a period after "δεδεμένῳ," making the quotation a separate sentence and implicitly a quotation of Ps 33:9 (LXX). Although the external evidence favors the reading "Χριστὸς," the internal evidence favors "χρηστὸς" as the original reading. The origin of the reading "Χριστὸς" may be explained by two factors. First, the transcriptional probability that a scribe misread "χρηστὸς" as "Χριστὸς" (or perhaps heard it wrongly due to a vocalic interchange of ι and η?), which later in the history of transmission became a *nomen sacrum*, would account for the origin of the latter reading. Second, intrinsic probabilities related to the context support the reading "χρηστὸς": (1) "τῷ κυρίῳ μήτε τῷ Παύλῳ, καὶ ταῦτα ὑπὲρ Χριστοῦ δεδεμένῳ" in all likelihood refers back to the preceding quotations from Jesus (Matt 4:17) and Paul (Phil 4:5 and agraphon or echo of other texts), and (2) "χρηστὸς" does in fact appear in Ps 33:9 (LXX), and the quotation in question is followed by quotations in sequence from Ps 33:12 and 13.

[39]Clem. *prot.* 9.88.2. The construction "οἱ μακράν . . . οἱ ἐγγύς" echoes language in Esth 9:20 (LXX), Dan 9:7 (Theodotian), and Isa 57:19 (LXX), but the most probable referent for this language is Eph 2:17, where Isa 57:19 is applied to the reconciling message Christ preached to both Jews and Gentiles; cf. John 1:9.

[40]Clem. *str.* 7.10.56.2; cf. Matt 5:20 and Rom 10:5.

[41]Clem. *str.* 7.10.56.3: "εἰς παιδείαν ὑπομένομεν." Cf. Heb 12:7: "εἰς παιδείαν ὑπομένετε." Although Stählin did not print this phrase as a quotation in the text and classified it as an allusion in the apparatus, the only difference from Heb 12:7 is the shift from the second person plural to the third person plural to accommodate Clement's customary mode of address in the *Stromata*.

[42]Clem. *str.* 7.10.56.5-57.1. The quotation of Matt 5:8 changes only the case and number of one word ("καθαροὶ" to "καθαρὸν"), and the phrases from 1 Cor 13:12 and 1 Thess 4:17 are verbatim quotations.

[43]Stählin, *Clemens Alexandrinus*, 3:41; Fenton John Anthony Hort and Joseph B. Mayor, *Clement of Alexandria Miscellanies Book VII: The Greek Text with Introduction, Translation, Notes, Dissertations and Indices* (London: Macmillan & Co., 1902), 101; *BibPatr* 1:418-19.

[44]Cf. Clem. *str.* 7.10.56.5, "προσμένει τῇ θεωρίᾳ τῇ ἀϊδίῳ ἀπο- κατάστασις," with Acts 3:21, "δέξασθαι ἄχρι χρόνων ἀποκαταστάσεως πάντων."

[45]Hort and Mayor, *Miscellanies Book VII*, 284.

[46]Clem. *str.* 7.10.56.1.

[47]Hort and Mayor, *Miscellanies Book VII*, 21; Stählin, *Clemens Alexandrinus*, 3:10. *BibPatr* 1:495 also listed Clem. *str.* 7.2.12.5 as an allusion to Eph 4:19.

[48]Kurt Aland, ed., *Vollständige Konkordanz zum griechischen Neuen Testament* (Berlin: Walter de Gruyter, 1983), 1:67.

[49]A search of TLG using the stems ἀπαλγ- and ἀπηλγ- and classified by century yielded the following results: eighth century B.C.E., 0; seventh century B.C.E., 0; sixth century B.C.E., 0; fifth century B.C.E., 1 (Thucydides); fourth century B.C.E., 1 (Theopompus); third century B.C.E., 4 (Polybius); second century B.C.E., 0; first century B.C.E., 2 (Philo, 1; Dionysius of Halicarnassus, 1); first century C.E., 3 (New Testament, 1; Plutarch, 1; Dio Chrysostom, 1); second century C.E. (to Clement of Alexandria), 8 (Aelius Aristides, 4; Clement of Alexandria, 4). The word appears in Philo with a meaning other than "to become devoid of feeling" or "to become hardened": in *De praemiis et poenis* 135.5, "ἀπαλγήσαντες" has the meaning "being despondent."

[50]Clem. *prot.* 9.83.3.7.

[51]Clem. *str.* 7.7.39.5. Hort and Mayor, *Miscellanies Book VII*, 69; Stählin, *Clemens Alexandrinus*, 3:30; and *BibPatr* 1:495 each identified here an allusion to Eph 4:19.

[52]Or. *Commentarii in Ephesios (frag.)* 18.18; ibid., 18.21; idem, *Homiliae in Ieremiam* 5.5.19; ibid., 20.9.18. See *BibPatr* 3:427.

[53]Clem. *str.* 7.12.78.3.

[54]*BibPatr* 1:500; Hort and Mayor, *Miscellanies Book VII*, 134-35; Stählin, *Clemens Alexandrinus*, 3:55; Wilson, "Stromata," ANF 2:545; Otto Stählin, *Des Clemens von Alexandreia ausgewählte Schriften*, vol. 5, BKV, 2d ser., vol. 20 (Munich: Kösel-Pustet, 1938), 81.

[55]Cf. Clem. *hyp.* (frg. in Stählin, *Clemens Alexandrinus*, 3:211), where Clement explicitly interpreted Phil 2:10 in this fashion.

[56]But see Carl Heussi, "Die Stromateis des Clemens Alexandrinus und ihr Verhältnis zum Protreptikos und Pädagogos," ZWT 45 (1902): 465-512; Johannes Munck, *Untersuchungen über Klemens von Alexandria*, FKGG, vol. 2 (Stuttgart: W. Kohlhammer, 1933), 9-38, 109-26; Friedrich Quatember, *Die christliche Lebenshaltung des Klemens von Alexandrien nach seinem Pädagogus* (Vienna: Herder, 1946); and Walter Wagner, "Another Look at the Literary Problem in Clement of Alexandria's Major Writings," CH 37, no. 3 (September 1968): 251-60, each of whom challenged the traditional view (based on Clem. *paed.* 1.3.3) that Clement planned the *Protrepticus, Paeda-*

gogus, and *Stromata* as a progressive trilogy, but with divergent counterproposals.

[57]Clem. *paed.* 1.7.53.3; cf. Hos 5:2 (LXX).

[58]Clem. *paed.* 1.8.66.3. Clement considered Sirach to be inspired Scripture, along with other books later classified as "deuterocanonical" (J. Ruwet, "Clément d'Alexandrie: Canon des Écritures et Apocryphes," *Bib* 29, nos. 1-2 [1948]: 93-4).

[59]Clem. *paed.* 1.8.66.4.

[60]Ibid., 1.8.66.5; cf. Exod 20:20 (LXX).

[61]Clem. *paed.* 1.8.67.2; cf. Sir 34:13.

[62]Clem. *paed.* 1.8.68.3. In a few passages dealing with eschatological punishment, it is the power of the fearful prospect of punishment to turn people from evil rather than its purifying effect that Clement emphasized as the salvific value of punishment: e.g., *paed.* 3.8.44.1-5, in which the punishment of the Sodomites in Genesis 19 continues to serve as an "example to people of prudent salvation (τῆς εὐλογίστου τοῖς ἀνθρώποις σωτηρίας εἰκών)" and illustrates the divine rationale for all punishment, including punishment after death: "It is for this reason that there are punishments and threats, so that fearing the penalties we may be kept from sinning (διὰ τοῦτο γὰρ αἱ κολάσεις καὶ αἱ ἀπειλαί, ἵνα δείσαντες τὰς δίκας τοῦ ἁμαρτάνειν ἀποσχώμεθα)." More work needs to be done on this aspect of Clement's thought to clarify its relationship to passages which portray eschatological punishment as being redemptive in some way without defining the manner in which such punishment is redemptive.

[63]Clem. *paed.* 1.8.68.3; cf. Sir 1:21 and 22 (v. 21 appears only in Codex Sinaiticus; Codicies Vaticanus and Alexandrinus have only v. 22 immediately following v. 20).

[64]Clem. *str.* 5.1.9.4. The quotation from Heraclitus is from frg. 28, and the subsequent allusion is to frg. 66. On Clement's use of βάβαρος as a reference to things Hebrew, see n. 19 above.

[65]Clem. *str.* 5.14.91.2. In *str.* 5.14.90.4-91.2, Clement quoted portions of and alluded to Plato *Respublica* 10.615E-616A. It is possible that 1 Thess 1:7-9 provided the conceptual background for linking Ps 103:4 (LXX) with Plato's concept of pedagogical punishment.

[66]Clem. *str.* 5.14.90.6.

[67]Ibid., 7.16.102.3; cf. Ps 57:5-6 (LXX). It should be noted that the punishment Clement wishes for these persons is to occur "before the judgment (πρὸ τῆς κρίσεως)."

[68]Hanson, *Allegory and Event*, 229-30; Mondésert, *Clément d'Alexandrie*, 166, n. 3.

[69]I.e., the roots of plants used as a medicine (LSJ, s.v. "ῥίζα, ης, ἡ," 1).

70. Clem. *paed.* 1.9.83.2-3; cf. Luke 5:31. Clement's use of "ὑγιαίνοντες" indicates a specific echo of Luke 5:31 rather than the Synoptic parallels in Matt 9:12 and Mark 2:17, which have "ἰσχύοντες" instead.

[71]Clem. *prot.* 1:8.2-3. Philo had compared the ideal teacher to the ἰατρὸς ἀγαθὸς whose chief concern is determining the specific remedy required for the healing of each patient in *De posteritate Caini* 141.8.

[72]Clem. *paed.* 3.8.44.2; see van Unnik, "'Wise Fire,'" 279-80.

[73]Cf. Clem. *str.* 1.28.179.3.

[74]Hort and Mayor, *Miscellanies Book VII*, 61. If "φρόνιμον πῦρ" is in fact an interpretive allusion to 1 Cor 3:13, the other passages in which Clement employs the expression may also need to be understood as conceptually dependent on that text. *BibPatr* 1:449, however, does not list *str.* 7.6.34.4 under references to 1 Cor 3:13. Hort and Mayor also suggested Isa 4:4 (LXX) as a possible referent of "φρόνιμον πῦρ" ("πνεύματι καύσεως"), but this seems much less plausible.

[75]Clem. *str.* 7.6.34.4; cf. Heb 4:12. The probability that this is a conscious allusion is strengthened not only by the striking verbal similarity between the two constructions (the present, deponent, singular participles from διικνέομαι differ only in gender and are both followed by ψυχῆς) but also by the fact that the occurrence of διικνέομαι in Heb 4:12 is a New Testament *hapax legomenon*.

[76]Clem. *str.* 7.6.34.4; cf. Isa 43.2 (LXX).

[77]Clem. *ecl.* 25.4.

[78]Karl Reinhardt, "Heraklits Lehre vom Feuer," in *Vermächtnis der Antike: Gesammelte Essays zur Philosophie und Geschichtsschreibung*, ed. Carl Becker (Göttingen: Vandenhoeck & Ruprecht, 1960), 70; van Unnik, "'Wise Fire,'" 280.

[79]Clem. *str.* 1.27.173.5; 4.24.154.1-3; 6.12.99.2; 7.2.12.1-5; 7.16.102.5.

[80]Clem. *paed.* 1.8.62.3-63.1.

[81]Wis 11:23-12:2.

[82]Clem. *paed.* 1.8.70.3; cf. Rom 12:17 and Luke 6:28. Oddly, neither Stählin, *Clemens Alexandrinus*, vol. 1, *Protrepticus und Paedagogus*, 3d rev. ed., GCS, no. 12 (Berlin: Akademie-Verlag, 1972), 131, nor *BibPatr* 1:442, noted an allusion to Rom 12:17 in *paed.* 1.8.70.3, but "ἀνταπόδοσις κακοῦ" is undoubtedly a conscious echo of "κακὸν ἀντὶ κακοῦ ἀποδιδόντες."

[83]Clem. *paed.* 1.8.72.1; cf. Sir 16:11b-12a. Cf. also *paed.* 1.9.81.3, where Clement made similar use of Sir 16:12a.

[84]Clem. *paed.* 1.8.72.2-3.

[85]Ibid., 1.8.73.2-3.

[86]Ibid., 1:418. Stählin, *Clemens Alexandrinus*, 3:114, also noted no reference to Acts 3:21 in *exc. Thdot.* 22.3.

[87]Robert Pierce Casey, *The Excerpta ex Theodoto of Clement of Alexandria*, SD, ed. Kirsopp Lake and Silva Lake, no. 1 (London: Christophers, 1934), 5, identified chapter 22 as a fragment of Theodotus.

[88]Cf. Steven R. Harmon, "A Note on the Critical Use of *Instrumenta* for the Retrieval of Patristic Biblical Exegesis," *JECS* 11, no. 1 (Spring 2003): 100.

[89]Ibid., 1:440.

[90]Clem. *exc. Thdot.* 56.

[91]Jer. *com. in Is.* 18.66.24.

[92]Stählin, *Clemens Alexandrinus*, 3:176; Henri Crouzel, "L'exégèse origénienne de I Cor 3, 11-15 et la purification eschatologique," in *Epektasis: Mélanges Patristiques Offerts au Cardinal Jean Daniélou*, ed. Jacques Fontaine and Charles Kannengiesser (N.p.: Éditions Beauchesne, 1972), 273, n. 4; *BibPatr* 1:449.

[93]Hort and Mayor, *Miscellanies Book VII*, 61, n. 2. If, however, 1 Cor 3:13 is behind Clement's use of this language, it may have a relationship to other passages in which Clement has employed some form of the expression φρόνιμον πῦρ.

[94]Joachim Gnilka, *Ist 1 Kor 3,10-15 ein Schriftzeugnis für das Fegfeuer? Eine exegetisch-historische Untersuchung* (Düsseldorf: Michael Triltsch Verlag, 1955), 17-18, after noting "Klemens von Alexandrien . . . ist der erste, der die Paulusstelle zitiert," lamented that "Leider erklärt Klemens die Feuerprüfung nicht weiter."

[95]Clem. *str.* 1.24.159.5.

[96]In *str.* 5.6.38.6, the text following ὄνομα is from Eph 1:21.

[97]Clem. *prot.* 9.85.3.

[98]Ibid., 1.7.2.

[99]Clem. *hyp.* (frg. in Stählin, *Clemens Alexandrinus*, 3:211).

[100]Clem. *paed.* 1.9.91.1.

[101]Stählin, *Clemens Alexandrinus*, vol. 2, *Stromata Buch I-VI*, 4th ed., GCS, no. 52 (15) (Berlin: Akademie-Verlag, 1985), 115; *BibPatr* 1:252. Cf. *str.* 2.2.4.3, "φοβοῦ δὲ τὸν μόνον δυνατὸν θεόν, . . . καὶ ἔκκλινον ἀπὸ παντὸς κακου," with Prov 3:7, "φοβοῦ δὲ τὸν θεὸν καὶ ἔκκλινε ἀπὸ παντὸς κακοῦ," and Matt 10:28, "φοβεῖσθε δὲ μᾶλλον τὸν δυνάμενον καὶ ψυχὴν καὶ σῶμα ἀπολέσαι ἐν γεέννῃ."

[102]So Stählin, *Clemens Alexandrinus*, 1:274; ibid., 3:175.

[103]Clem. *paed.* 1.5.14.2; ibid., 1.8.71.3; idem, *str.* 4.4.15.6; ibid., 4.6.30.1; idem, *exc. Thdot.* 18.1.

[104]In *str.* 3.6.54.3, vv. 35 and 40 provide biblical evidence that it is not inherently wrong to have material possessions, for one must have food, drink, shelter, and clothing to be able to give these things to those in need and thus to God. Clement quoted v. 40 in *paed.* 3.4.30.2 against wealthy women who seemed to value their exotic pets over "rational" old men. Clement also alluded to v. 40 in writing of the salvation that is to be found in working for the help and improvement of people, which is reckoned as done to God (*str.* 7.3.21.4); for Clement, the Christian Gnostic was one who recognized this truth (*str.* 7.9.52.2).

[105]In *str.* 2.16.73.1, Clement quoted vv. 35 and 40 to illustrate the true nature of the anthropomorphisms applied to God in Scripture: just as God can be said to be nourished without literally being nourished, so references to God's experience of joy do not mean that God is really subject to human passions.

[106]Clement may have lifted the expression "σκότος τὸ ἐξώτερον" from identical language in Matt 8:12, 22:13, and 25:30, (contra *BibPatr* 1:246-47, 275, 283, which does not note any citations of or allusions to these texts in *q.d.s.* 13.4).

[107]Clem. *paed.* 2.10.105.1.

[108]A limit to this "partaking of fire" might be suggested by the translation of Ferguson, *Clement of Alexandria*, 180 ("The one, the rich man, was punished in hell and had his share of its fire"), but such a limit is not suggested by "μετέχων."

[109]Clem. *paed.* 3.6.334.4.

[110]So the translation of Ferguson, *Clement of Alexandria*, 228: "he . . . will never find true life."

[111]*BibPatr* 1:509.

[112]Stählin, *Clemens Alexandrinus*, 2:246; *BibPatr* 1:543.

[113]Clement approvingly cited the teachings of Heraclitus and Plato on the pedagogical nature of punishment in *str.* 5.1.9.4 and 5.14.90.4-91.2, claiming that they were dependent on Hebrew thought. At the very least this indicates that Clement believed elements of Greek philosophy to be consistent with Scripture; it may suggest a more pervasive reading of Scripture in light of philosophical presuppositions, and Clement himself may not have been conscious that he was reading Scripture in such a manner.

Chapter 3

"That God May Be All in All": Origen

Studies of Origen's theology underwent a major paradigm shift in the middle of the twentieth century.[1] Scholarship in the first three decades of the century[2] tended to portray Origen as a Hellenistic philosopher and speculative systematician with nominally Christian theological commitments, and it routinely ascribed to Origen the systematized dogmas of later Origenism as represented by the literary remains of the Origenist controversies of the fourth through sixth centuries.[3] Between 1930 and 1950, however, significant advances in research on Origen "restored, at least to the consciousness of scholars, the reputation of Origen as the towering figure of early Christian spiritual and biblical theology"[4] and made him currently "after Augustine, the most widely read of the ecclesiastical writers of antiquity."[5] This new perspective on Origen was achieved principally through the contributions of Walther Völker, Henri de Lubac, Hans Urs von Balthasar, and Jean Daniélou. Völker argued that conclusions about Origen's thought must be based on the whole of Origen's corpus, including those works extant only in Latin translation, and called attention to the importance of Origen's thoroughgoing concern for spirituality for understanding his thought. De Lubac continued Völker's methodology of critical attention to the Latin translations as well as the surviving Greek writings and cultivated fresh appreciation for Origen's biblical exegesis, and von Balthasar and Daniélou joined Völker and de Lubac in seeking to paint a holistic portrait of Origen as churchman, exegete, and mystic as well as speculative theologian.[6]

This revised understanding of Origen has special relevance for the subject of our investigation. In the framework of the earlier approach to Origen, the concept of an *apokatastasis* in which all intelligent beings are restored to their original, pristine contemplation of the divine through a process of remedial punishment could easily be attributed to the sway Middle Platonism held over his thought. While Origen's philosophical orientation certainly influenced his eschatology, the recent reappraisal of his commitment to the exposition of Scripture within the parameters of the church's rule of faith in the context of the catechumenate requires that the possibility that Origen's universalism was deeply rooted in biblical sources be taken seriously.

I. *Apokatastasis* in the Thought of Origen

A. The Universal Restoration

Origen's hope for the ultimate salvation of all rational creatures is most clearly expressed in sections of *De principiis* and *Contra Celsum*, his two most uncharacteristic works. If the concept were confined to these writings, one could easily place it on the periphery of his thought along with other cautiously advanced philosophical and theological speculations. Indications of the idea are also present, however, in the commentaries on John and Romans and in homilies on Joshua and Jeremiah, suggesting a more central position for the *apokatastasis* in Origen's thought. Since these genres of Origen's works have different purposes and intended audiences, his expressions of the concept will be examined by genre in the following order: tractates, which were more speculative and/or philosophical in nature and seem to have been intended for the most advanced class of Christians (or, in the case of *Contra Celsum*, for the philosophically inclined non-Christian); commentaries, which were less speculative than the tractates but still were "explanations at the 'scholarly' level of books of Scripture";[7] and homilies, which were "sermons expounding a scriptural text verse by verse, but in a way better suited to the general public in Christian congregations."[8]

1. The Universal Restoration in the Tractates. The most explicit affirmations of eschatological universalism appear in sections of books 1 and 3 of *De principiis*. The entirety of chapter 6 of book 1 is an extended discussion of "the end or consummation (*finis vel consummatio*)."[9] Origen felt it necessary to make clear in the first paragraph that the ensuing discussion was a provisional venture dealing with issues concerning which the rule of faith did not mandate precise formulations:

> However, we say these things with great fear and caution, more by way of discussing and investigating than by settling matters certainly and definitely. For we have indicated above which things are matters clearly delimited by dogma; and I believe we have done this to the best of our ability when we discussed the Trinity. But concerning the present matters, as much as we are able we are engaging in discussion rather than definition.[10]

In light of Origen's expressed lack of certainty about eschatological matters and reluctance to advance his opinions on them as the official teaching of the church, this aspect of Origen's thought must be regarded as a suggested possibility rather than settled conclusion.

Origen affirmed both the reality of eschatological punishment for all people and the ultimate restoration of all people to God. The rationale for this restoration is the equation of the final subjection of all to Christ promised in the Scriptures with salvation:

> Therefore the end of the world and the consummation will come about when everyone will yet be subjected to punishments as the deserved consequence of sins, at the time which God alone knows, when he will pay each one what is deserved. But we believe that the goodness of God through Christ may restore[11] his whole creation to one end, with even the enemies being subjugated and subdued. For so says Holy Scripture: "The Lord said to my Lord,[12] sit at my right hand, until I make your enemies your footstool." And if it is less clear to us what the prophetic language proclaims in this instance, we may learn from the Apostle Paul, who says more straightforwardly that "Christ must reign, until he has put all his enemies under his feet."[13] And if not even such a straightforward proposition as the Apostle's sufficiently instructs us as to what it means for enemies to be placed under the feet, listen also to the following: "For all things must be subjected to him."[14] What then is the subjection by which all things must be subjected to Christ? I think that this is the same as that by which we too wish to be subjected to him, by which both the apostles and all the saints who were followers of Christ were subjected to him. For the term subjection—which has to do with our subjection to Christ—indicates

> the salvation of those who are subject, which is from Christ, as also
> David said: "Will not my soul be subject to God? For from him is
> my salvation."[15]

The achievement of this "end" of "subjection to Christ" may be said to
be a "restoration" on the basis of the eschatological correspondence
between beginning and end in Origen's thought. Origen expressed this
concept in terms of a formula employed here and elsewhere: "For the
end is always like the beginning (*Semper enim similis est finis ini-
tiis*)."[16] The eschatological subjection of all to Christ, of which both
Paul and the prophetic psalmist wrote, is a restoration to an original
condition of subjection to Christ and unity with the Holy Spirit which
all rational creatures possessed in the beginning.[17]

Origen returned to eschatology in book 3, chapter 6 of *De principiis*, characterizing the previous discussion in *princ.* 1.6 as consistent
with biblical authority and appropriate for catechesis: "But concerning
the end and consummation of all things we have already in the preceding pages discussed to the best of our abilities, in accordance with what
the authority of divine Scripture has allowed, those things which we
consider to be adequate for instruction."[18] In *princ.* 3.6 he reaffirmed
belief in the universal extent of this restoration of the original state as
the implication of 1 Cor 15:28: the "all" in which God will ultimately
be "all" will exclude evil and irrational animals[19] but will include "each
individual person (*singulis eum*)."[20]

Origen's belief in the universal restoration of rational creatures is
attested also by a passage near the end of *Contra Celsum*. In response
to the charge of Celsus that it would be impossible for all the inhabitants of the earth to come under one law, Origen contended that such a
state of affairs is not only possible but will in fact be the destiny of
"every rational creature (πᾶν τὸ λογικόν)":

> Whereas the Stoics suppose that the conflagration in which all
> things are changed into fire will take place when the strongest of
> the elements prevails over the others, we say that the Word will
> prevail over the whole rational nature and will refashion every soul
> into his own perfection when everyone exercising simple authority
> will choose what each one wishes and wills to happen. And we say
> that although there are some diseases and wounds in the body
> which happen to be stronger than all medical skill, in the case of
> souls it is not likely that there is any evil which cannot be healed by
> the one who is Word and God over all. For the Word is more pow-
> erful than all the evils in the soul, and the healing which is in him
> comes to be applied to each one in accordance with the very will of

God, and the end of things is for evil to be destroyed. But as to
whether or not it is impossible for it to return to the previous state,
it is not the place of the present discourse to teach.[21]

Origen supported these assertions by going on to quote Zeph 3:7-13.[22]
The evasive allusion to the possibility of declension from the restored
state at the end of the passage quoted above reflects an aspect of Origen's doctrine of the *apokatastasis* that distinguishes it from similar
expressions of the idea in Clement of Alexandria and Gregory of
Nyssa. In Origen's system, the restoration of all rational creatures to
their pre-fall state does not appear to preclude the possibility of an endless cycle of falls and restorations. There are other texts in Origen that
appear to contradict such an interpretation of Origen's thought.[23] Nevertheless, the strong hints in *De principiis* that Origen allowed for this
possibility,[24] coupled with accusations of his opponents to that effect,[25]
require one to conclude that Origen's understanding of the restoration
of all things to the state of affairs at the beginning of this present age
did not rule out the existence of succeeding ages. This distinctive feature of Origen's version of the *apokatastasis* may be explained in terms
of his anthropology, which emphasized the freedom of rational creatures,[26] as well as his protology, in which the present corporeal existence of rational souls is the consequence of an inattentive fall away
from the contemplation of God on the part of preexistent, disembodied
souls.[27] What is restored in the *apokatastasis* is this state of disembodied contemplation. Since the restoration does not revoke the freedom
of these souls, they may conceivably turn away from contemplation
once again.

2. The Universal Restoration in the Commentaries. Origen's universalism is also apparent in the *Commentarii in Epistulam ad Romanos* and
the *Commentarii in Iohannem*. In commenting on Romans chapter 11,
Origen found the ultimate redemption of all people promised there:
"the fullness of the Gentiles (*plenitudo gentium*)" as well as "all Israel
(*omnis Israel*)."[28] This will come to pass on account of the insuppres-
sible power of the redeeming work of Christ:

> But we maintain that the power of the cross of Christ and of his
> death is so great that it brings to health and remedy not only the
> things of the present and future but also the things of previous ages,
> and it is sufficient not only for our human order, but also for the
> heavenly powers and orders. For according to the opinion of the
> apostle Paul himself, Christ has made peace "through the blood of

his cross" not only with "those things which are on the earth" but also with "those things which are in heaven."[29]

Origen's confidence in the universality of the *apokatastasis* was therefore partially rooted in his belief in the universal efficacy of the atonement.

The reconciling power of the cross would eventually lead all to become subject to God and therefore be saved, with their worship of God serving as the evidence of their salvation. Origen developed this core concept of his understanding of the universal restoration at length in his exposition of Rom 14:11.[30] The main features of the position Origen articulated in *De principiis* are evident in this passage: all will be saved; the salvation of all is assured by the eventual subjection of all to Christ promised by Scripture; this subjection includes even the enemies of God; the salvation of all does not exempt anyone from judgment; and although all will be saved, some will require longer periods of time to arrive at salvation than others.[31]

The *Commentarii in Iohannem*, which fortunately survived in its entirety in Greek, is replete with passages in which Origen expressed his conviction that all people would in the end be saved.[32] In the course of an explanation of the meaning of "beginning" in John 1:1 early in book 1 of the commentary, Origen identified the goal of the beginning as "that which is called the restoration (τῇ λεγομένῃ ἀποκαταστάσει),"[33] in which "no one is left then as an enemy, if indeed it is true that 'he must reign until he has put all his enemies under his feet; and the last enemy to be destroyed is death.'"[34] Later in book 1 Origen identified not only human beings but also all "rational beings" or "spiritual beings" as the beneficiaries of Christ's "sacrifice offered once for all" (Heb 9:28) and Christ's tasting of death "for all" (Heb 2:9).[35] Twice Origen insisted that the "world" whose sin the Lamb of God takes away (John 1:29) should not be limited to the church on the basis of 1 John 2:2 and 1 Tim 4:10.[36] In book 13 Origen contemplated the possibility that the evil spiritual powers might be included in the scope of Christ's salvation. In an allegorical interpretation of the two sojourns of Jesus in Cana (John 2:1 and 4:46) as two sojourns of Christ in the world,[37] the royal official in the second sojourn is "an image of a certain power of the rulers of this age," who are capable of conversion.[38] Origen's exposition of the prophecy of Caiaphas in John 11:50 that "it is advantageous for you that one man should die on behalf of the people so that the whole nation might not be destroyed" in book 28 of the commentary also pointed toward the universality of salvation:

Now the one who wishes that what is at work in Caiaphas might be true also in this instance (I am referring to his declaration that "it is advantageous for us[39] that one man should die on behalf of the people") will understand the phrase "it is advantageous for us" in a deeper sense on account of the statement concerning the goal. He will make use of the passage "so that by the grace of God (or, apart from God) he might taste death on behalf of all," and he will understand the words "on behalf of all" and "apart from God on behalf of all."[40] And that one will also make use of the text "who is the savior of all people, especially of those who believe";[41] but because this is "the lamb of God who takes away the sin of the world,"[42] he will understand in a unique sense the taking away of the sin of the world, and not a portion of it.[43]

The final book of the commentary contains a running commentary on 1 Cor 15:22-27 in which Origen argued that since "all things" which will become subject to Christ include the enemies of God, even the enemies of God will be saved.[44] Although all will be made alive in Christ (v. 22), this does not contradict the justice of God, for each person will be judged as he or she deserves, as indicated by the phrase "but each in one's own order" in v. 23.[45]

3. The Universal Restoration in the Homilies. Origen touched upon aspects of his eschatological universalism in two of his homilies. In the fourteenth homily of the *Homiliae in Ieremiam*, preserved in Greek, Origen employed both ἀποκατάστασις and ἀποκαθίστημι in such a way as to suggest the concepts signified by his use of this language elsewhere:

"Therefore the Lord says this: if you return, I will also restore you."[46] Again these things are said to each one whom God will invite to return to him; but a mystery seems to me to be disclosed here in the words "I will restore you." No one is restored to a place where he has never been before; rather, the restoration is to things that have to do with one's own home. For example, if my limb has become dislocated, the physician will attempt to restore the dislocation. When someone has come to be outside his homeland, whether justly or unjustly, but regains the ability to be again in his homeland legally, he is restored to his own homeland. The same thing in my mind applies to the case of a soldier who has been expelled from his own unit and is restored. Therefore he says here to us who have turned away that, if we return, he will restore us. For such also is the goal of the promise, as it is written in the Acts of the Apostles in the words "until the times of the restoration of all which God announced by the mouth of his holy prophets from of old"[47] in Christ Jesus, "to whom is the glory and the power forever. Amen."[48]

Although this passage does not explicitly affirm a necessarily universal restoration, Origen's use of ἀποκατάστασις and ἀποκαθίστημι therein indicates that he employed the terms in the sense of a restoration to a previous state rather than the achievement of a goal.[49] In light of Origen's portrayal of the previous state as one which has been previously experienced, his protological assumption of the preexistence of the soul seems implicit in his explanation of the sense in which Jeremiah spoke of the restoration of people to God.[50]

Origen's universalism is more explicit in the eighth homily of the *In Iesu Nave homiliae*. He applied the conviction of Paul that "all Israel will be saved" (Rom 11:26) to "every soul (*omni animae*)"; all will be saved after the remedy of the eternal fire of Matt 25:41 has been applied to those in need of it.[51] The universality of the *apokatastasis* in Origen's thought was therefore inseparable from its corollary of remedial punishment.

Origen clearly expressed the idea of an eventual restoration of all rational creatures to their primitive state in the tractates, the commentaries, and the homilies. The presence of the idea in all three major genres of Origen's writings, with intended audiences both learned and common, leads to the conclusion that the universal restoration was a conviction more basic to his thought than the disclaimer about venturing beyond dogmatic definition in *princ.* 1.6.1 might initially suggest.[52]

B. The Nature and Duration of Punishment after Death

The corollary to Origen's hope for the universal restoration was his understanding of punishment after death as fundamentally redemptive and its duration as limited by its redemptive goal. This aspect of Origen's individual eschatology will again be examined by genre—tractates, commentaries, and homilies—to determine whether audience might have had some impact on the expression of his thoughts about the nature of eschatological punishment.

1. Punishment after Death in the Tractates. Discussion of the nature and duration of punishment after death appears in *De oratione* and *De principiis* among the tractates. In his exposition of the petition "and lead us not into temptation, but deliver us from evil" from the Lord's

Prayer in the treatise *De oratione*, Origen dealt with the nature of the punishment of those who have succumbed to temptation:

> But receiving "in the fire"[53] and "in the prison"[54] not "a penalty for error"[55] but rather a benefit for the purification of the evils that belong to the error along with the salvation that comes from the sufferings which follow those who love pleasure, they are delivered from all "filth" and "blood" with which they were stained and defiled, with the result that they were not able to think about being saved from their own destruction. For that very reason God "will wash away the filth of the sons and the daughters of Zion and will cleanse the blood from their midst with a spirit of judgment and a spirit of burning."[56] For "he is coming like the fire of a smelting furnace and like the soap of fullers,"[57] washing and purifying those who have need of such medicines because they did not think it fit to wish "to have God in their understanding," regarding which after they have yielded they will hate the "reprobate mind."[58] For God does not wish for what is good to transpire for anyone under compulsion but rather voluntarily, perhaps for the benefit of some who have consorted with evil for so long that they perceive its shame and turn away from it only with much toil and pain, since they had falsely taken it to be good.[59]

Origen thus viewed punishment after death as primarily purifying, medicinal, and redemptive rather than retributive in nature and purpose. Lest there be a conflict between the idea of a universal restoration achieved through remedial punishment and his emphasis on human freedom, Origen was careful to point out the persuasive nature of such punishment: it does not make people good against their will, but rather they are ultimately persuaded by it to choose the good freely.

De principiis contains several passages in which Origen addressed the nature of eschatological punishment. In his account of the church's rule of faith in the preface to the treatise, Origen attributed to the apostles the teaching that "the soul, having its own particular substance and life, after its departure from this world will be rewarded for its merits, whether obtaining an inheritance of eternal life and beatitude if its deeds warrant it, or being delivered to eternal fire and punishment if the guilt of its wickedness is directed toward this."[60] He treated this aspect of the apostolic teaching in chapter 10 of book 2, affirming at the outset of his discussion that both the "Holy Scriptures" and the "proclamation of the Church" taught that "at the time of the judgment 'eternal fire' and the 'outer darkness' and a 'prison' and a 'furnace' and other things similar to these have been prepared for sinners."[61] After a discussion of the nature of the resurrection body (*princ.* 2.10.1-3), Origen turned to the question of the meaning of the "eternal fire" threatened by Matt 25:41. The fires of hell, which are kindled not by God but by each individual human,[62] point not to literal fires but rather to the pain experienced by the soul when the conscience recalls every act of evil.[63] The soul brings punishment upon itself when it moves away from the original harmony of its creation, but the punishment of the painful experience of disharmony leads it to seek harmony and order once again.[64] Origen compared such punishment to the painful cures administered by a physician and understood them as beneficial in intent, even when portrayed in Scripture by means of such an image as fire.[65] The "outer darkness" of Matt 8:12 likewise did not signify for Origen a literal dark place but rather described "those who through immersion in the darkness of profound ignorance are made to be outside of every light of reason and intelligence."[66] Origen advocated a similarly non-literal interpretation of the "prison" of 1 Pet 3:19.[67] As to the duration of this punishment, a fragment of questionable authenticity (possibly omitted by Rufinus from the conclusion of the chapter but preserved by Justinian and Pseudo-Leontius of Byzantium) maintains that punishment is not everlasting, ends when the soul has finally become purified, and is applied redemptively to demons as well as humans.[68]

Less extensive treatments of punishment after death appear elsewhere in *De principiis*. Origen speculated that the process of pedagogical punishment could extend over several ages.[69] Some, however, might make much swifter progress in responding to correction.[70] The end result of this process will be subjection to God, so that God becomes "all in all."[71]

2. Punishment after Death in the Commentaries. Origen occasionally reflected upon the nature and duration of punishment after death in his commentaries on biblical books. Most of the relevant discussions occur in the two extant portions of his commentary on Matthew: the Greek *Commentarii in Matthaeum*, of which only books 10-17 on Matt 13:36-22:33 have been preserved, and an anonymous Latin translation of the *Commentariorum series in Matthaeum* on Matt 22:34-27:63.[72] In the *Commentarii in Matthaeum*, Origen understood the punishment of drowning with a millstone the one who has caused a "little one" to stumble (Matt 18:6) as medicinal in nature (it is for the "θεραπείαν" of his sin) and ultimately limited in duration (when he has been punished enough, he will be free of suffering).[73] Origen reconciled the conflict between this understanding of the duration of punishment after death

and the biblical description of this punishment as "eternal" by main-
taining that the adjective αἰώνιος described long rather than everlasting
periods of time.[74] Although Origen questioned the propriety of defining the nature of Gehenna in the *Commentariorum series in Matthaeum*,[75] he nevertheless in the same commentary portrayed
punishment after death as both purificatory and pedagogical.[76]

Isolated references to punishment after death appear in other
commentaries. Origen expressed some uncertainty as to whether the
punishment of souls in hell would continue throughout eternity in the
Commentarii in Iohannem,[77] and in the *Commentarii in Epistulam ad
Romanos* he advocated a non-literal interpretation of the flames of hell
as the torments of consciences confronted by the memory of their evil
deeds.[78] Eschatological punishment is portrayed as having a purifying
function in the *Commentarii in Iohannem*, the *Libri in Canticum canticorum*, and the *Fragmenta in Proverbia* preserved in the *Apologia pro
Origene* of Pamphilius.[79]

3. Punishment after Death in the Homilies. Eschatological punishment
was a frequent theme in the homilies of Origen. Often Origen referred
to the punishment of eternal fire in such a way as to suggest a more
traditional perspective on the nature and duration of punishment after
death.[80] The prospect of punishment described as everlasting torment
had a pedagogical function in the present earthly life by warning people
away from sinful behavior, and Origen was accordingly loath to part
entirely with this traditional language and imagery in his preaching.[81]
In the fourth homily of the *In Ezechielem homiliae* he found it necessary to appeal to the "common sense (*communem sensum*)" in which
punishment in Gehenna was understood to be eternal in order to refute
unidentified persons who believed that the prayer of a "*martyr pater*"
could deliver a person from Gehenna.[82] The frequency with which
Origen openly identified purposes for punishment after death other than
pure retribution in his sermons, however, suggests that although he
viewed punishment in Gehenna as fearful and unavoidable, he understood it as eternal in effect rather than eternal in duration. Just as the
smelting furnace removes impurities from precious metals, so the fires
of hell purify those souls who are punished by them.[83] The "baptism
with fire" of which John the Baptizer spoke in Matt 3:11 and Luke 3:16
is the means of purification which those who had not been baptized
"with the Holy Spirit" during their earthly lives would have to undergo
in the next life.[84] Origen also depicted punishment after death as pedagogical and medicinal in character in the homilies.[85] In commenting

upon Jer 20:7 (LXX), "You have deceived me, O Lord, and I was deceived," Origen compared God to a physician who sometimes must deceive or withhold information from a patient in order to bring about healing. In this case, the information withheld is the remedial nature of punishment, which must be concealed if the biblical references to eternal fire are to have their pedagogical effect.[86] Nevertheless, Origen did on occasion proclaim the salvific purpose of eschatological punishment in his homilies.[87]

Origen thus explained the nature and purpose of punishment after death as medicinal, purificatory, pedagogical, and redemptive (and therefore limited in duration) rather than merely retributive in the tractates, commentaries, and homilies. As was the case with his affirmations of the universal restoration, Origen's consistent portrayal of the character of divine punishment as remedial in different genres with intended audiences differing widely in spiritual maturity and theological sophistication indicates its importance as an integral feature of his theology.

II. *Apokatastasis* and Exegesis

A. The Use of Scripture in the Articulation of Apokatastasis

The frequency and importance of biblical texts in the extant expressions of Origen's concept of the *apokatastasis* is readily apparent in the preceding examination of this aspect of his eschatology. We turn now to the role of these biblical citations and allusions in the passages from Origen's works in which the universal restoration and its accomplishment through remedial punishment were explicitly affirmed.

1. The Universal Restoration. Origen's belief in the restoration of all rational creatures to their condition prior to the Fall manifested itself in five interrelated convictions: (1) the ultimate subjection of all, including the enemies of God, to Christ; (2) the ultimate worship of God by all as the evidence of this subjection; (3) the equation of the subjection of all with the salvation of all; (4) the certainty of the final reconciliation of all; and (5) the ultimate exclusion of evil from the universe. Origen connected each of these convictions directly to biblical texts.

Origen was convinced that all rational creatures, including those presently opposed to God, would eventually become subject to Christ on the basis of 1 Cor 15:22-28[88] and his Christological interpretation of Ps 109:1 (LXX).[89] He found biblical corroboration of the subjection of all to Christ in texts which anticipated the worship which all creatures would one day offer to God: Isa 45:23 and its quotation in Rom 14:11,[90] Zeph 3:7-13,[91] and Phil 2:10-11.[92] That all would become subject to Christ and would therefore be saved was not only suggested by the biblical assurances of universal worship; it was explicitly taught, Origen maintained, by the psalmist's equation of his own subjection to God with salvation in Ps 61:2 (LXX).[93] Passages of Scripture which employed universalistic language such as "all" or "whole" in describing the objects of salvation assured the universal outcome of God's work of redemption. These texts included John 1:29,[94] John 11:50,[95] Rom 11:25-26,[96] 2 Cor 5:19,[97] Col 1:20,[98] 1 Tim 4:10,[99] Heb 2:9,[100] Heb 9:28,[101] and 1 John 2:2.[102] Finally, Origen believed that 1 Cor 15:28 with its promise that God would become "all in all" completely excluded the continued existence of evil in the universe; evil would therefore be eradicated from everyone so that all would experience God's salvation.[103]

Frequently Origen linked together several of these texts in a manner reminiscent of earlier Jewish-Christian midrashic exegesis, in which the meaning of a given text was explained in terms of similar words or concepts in other texts. Two groups of texts often appeared together in Origen's works in connection with the universal restoration. One such group involved some combination of 1 Cor 15:22-28, Phil 2:10, Isa 45:23/Rom 14:11, and Ps 61:2 (LXX).[104] The combined testimony of these texts enabled Origen to argue that becoming subject to God was the equivalent of being saved by God and resulted in the worship of God by all. Another grouping of texts included some combination of John 1:29, John 11:50, 1 Tim 4:10, Heb 2:9, and 1 John 2:2.[105] Origen combined these texts in order to demonstrate that universalistic language in one text had the same inclusive meaning as universalistic language in other texts.

2. The Nature and Duration of Punishment after Death. At the core of Origen's understanding of punishment after death as remedial in nature and limited in duration was his interpretation of the biblical image of the fires of divine judgment and eternal punishment as purificatory in purpose. His primary textual rationale was 1 Cor 3:10-15;[106] he found additional support for understanding these fires as beneficial in nature in John the Baptizer's reference to the "baptism with fire" which Jesus would bestow (Matt 3:11 and Luke 3:16).[107] On the basis of this interpretation of these texts, Origen could link purificatory punishment to the comparisons of divine judgment to fire in Deut 28:22,[108] Isa 4:4

(LXX),[109] Isa 47:14-15,[110] Isa 66:16-17,[111] and Mal 3:2-3.[112] A passage in the first homily of the *In Ezechielem homiliae* connected Ezek 1:27 with Heb 12:29, 1 Cor 3:12-13, Luke 12:49, Isa 10:16-17, and Isa 47:14-15 in an extended explanation of the purifying function of divine punishment.[113] Romans 2:15-16 suggested the interpretation of fiery punishment as a metaphor for the role of the memory of the conscience in purging departed souls of evil.[114]

Although the image of Christ as physician in Matt 9:12, Mark 2:7, and Luke 5:31 did not figure prominently in passages in which Origen dealt directly with the nature of punishment after death, Origen associated the comparison of God to a physician and divine punishment to a physician's painful cure with biblical texts.[115] In Jer 15:15-16 and 27-29 he found support for depicting punishment as a bitter medicine that, though difficult to swallow, brings about healing.[116] From Jer 20:7 (LXX) Origen derived his portrayal of God as a physician who must on occasion deceive or withhold information from a patient for the patient's benefit.[117]

A number of biblical images of eternal punishment did not directly furnish Origen with an exegetical rationale for his perspective on punishment after death but rather were reinterpreted by him in keeping with the perspectives he had established on the basis of other texts. These images include the "prison" of Matt 5:25-26[118] and 1 Pet 3:19,[119] the "outer darkness" of Matt 8:12,[120] the "eternal fire" of Matt 25:41,[121] the "furnace of fire" of Matt 13:42,[122] and the burning up of the works of the earth mentioned in 2 Pet 3:10.[123]

B. Apokatastasis and the Interpretation of Other Selected Biblical Texts

1. Universalistic Texts

(a) John 12:32. Origen quoted or alluded to John 12:32 on ten occasions.[124] None of his uses of this text suggests his hope for the salvation of all rational creatures.

(b) Acts 3:21. According to the compilers of *Biblia Patristica*, Origen made reference to Acts 3:21 eight times.[125] There is no apparent reference, even at the level of allusion, in one of the passages listed in *Biblia Patristica*,[126] and the quotations or allusions in three others have no universalistic overtones.[127] A possible allusion appears in the commentary on John in a reference to "that which is called the restoration (τῇ λεγομένη ἀποκαταστάσει),"[128] but this was more likely employed as a

technical designation.[129] If this were conclusively shown to be a reference to Acts 3:21, it would be an explicitly universalistic use of that text; in all probability, however, Origen intended no allusion to Acts 3:21 here. A better candidate for an intentional verbal echo or allusion is a reference to the "restoration of all things (*restitutione omnium*)" in book 2 of the *De principiis*,[130] but while nothing in the immediate context excludes a universalistic interpretation of this text, neither does anything in the immediate context require it. Origen explicitly quoted Acts 3:21 at the end of the fourteenth homily of the *Homiliae in Ieremiam* in connection with his definition of the term ἀποκατάστασις as the restoration of a previous condition, but in this passage he did not address the question of whether the restoration extended to all rational creatures or only to those who responded faithfully to God in their earthly existence.[131] It seems then that while it is probable that Origen understood the "ἀποκαταστάσεως πάντων" of Acts 3:21 to be universal, the text played no significant role in the explicit articulation of his eschatological universalism.

(c) Romans 5:18-21. Quotations of or allusions to portions of Rom 5:18-21 appear forty-nine times in the extant Origenian corpus.[132] In most of these uses of Rom 5:18-21, Origen's emphasis is Christological rather than soteriological or eschatological. In the *Commentarii in Epistulam ad Romanos*, however, Origen took up the question of the precise meanings of "πάντας/*omnes*" in v. 18 and "πολλοί/*plures*" in v. 19. Origen acknowledged the position of those who distinguished between "πάντας/*omnes*" and "πολλοί/*plures*" so that it is only a portion of "all" rather than the totality of "all" who are made righteous,[133] but he himself argued for the equivalence of the two terms so that in his understanding "all" are in the end made righteous.[134]

(d) Romans 11:25-26a. On fifty-nine occasions Origen made use of Rom 11:25-26a.[135] As Peter Gorday notes in his study of Origen's exegesis of Romans, Rom 11:25-26 "always . . . serves Origen as a means of witnessing to the outcome of the historical and cosmic process of salvation"[136] and expressed for Origen "the absolute conviction that God intends to redeem and will redeem even the most recalcitrant members of his creation."[137] Jerome's complaint that some persons had appealed to Rom 11:25-26a as a prooftext for their belief in an end to the torments of hell seems to have been directed primarily, if not entirely, against Origen.[138]

(e) Romans 11:32. Six references to Rom 11:32 appear in Origen's writings.[139] In a trio of quotations of this text in the *Commentarii in Epistulam ad Romanos*, Origen interpreted it as teaching the inclusion of all people in both sin and redemption.[140] The remaining references are not explicitly related to the universality of redemption.

(f) 1 Corinthians 3:12-15. Origen quoted or alluded to some portion of 1 Cor 3:12-15 sixty times.[141] His interpretation of the refiner's fire as one which purifies all of humanity rather than only Christian believers makes 1 Cor 3:12-15 the key text in his biblical argument for the reme-dial nature of punishment after death.[142] Virtually all of the sixty refer-ences to this text relate to this understanding of punishment, with reference to either the purification resulting from the divine discipline of believers in the present life or the purification of evil from the soul after death.[143]

(g) 1 Corinthians 15:22-28. Among those texts examined herein, the passage cited most often by Origen was 1 Cor 15:22-28. Origen made use of all or part of this passage 209 times.[144] This text was so signifi-cant for Origen's thought that Peter Nemeshegyi suggested that the whole of Origen's eschatology might be viewed as a commentary on 1 Cor 15:24-28.[145] The all-inclusive understanding of the "all" who are made alive in Christ (v. 22), the emphasis on the inclusion of even the enemies of God in the subjection of all to Christ (vv. 26-27), and the understanding of the phrase "that God may be all in all" as excluding the existence of evil (v. 28) furnished Origen with his primary source of biblical support for the universality of the *apokatastasis*.

(h) 2 Corinthians 5:19. Origen referred to 2 Cor 5:19 on fifteen occa-sions, not including a lone reference in a passage dubiously attributed to Origen in a catena of patristic commentaries on the Psalms.[146] In most of these references this text served as evidence for the universal outcome of God's work of redemption.[147]

(i) Ephesians 1:10. According to the compilers of *Biblia Patristica*, quotations of Eph 1:10 appear five times in Origen's works, not includ-ing a citation in a passage of doubtful authenticity in a catena on the Psalms.[148] In two references from a lost commentary on Ephesians preserved in catenae, Origen commented only on the phrase "τοῦ πληρώματος τῶν καιρῶν."[149] In another quotation of the verse in the remains of the commentary, he mentioned the "ἀνακεφαλαίωσις ἐν τῷ

Χριστῷ" but did not include "τὰ πάντα" as the object of "ἀνακεφαλαιώσασθαι."[150] Two additional references listed in *Biblia Patristica* are only possible allusions to Eph 1:10 and appear in contexts
which do not suggest a connection with Origen's eschatological universalism.[151] One must therefore conclude that despite the presence of
Pauline "πᾶς" language in Eph 1:10, Origen did not relate this text to
his concept of *apokatastasis* in what remains of his writings.

(j) Philippians 2:9-11. Origen cited or alluded to portions of Phil 2:9-
11 fifty-six times, often in conjunction with 1 Cor 15:22-28.[152] As we
have already noted, Phil 2:9-11 was a key text in Origen's exegetical
case for a universal restoration.

(k) Colossians 1:20. Origen made use of Col 1:20 on twenty-six occasions.[153] Paul's use of "τὰ πάντα" with reference to the objects of the
reconciling work of God that is accomplished though the cross led Origen to employ this text as an assertion of the universal efficacy of the
work of Christ. This interpretation accords with Origen's consistent
interpretation of πᾶς as universally inclusive in soteriological contexts
in Paul's letter to the Romans.[154]

(l) 1 Timothy 2:4. There are three citations of 1 Tim 2:4 in Origen's
surviving works (apart from a pair of references in passages of catenae
on Matthew and the Psalms which in all likelihood were falsely attributed to Origen).[155] One reference in the portion of the commentary on
Matthew preserved only in Latin has no connection to Origen's concept
of *apokatastasis*.[156] In a homily on Exodus, however, Origen linked a
quotation of 1 Tim 2:4 not only with the idea of a universal restoration
but also with his redemptive understanding of the nature of punishment
after death: "Therefore since God is merciful and 'wants all people to
be saved,' for that reason he says, 'I will visit their evil deeds with an
iron rod and their sins with whips, but I will not take away my mercy
from them.'"[157] Origen made the same connection also in the *Commentarii in Epistulam ad Romanos*, juxtaposing a universalistic interpretation of 1 Tim 2:4 with an explanation of the purgative character of the
"*ignis gehennae*."[158]

(m) Titus 2:11. Origen referred to Tit 2:11 only once.[159] A quotation
of this text appears in the fourteenth homily of the *In Iesu Naue
homiliae*, but without the reference to "all people" as the beneficiaries
of salvation.[160] Instead, the translation of Rufinus substituted "*sal-*

vatoris nostri" for "σωτήριος πᾶσιν ἀνθρώποις"; the former reading occurs also in a number of Greek MSS as well as in some MSS of the Vulgate.[161]

(n) 2 Peter 3:9. Twice Origen alluded to 2 Pet 3:9.[162] In neither instance did Origen employ this text as a witness to the universality of repentance.[163]

(o) 1 John 2:2. In comparison with his predecessor Clement of Alexandria and his later admirer Gregory of Nyssa, Origen made frequent reference to 1 John 2:2. Thirty-three citations of or allusions to 1 John 2:2 appear in Origen's writings.[164] Like Clement before him, Origen clearly understood the sacrifice of Christ "for the sins of the whole world" to be universally efficacious.

2. Texts Suggesting Eternal Punishment. Origen neither quoted nor alluded to Rev 20:14-15, but he did interact with the following texts traditionally understood in terms of eternal punishment as the everlasting torment of the wicked.

(a) Matthew 5:29-30. Origen quoted or alluded to Matt 5:29 and/or v. 30 in eight extant passages.[165] In one instance he quoted phrases from both verses but did not include the crucial references to punishment "εἰς γέενναν."[166] In the remainder of his uses of this text, Origen presented such punishment as a real prospect[167] and even placed literal emphasis on the "whole body" as the object of punishment in Gehenna.[168] Origen then appealed to the punishment threatened in Matt 5:29-20 as a motivation for moral conduct in the present without defining the nature or duration of such punishment.

(b) Matthew 8:12. Origen referred to Matt 8:12 twenty-two times (or twenty times if references in questionably genuine catena fragments on the Psalms and Proverbs are excluded).[169] His previously noted use of this text indicates that he understood "the outer darkness (τὸ σκότος τὸ ἐξώτερον)" not as purely retributive and everlasting but rather as having a remedial function, upon the completion of which it would cease to exist.

(c) Matthew 10:28/Luke 12:5. There are twenty-four references to Matt 10:28 and/or its parallel in Luke 12:5 (or twenty-one references when one reference in a probably spurious fragment and two references in

dubiously attributed passages in a catena on Proverbs are excluded from consideration).[170] Origen put this text to a wide variety of uses. In the *Commentarii in Iohannem* he mentioned Heracleon's contention that it precluded the immortality of the soul, and in the *Commentarii in Epistulam ad Romanos* he made reference to it in a discussion of whether or not the body was the object of redemption.[171] He cited Matt 10:28 three times in a chapter of the *Exhortatio ad Martyrium* as evidence that Jesus had predicted martyrdom for those who followed him.[172] In the remainder of his interaction with Matt 10:28/Luke 12:5, Origen seems to have presented destruction in Gehenna as a real threat.[173] He did not, however, offer any additional theological commentary that would clarify his understanding of the nature or duration of this threatened destruction.

(d) Matthew 18:8-9/Mark 9:42-48. There are thirteen instances in which Origen interacted with Matt 18:8-9, all of which appear in the portion of the *Commentarii in Matthaeum* extant in Greek.[174] These quotations or allusions mention the threat of the "eternal fire" (v. 8) or the "fire of Gehenna" (v. 9) most often as a motivation for ethics, but without elaborating on the meaning of these expressions.[175] A reference to Mark 9:42 (or Matt 18:6) earlier in the commentary does interpret the "millstone" as "θεραπείαν" for the sins of the one who has caused others to stumble.[176] Origen therefore made use of this text to portray eschatological punishment as medicinal in nature.

(e) Matthew 25:31-46. Origen referred to some portion of Matt 25:31-46 on 196 occasions.[177] The frequency with which he made reference to this passage attests to his keen interest in the reality of eschatological punishment and his quest for the best possible understanding of its nature. In the majority of these uses of Matt 25:31-46, it is clear that Origen interpreted the "eternal fire" to which the "goats" will be condemned in terms of his own understanding of the nature of punishment after death as essentially redemptive.[178]

(f) Luke 16:19-31. Origen's interest in biblical texts related to individual eschatology is also apparent in the seventy-nine references (or seventy-six when a reference in a doubtfully attributed section in a catena on Proverbs and two references in a collection of probably spurious homilies on the Psalms are subtracted) to all or part of the parable of the rich man and Lazarus in Luke 16:19-31.[179] Thirty-nine homilies on Luke are extant in a Latin translation by Jerome, but no homily on

Luke 16:19-31 survived among them.[180] Two fragments from a lost homily on this passage deal only with portions of vv. 19 and 23 that are of little relevance for Origen's understanding of the nature of punishment after death.[181] Most of the remainder of the references either use the parable as a whole as a motivation for morality in the present life by underscoring the eschatological reversal of the lots of Lazarus and the rich man[182] or focus on the interpretation of some detail of the parable such as the "bosom of Abraham" (vv. 21-22)[183] or "Moses and the prophets" (v. 29).[184] The nearest Origen comes to offering an interpretation of the parable in light of his theology of eschatological punishment appears in a general allusion to the passage in the fourteenth homily of the *In Leviticum homiliae*, in which Origen suggested that those who willingly receive suffering in the present life will not have to endure it in the next life.[185] For Origen, asceticism was a voluntary anticipation in one's earthly life of the purificatory nature of punishment after death and a possible means for averting eschatological punishment altogether.

(g) 2 Thessalonians 1:7-9. Origen made use of 2 Thess 1:7-9 only once, in the portion of the commentary on Matthew preserved in Latin.[186] This lone reference functioned as a warning about the prospect of punishment, but Origen did not explain the nature of the "punishment of eternal destruction" (v. 9).[187]

(h) Revelation 21:8. Origen referred to Rev 21:8 twice (not counting a quotation in a passage of a catena on the Psalms wrongly attributed to Origen).[188] Neither reference sheds much light on Origen's perspective on the nature or duration of the "lake of fire" or the "second death."[189]

III. Conclusions

In spite of the tendency of early twentieth-century patristic scholarship to portray Origen as a nominally Christian Middle Platonist, even a cursory reading of the passages in which Origen expresses his hope for universal salvation reveals a mind steeped in the Christian Scriptures. A careful investigation of the relevant portions of Origen's works uncovers a solid exegetical substructure for his vision of a universal *apokatastasis*. The core of this substructure was 1 Cor 15:22-28, which promised the ultimate subjection of all to Christ and the exclusion from the universe of anything which is not permeated by the divine good. All other texts to which Origen appealed in this connection have their place in the substructure as confirmation or elaboration of the ideas he found in 1 Cor 15:22-28. Psalm 109:1 (LXX), Isa 45:23, Rom 14:11, Zeph 3:7-13, and Phil 2:10-11 confirmed for Origen the total universality of the eschatological subjection to Christ foretold by 1 Cor 15:22-28, a subjection which would even include those who had lived as the enemies of God during their earthly existence. Psalm 61:2 (LXX) showed that this subjection would not be a servile admission of defeat forced from those condemned to eternal retribution but rather would be the result of the free response to divine pedagogy of those who on account of their salvation will worship God forever. Origen also found universal participation in salvific subjection attested in John 1:29, John 11:50, Rom 11:25-26, 2 Cor 5:19, Col 1:20, 1 Tim 4:10, Heb 2:9, Heb 9:28, and 1 John 2:2.

The core of a supporting substructure underlying the corollary concept of the remedial nature of eschatological punishment was 1 Cor 3:10-15, which Origen read as a witness to the role of punishment in removing accretions of evil from those who must be brought to the point of saving subjection "only as through fire." He found the same idea elsewhere in the Scriptures: Deut 28:22, Isa 4:4 (LXX), Isa 10:16-17, Isa 47:14-15, Isa 66:16-17, Ezek 1:27, Mal 3:2-3, Matt 3:1, Luke 3:16, Luke 12:49, and Heb 12:29. These texts, coupled with the purgative function of the conscience when tormented by the memory of evil deeds throughout the period of punishment suggested to Origen by Rom 2:15-16, enabled him to interpret apparent biblical references to eternal, retributive punishment in other than literal terms (Matt 5:25-26, Matt 8:12, Matt 13:42, Matt 25:41, 1 Pet 3:19, and 2 Pet 3:10).

Origen's references to the texts selected as test cases for the impact of his eschatological universalism upon his biblical interpretation indicate that his vision of the universal *apokatastasis* both was derived from biblical texts and functioned as part of the hermeneutical pre-understanding that influenced his reading of a number of texts. Romans 5:18-21, Rom 11:25-26a, Rom 11:32, 1 Cor 3:12-15, 1 Cor 15:22-28, 2 Cor 5:19, Phil 2:9-11, Col 1:20, 1 Tim 2:4, and 1 John 2:2 received a universalistic interpretation. Origen's references to John 12:32, Eph 1:10, Tit 2:11, and 2 Pet 3:9, on the other hand, show no traces of the influence of a universalistic hermeneutic, and even Acts 3:21 with its reference to an "ἀποκαταστάσεως πάντων" is not explicitly interpreted in light of his technical use of that language elsewhere.

References to passages that are more suggestive of an understanding of eschatological punishment as retributive and eternal reveal a tension Origen intentionally maintained between two seemingly mutually exclusive ways of portraying such punishment. The references to Matt 5:29-30 and Matt 10:28/Luke 12:5 highlight the retributive elements of these texts as real threats which warn of terrible punishment if one does not repent, but the language of eternal retribution in the references to Matt 8:12 and 2 Thess 1:7-9 is accommodated to Origen's remedial understanding of punishment. Origen could make use of Matt 18:8-9/Mark 9:42-48, Matt 25:31-46, and Luke 16:19-31 to communicate one perspective on the nature of punishment in some contexts and another perspective in other contexts. He does not seem to have seen any contradiction in presenting both pictures of punishment. It was important for him to preserve the biblical language of threatened eternal retribution on account of its power to motivate moral transformation; it was also important for him to speak of the dealings of God with humanity in the manner which best lent coherence to the biblical portrayals of these dealings vis-à-vis the Gnostic denials of such coherence. Using these texts in seemingly contradictory ways enabled him to meet both objectives, as did his hermeneutical theory, which allowed him to find truth in both the "literal sense" and the "spiritual sense" of the text.

The philosophical underpinnings of Origen's eschatological universalism, which were certainly present along with the exegetical substructure, are not as visible as was the case with Clement of Alexandria. Clement could mention the consistency of his view of punishment with that of Plato while citing comparatively fewer biblical texts in support of his ideas, but Origen eschewed references to philosophical literature in this connection while saturating his discussions of the *apokatastasis* with references to Scripture. There is nevertheless so extensive an interplay between Origen's implicit philosophical presuppositions and his explicit appeals to Scripture that it is impossible to determine conclusively whether Origen derived his universalism directly from Scripture or read the Scriptures in light of the universal salvation of which he had already become convinced on philosophical grounds. The latter possibility is probably the more accurate description of the relationship between *apokatastasis* and exegesis in Origen's thought, but this conjecture must not be allowed to obscure the importance of Scripture for this aspect of Origen's thought.

Notes

[1]The best account of these developments is the section on "Die Origenesforschung im zwanzigsten Jahrhundert" in Henri Crouzel, "Die Patrologie und die Erneuerung der patristischen Studien," in *Bilanz der Theologie im 20. Jahrhundert: Perspektiven, Strömungen, Motive in der christlichen und nichtchristlichen Welt*, ed. Herbert Vorgrimler and Robert Vander Gucht (Freiburg: Herder, 1970), 3:515-21. See also idem, "The Literature on Origen 1970-1988," *TS* 49, no. 3 (September 1988): 499-516; Robert J. Daly, "Translator's Epilogue," in Hans Urs von Balthasar, *Origen, Spirit and Fire: A Thematic Anthology of His Writings*, trans. Robert J. Daly (Washington, D. C.: The Catholic University of America Press, 1984), 371-73; Joseph W. Trigg, "A Decade of Origen Studies," *RelSRev* 7, no. 1 (January 1981): 21-27. As Daly, "Epilogue," 372, suggests, a survey of the papers of the quadrennial International Origen Congresses (Henri Crouzel, Gennaro Lomiento, and Josep Rius-Camps, eds., *Origeniana: Premier colloque international des études origéniennes*, QVC, no. 12 [Bari: Istituto di Letteratura Cristiana Antica, 1975]; Henri Crouzel and Antonio Quacquarelli, eds., *Origeniana Secunda: Second colloque international des études origéniennes*, QVC, no. 15 [Rome: Edizioni dell'Ateneo, 1980]; Richard Hanson and Henri Crouzel, eds., *Origeniana Tertia: The Third International Colloquium for Origen Studies* [Rome: Edizioni dell'Ateneo, 1985]; Lothar Lies, ed., *Origeniana Quarta: Die Referate des 4. Internationalen Origeneskongress*, ITS, no. 19 [Innsbruck: Tyrolia-Verlag, 1987]; Robert J. Daly, ed., *Origeniana Quinta: Papers of the 5th International Origen Congress*, BETL, vol. 105 [Leuven: Leuven University Press, 1992]; Gilles Dorival and Alain Le Boulluec, eds., *Origeniana Sexta: Origène et la Bible. actes du Colloquium Origenianum Sextum, Chantilly, 30 Septembre 1993*, BETL, vol. 118 (Leuven: Leuven University Press, 1995]; Wolfgang Bienert, ed., *Origeniana Septima: Origenes in den Auseinandersetzung des 4. Jahrhunderts*, BETL, vol. 137 [Leuven: Leuven University Press, 1999]) and the papers on Origen presented at the Oxford Patristic Conferences (also held quadrennially; published in *StudPat*, vols. 1-38) provides an excellent orientation to the status of contemporary Origen studies.

[2]According to Crouzel's characterization of the general consensus among Origen scholars in the late nineteenth and early twentieth centuries, " . . . sie ihre Aufmerksamkeit mehr dem Griechen als dem Christen, mehr dem systematischen Philosophen als dem Mann der Kirche zuwendet, unterscheidet sie kaum zwischen der Lehre des Origenes selbst und dem späteren Origenismus, das heißt dem theologischen System, das Evagrius Pontikus und seine Freunde auf gewissen Gedankengängen des Alexandriners aufbauten und das die origenistischen Streitigkeiten des vierten und fünften Jahrhunderts hervorrief, die zu den Anathematismen des Fünften Ökumenischen Konzils führte. Dieses System ist hauptsächlich dem Traktat *De principiis* entnommen. Die Übertragung Rufins wird scharf kritisiert und radikal disqualifiziert, da man ihr vorwirft, Origenes möglichst von allen Irrtümern reinwaschen zu wollen; die von den Gegnern Hieronymus und Justinian zitierten Stellen hingegen werden

kritiklos übernommen. Alle spätern Texte, die den Origenismus betreffen, werden zur Erklärung dieser Schrift verwendet, wie wenn die Lehre der Origenisten oder die von den Antiorigenisten vorausgesetzte Lehre in allen Punkten mit der des Origenes übereinstimmte" (Crouzel, "Patrologie," 3:518). Crouzel placed in this category the work of Paul Koetschau, whose portrayal of Origen's thought in his critical edition of *De Principiis* confused Origen with later Origenism (Paul Koetschau, *Origenes Werke*, vol. 5, *De Principiis (Περὶ ἀρχῶν)*, GCS, no. 22 [Leipzig: Hinrichs'sche Buchhandlung, 1913]); Eugène de Faye, whose multivolume study on Origen was based on the premise that only those works extant in Greek were reliable sources for reconstructing Origen's thought, a methodology which eliminated from consideration most of the homiletic literature and focused attention on Origen's more speculative works (Eugène de Faye, *Origène, sa vie, son, oeuvre, sa pensée*, 3 vols. [Paris: E. Leroux, 1923-28]); and Hal Koch, whose monograph on the Platonic background of Origen's concepts of providence and pedagogical discipline emphasized the philosophical influences on the thought of Origen while minimizing its biblical sources (Hal Koch, *Pronoia und Paideusis: Studien über Origenes und sein Verhältnis zum Platonismus*, AKG, ed. Emanuel Hirsch and Hans Lietzmann, no. 22 [Berlin: Walter de Gruyter, 1932]). The interpretation of Origen as Greek philosopher had its roots in the nineteenth-century labors of Ferdinand Christian Baur, who placed Origen at the extreme Hellenistic pole of a dialectical reconstruction of early Christian history in which Jewish Christianity provided the thesis, Hellenistic Christianity the antithesis, and early catholic Christianity the synthesis (Trigg, "Decade of Origen Studies," 22).

³Henri Crouzel, "Origenism," in *Encyclopedia of the Early Church*, ed. Angelo Di Berardino, trans. Adrian Walford (New York: Oxford University Press, 1992), 2:623-24, identified six "moments" in Origenism which should be distinguished from one another: first, the positions of Origen himself; second, the representation of Origen's positions by his detractors in the third and fourth centuries (e.g., Methodius, Peter of Alexandria, and Eustathius of Antioch); third, the scholastic Origenism of Egyptian and Palestinian monks in the late fourth century (e.g., Evagrius of Pontus); fourth, the representation of Origenism by anti-Origenist writers in the late fourth and fifth centuries (e.g., Epiphanius, Jerome, and Theophilus of Alexandria); fifth, the Evagrian Origenism of sixth-century Palestinian monks (e.g., Stephen bar Sudayle), which tended toward a radical pantheism; sixth, the representation of Origenism in its condemnations by the emperor Justinian in 543 and 553. On the history of the controversies in which these later "moments" find their place, see Elizabeth A. Clark, *The Origenist Controversy: The Cultural Construction of an Early Christian Debate* (Princeton, N.J.: Princeton University Press, 1992; James Walter Armantage, *Will the Body Be Raised? Origen and the Origenist Controversies* (Ph.D. diss., Yale University, 1970); Antoine Guillaumont, *Les "Kephalaia Gnostica" d'Evagre le Pontique et l'histoire de l'Origénisme chez les Grecs et chez les Syriens*, PatSorb, no. 5 (Paris: Éditions du Seuil, 1962); Franz Diekamp, *Die origenistischen Streitigkeiten im sechsten Jahrhundert und das fünfte allgemeine Concil* (Münster: Verlag Aschendorff, 1899).

[4]Daly, "Epilogue," 371-72.

[5]Crouzel, "Origenism," 2:624.

[6]Walther Völker, *Das Vollkommenheitsideal des Origenes: eine Untersuchung zur Geschichte der Frömmigkeit und zu den Anfangen christlicher Mystik*, BHT, no. 7 (Tübingen: J. C. B. Mohr, 1931); Henri de Lubac, *Histoire et Esprit: L'intelligence de l'Écriture d'après Origène*, Théologie, no. 16 (Paris: Aubier, 1950); Hans Urs von Balthasar, "Le mystérion d'Origène," *RSR* 26 (1936): 513-62; 27 (1937): 38-64 (= idem, *Parole et mystère chez Origène* [Paris: Éditions du Cerf, 1957]); idem, *Geist und Feuer: Ein Aufbau aus seinen Schriften* (Salzburg: Otto Müller Verlag, 1938); ET, *Origen, Spirit and Fire: A Thematic Anthology of His Writings*, trans. Robert J. Daly (Washington, D. C.: The Catholic University of America Press, 1984); Jean Daniélou, *Origène* (Paris: La Table Ronde, 1948); ET, *Origen*, trans. Walter Mitchell (New York: Sheed and Ward, 1955). Trigg, "Decade of Origen Studies," 22, noted the anticipation of this perspective in Ernst Rudolf Redepenning's response to Baur's assessment of Origen (Ernst Rudolf Redepenning, *Origenes: eine Darstelling seines Lebens und seiner Lehre*, 2 vols. [Bonn: Eduard Weber, 1841-46]) and its continuation in the many works of Henri Crouzel on Origen (e.g., Henri Crouzel, *Origène* [Paris, Éditions Lethielleux, 1985]; ET, *Origen*, trans. A. S. Worrall [San Francisco: Harper & Row, 1989]); according to Trigg, Crouzel "is currently the leading exponent of this position."

[7]Crouzel, *Origen*, 40.

[8]Ibid. According to Eusebius (*h.e.* 6.36.1), the bulk of these were delivered and committed to writing in Caesarea sometime after Origen had reached the age of sixty, when for the first time he permitted stenographers to record his extemporaneously delivered homilies.

[9]Or. *princ.* 1.6.1 (translation of Rufinus).

[10]Ibid.

[11]Given the context, it seems probable that *revoco* is Rufinus's translation of ἀποκαθίστημι.

[12]Although the original referent of "τῷ κυρίῳ μου" in Ps 109:1 (LXX), or "לַאדֹנִי" in Ps 110:1 (MT), was the Davidic king on the occasion of the festival of his enthronement (see Sigmund Mowinckel, *The Psalms in Israel's Worship*, trans. D. R. Ap-Thomas [New York: Abingdon Press, 1962], 1:47-48, 63-65), Origen here continued the early Christian Christological interpretation of this psalm (see Matt 22:41-46, Acts 2:34-35, Heb 1:13 and 10:12-13, and the patristic literature cited in Marie-Josèph Rondeau, *Les Commentaires Patristiques du Psautier (IIIe-Ve siècles)*, OCA, no. 219 [Rome: Pontificium Institutum Studiorum Orientalium, 1985], 2:12, 21-23, 28-30, 32-33, 60). The translation of "*domino*" as "Lord" must therefore be capitalized in this instance.

[13]1 Cor 15:25.

[14]Quoted loosely from 1 Cor 15:27 and/or v. 28.

[15]Or. *princ.* 1.6.1. The quotation attributed to David is from Ps 61:2 (LXX).

[16]Ibid., 1.6.2.; cf. ibid, 2.1.1; ibid., 2.1.3; ibid., 3.6.3; idem, *Jo.* 13.37.244; idem, *Cels.* 8.72. According to Henri Crouzel and Manlio Simonetti, *Origène:*

Traité des Princeps, SC, no. 253 (Paris: Les Éditions du Cerf, 1978), 2:92-93, this idea had philosophical roots: "Le principe de la fin semblable au commencement, hérité de la philosophie grecque, détermine les doctrines de la préexistence et de l'apocatastase." The antecedents of the concept of an eschatological correspondence between beginning and end are not confined to pagan philosophical literature, however, for Ps.-Barn. *Barn.* 6.13 gives evidence of the presence of the idea in early second-century Jewish Christianity: "The Lord says, 'Behold, I am making the last things like the first things' (λέγει δὲ κύριος· Ἰδού, ποιῶ τὰ ἔσχατα ὡς τὰ πρῶτα)."

[17]Or. *princ.* 1.6.2.

[18]Ibid., 3.6.1. In light of Origen's previously stated reluctance to advance his eschatological perspectives as the dogma of the church (ibid., 1.6.1), it seems that he did not limit that which was appropriate for catechetical instruction to the exposition of the *regula fidei*. On the role of the *regula* in Origen's thought and writings, see Albert C. Outler, "Origen and the *Regula Fidei*," *SecCent* 4 (1984): 133-41.

[19]Ibid., 3.6.2. The Latin translation of Rufinus and the Greek fragment preserved in Justinian *Epistula ad Menam* (frg. 27) are in agreement at this point.

[20]Or. *princ.* 3.6.3.

[21]Or. *Cels.* 8.72.

[22]Ibid.

[23]Daley, *Hope of the Early Church*, 58, cited as evidence that Origen conceived of salvation as "the permanent stability of rational creatures in loving union with God" Or. *Jo.* 10.295; idem, *hom. in 1 Reg.* 1.4; and idem, *dial.* 27. Daley also pointed to Or. *comm. in Rom.* 5.10 as an explicit rejection of an ongoing series of falls and restorations but acknowledged that "[t]his work . . . is preserved only in a translation by the 'friendly witness' Rufinus" (Daley, *Hope of the Early Church*, 237, n. 28).

[24]Or. *princ.* 2.3.1-2.

[25]Jer. *ep.* 124.5,10; Just. *ep. ad Men.* (frgs. 16 and 20).

[26]Or. *princ.* praef.; ibid., 3.1.1.

[27]Ibid., 1.81.; ibid., 3.1.21-22.

[28]Or. *comm. in Rom.* 8.12 (FontChr 2,4:300-8; PG 14:1195-98), passim. As translated by Rufinus, Origen seems to vacillate in this section between an inclusive interpretation of "the fullness of the Gentiles" and "all Israel" and a restrictive interpretation of these phrases as referring to those among the Gentiles and Israel who come to believe (Peter Gorday, *Principles of Patristic Exegesis: Romans 9-11 in Origen, John Chrysostom, and Augustine*, SBEC, vol. 4 [New York: Edwin Mellen Press, 1983], 80-82; 87-88; 296, n. 148; 297, n. 151; 299, n. 159). It is possible that Rufinus modified some of Origen's more explicitly universalistic statements in translating this section. On the problematic textual history of this work, see Charles P. Hammond, "Notes on the Manuscripts and Editions of Origen's Commentary on the Epistle to the Romans in the Latin Translation by Rufinus," *JTS* n.s. 16 (1965): 338-57, and Theresia

Heither, *Origenes: Commentarii in Epistulam ad Romanos, Römerbriefkommentar*, FontChr 2, pt. 1 (Freiburg: Herder, 1990), 11-16.

[29]Or. *comm. in Rom.* 5.10 (FontChr 2,3:182; PG 14:1053). The quoted material is from Col 1:20.

[30]Or. *comm. in Rom.* 9.41 (FontChr 2,5:140-42; PG 14:1243-44).

[31]It is unclear whether Origen had in mind a period of purgatorial punishment in this reference to "a longer period of time" required for the salvation of those who have neglected the improvement of their souls. Such an intention would be consistent with Origen's thoughts on the nature of punishment after death expressed elsewhere, but the idea is not explicit in this passage.

[32]Daley, *Hope of the Early Church*, 237, n. 25, noted with reference to Origen's eschatological universalism that "[t]his conception of the 'end' (τέλος) of history is particularly strong in the *Commentary on John*."

[33]The description of the *apokatastasis* as "τῇ λεγομένη" might indicate that the word had already assumed a technical meaning which would have been familiar to Origen's readers, as Daley (ibid., 58) suggested.

[34]Or. *Jo.* 1.16.91. The biblical quotation is from 1 Cor 15:25-26.

[35]Or. *Jo.* 1.35.255-56.

[36]Ibid., 6.55.284-85; ibid., 6.59.304-5.

[37]Ibid., 13.57.391.

[38]Ibid., 13.59.411-13. The opposition of "ἄνθρωποι" and "τῶν δυνάμεων" (ibid., 13.59.412) suggests that Origen conceived of these "rulers" as spiritual rather than human powers; this passage is then possible evidence for Origen's belief in the possibility of the ultimate salvation of Satan and the demons (cf. ibid., 1.35.255-56). On the other hand, in the *Epistula ad quosdam caros suos Alexandriam*, substantial fragments of which were preserved in Latin translation by Jerome and Rufinus, Origen vigorously denied having taught such a thing. Perhaps the resolution of the apparent conflict between passages in which Origen hinted that even the most evil spiritual beings were not beyond salvation and Origen's denial that he had ever taught the ultimate salvation of the devil lies in his distinction between teaching as the exposition of the church's rule of faith and the discussion of matters concerning which speculation was permissible (*princ.* 1.6.1). For the Latin text, English translation, and analysis of the fragments of the *Epistula ad quosdam caros suos Alexandriam*, see Henri Crouzel, "A Letter from Origen 'To Friends in Alexandria,'" trans. Joseph D. Gauthier, in *The Heritage of the Early Church: Essays in Honor of the Very Reverend Georges Vasilievich Florovsky*, ed. David Neiman and Margaret Schatkin, OCA, no. 195 (Rome: Pontificium Intstitutum Studiorum Orientalium, 1973), 135-50.

[39]Origen is a witness to the variant reading "ἡμῖν" present in Codex Alexandrinus and other MSS of John.

[40]Heb 2:9. Origen had earlier noted the presence of variant readings for this verse in MSS of Hebrews with which he was acquainted (Or. *Jo.* 1.35.255).

[41]The quotation is from 1 Tim 4:10.

[42]John 1:29.

[43]Or. *Jo.* 28.18.154-55.

[44]Ibid., 32.3.26-33.
[45]Ibid., 32.3.28.
[46]Jer 15:19.
[47]Acts 3:21.
[48]Or. *hom. in Jer.* 14.18. The final biblical quotation is from 1 Pet 4:11.

[49]On the differing connotations of this language in Origen and his predecessors, see Méhat, "'Apocatastase,'" 196-214, in conjunction with the qualifications of Méhat's conclusions offered by Siniscalco, "'Ἀποκατάστασις e ἀποκαθίστημι," 395.

[50]On Origen's conception of the preexistence of the soul, see Marguerite Harl, "La préexistence des âmes dans l'oeuvre d'Origène," in *Origeniana Quarta: Die Referate des 4. Internationalen Origeneskongress*, ed. Lothar Lies, ITS, no. 19 (Innsbruck: Tyrolia-Verlag, 1987), 238-58, and D. Gerald Bostock, "The Sources of Origen's Doctrine of Pre-existence," in *Origeniana Quarta*, 259-64.

[51]Or. *hom. in Jos.* 8.5.

[52]On the other hand, Frederick W. Norris, "Universal Salvation in Origen and Maximus," in *Universalism and the Doctrine of Hell: Papers Presented at the Fourth Edinburgh Conference in Christian Dogmatics, 1991*, ed. Nigel M. de S. Cameron (Carlisle, U.K.: Paternoster Press, 1993; Grand Rapids: Baker Book House, 1993), 35-72, has proposed on the basis of the tension between passages in Origen which seem to suggest universal salvation and passages which seem to suggest eternal punishment that Origen actually taught "two views for his readers to choose . . . : universal salvation and a limited hell as well as salvation only for those who live the gospel and eternal damnation, perhaps even annihilation, for those like the devil who continuously refuse" (ibid., 62). Although Norris defended his case thoroughly, the combined evidence of the universalistic passages in Origen and the observations of such a tendency by his relative contemporaries requires one to conclude that, at the very least, Origen openly speculated that a universal restoration was consistent with the Scriptures, the character of God, and the broad parameters of the teaching of the Church. One should nevertheless heed the cautions of Norris against systematically stripping Origen of his ambiguities and inconsistencies.

[53]The phrase "ἐν . . . τῷ πυρὶ" refers back to the expression "τῷ φρονίμῳ πυρὶ" earlier in *or.* 29.15, which in turn is a possible allusion to Isa 4:4, Mal 3:2, and/or 1 Cor 3:13 (so John J. O'Meara, *Origen: Prayer, Exhortation to Martyrdom*, ACW, ed. Johannes Quasten and Joseph C. Plumpe, no. 19 [New York: Newman Press, 1954], 224, n. 620). On the recurring image of the "wise" or "discerning" fire (employed previously by Clement of Alexandria) in Origen's eschatology, see van Unnik, "'Wise Fire,'" 281-82, 285. In Origen the φρόνιμον πῦρ "purifies the souls for the *apokatastasis* and is 'wise,' because it makes a distinction between good and evil" (ibid., 285).

[54]Cf. Matt 5:25-26.
[55]Rom 1:27.
[56]Isa 4:4 (LXX).
[57]Mal 3:2 (LXX).

[58]Rom 1:28.

[59]Or. *or.* 29.15.

[60]Or. *princ.* praef. 5.

[61]Ibid., 2.10.1. The brief echoes of "that which the Holy Scriptures threaten" are from Matt 25:41, Matt 8:12, 1 Pet 3:10, and Matt 13:42.

[62]Origen appealed to Isa 50:11, "Walk in the light of your fire and in the flame which you have kindled for yourselves," as evidence for this perspective. The materials by which each kindles one's own fire are "wood, hay, and stubble" (1 Cor 3:12).

[63]Or. *princ.* 2.10.6. Origen based this psychological interpretation of "eternal fire" in part on Rom 2:15-16, "their thoughts among themselves either accusing or defending them on the day in which God will judge the secrets of people, according to my gospel, through Jesus Christ."

[64]Or. *princ.* 2.10.5.

[65]Ibid., 2.10.6. Origen cited Deut 28:22,28-29; Jer 15:15-16, 27-29; Isa 4:4; Isa 47:14-15 (LXX); Isa 66:16-17; and Mal 3:3 as teaching the medicinal and purifying nature of punishment.

[66]Or. *princ.* 2.10.8.

[67]Ibid.

[68]G. W. Butterworth, *Origen: On First Principles* (Gloucester, Mass.: Peter Smith, 1973), 146, deemed the testimonies of Justinian and Pseudo-Leontius trustworthy and included the fragment in the text at the conclusion of *princ.* 2.10. On the other hand, Crouzel and Simonetti, *Traité des Principes*, 2:241-42, denied the authenticity of the fragment and in the text of their edition ended the chapter with the conclusion of Rufinus's translation: "*Sed sufficient ista in praesenti loco, quae interim nunc, ut dicendi ordo seruaretur, quam paucissimis dicta sunt*" (ibid., 1:394).

[69]Or. *princ.* 1.6.3.

[70]Ibid., 3.6.6.

[71]Ibid., 3.6.9, quoting 1 Cor 15:28.

[72]In addition to the *Commentarii in Matthaeum* and the *Commentariorum series*, there are a number of short fragments of varying degrees of certainty of authenticity printed in Erich Klostermann and Ludwig Früchtel, eds., *Origenes Werke*, vol. 12, *Origenes Matthäuserklärung*, pt. 3, *Fragmente und Indices*, GCS, vol. 41, pt. 2 (Berlin: Akademie-Verlag, 1968). On the textual evidence for Origen's commentaries on Matthew, see Charles P. Hammond, "Some Textual Points in Origen's Commentary on Matthew," *JTS* n.s. 24 (1973): 380-404.

[73]Or. *comm. in Mt.* 13.7.

[74]Ibid., 15.31.

[75]Or. *comm. ser. in Mt.* 16.

[76]Ibid., 20.

[77]Or. *Jo.* 28.8.63-66.

[78]Or. *comm. in Rom.* 7.5; cf. idem, *princ.* 2.10.4-6.

[79]Or. *Jo.* 13.23.138; idem, *Cant.* 3 (GCS 33:238); idem, *fr. in Pr.* (PG 17:615-16).

[80]E.g., Or. *hom. in Jer.* 19.15; idem, *hom. in Lev.* 3.4; ibid., 14.4.

[81]See Or. *hom. in Jer.* 12.4-5; ibid., 19.15; ibid., 20.4.

[82]Or. *hom. in Ez.* 4.8.

[83]E.g., Or. *hom. in Jer.* 19.15; ibid., 20.8; idem, *hom. in Ez.* 5.1. Origen frequently cited or alluded to 1 Cor 3:11-15 in this connection.

[84]Or. *hom. in Ez.* 1.13; idem, *hom. in Jer.* 1.3; ibid., 2.3.

[85]E.g., Or. *hom. in Ez.* 1.3; idem, *hom. in Jer.* 20.3. In the former passage, Origen classified this view of punishment as ultimately salvific as one of the mysteries normally hidden from the simple Christian but which must occasionally be proclaimed publicly in order to correct inadequate views of God and the divine purposes in punishment. *"Parvuli"* is a verbal echo of 1 Cor 3:1.

[86]Or. *hom. in Jer.* 20.3. One motive for the use of this analogy ("ἐκ τοῦ ἀνὰ λόγον πατρὶ καὶ ἰατρῷ ὁ θεός," ibid.) was the refutation of Gnostic arguments for an "evil God" of the Old Testament distinct from the "good God" of the New Testament that appealed to Old Testament depictions of God as vengeful in executing punishment and immoral in dealings with humanity—e.g., in "deceiving" them. On the role of theodicy vis-à-vis Gnosticism in Origen's eschatological universalism, see the not disinterested study of Harold E. Babcock, "Origen's Anti-Gnostic Polemic and the Doctrine of Universalism," *UUC* 38, no. 3-4 (Fall-Winter 1983): 53-59, a Universalist of the North American denominational variety who concluded that Origen's universalism was much less certain and systematized than commonly supposed.

[87]Or. *hom. in Ex.* 6.4; idem, *hom. in Ez.* 1.3; idem, *hom. in Jer.* 20.3; idem, *hom. in Num.* 25.6.

[88]E.g., Or. *princ.* 1.6.1; idem, *comm. in Rom.* 9.41 (FontChr 2,5:140-42; PG 14:1243-44); idem, *Jo.* 32.3.26-33.

[89]Or. *princ.* 1.6.1.

[90]Or. *comm. in Rom.* 9.41 (FontChr 2,5:140-42; PG 14:1243-44).

[91]Or. *Cels.* 8.72.

[92]E.g., Or. *comm. in Rom.* (FontChr 2,5:140-42; PG 14:1243-44).

[93]Or. *princ.* 1.6.1; idem, *hom. in Ez.* 1.15.

[94]E.g., Or. *Jo.* 6.55.284-85; ibid., 6.59.304-5; ibid., 28.18.154-55.

[95]Ibid.

[96]E.g., Or. *comm. in Rom.* 8.12 (FontChr 2,4:300-8; PG 14:1195-98); idem, *hom. in Jos.* 8.5.

[97]E.g., Or. *comm. in Rom.* 9.41 (FontChr 2,5:140-42; PG 14:1243-44).

[98]E.g., ibid., 5.10 (FontChr 2,3:182; PG 14:1053).

[99]Or. *Jo.* 6.55.284-85; ibid., 6.59.304-5; ibid., 28.18.154-55.

[100]Ibid., 1.35.255-56; ibid., 28.18.154-55.

[101]Ibid., 13.57.391.

[102]E.g., ibid., 6.55.284-85; ibid., 6.59.304-5.

[103]Or. *princ.* 3.6.3.

[104]Or. *comm. in Rom.* 9.41 (FontChr 2,5:140-42; PG 14:1243-44); ibid., 7.4 (FontChr 2,4:56-58; PG 14:1112); idem, *princ.* 1.6.1-2; idem, *hom. in Ez.* 1.15.

[105]Or. *Jo.* 6.55.284-85; ibid., 6.59.304-5; ibid., 28.18.154-55.

[106]E.g., Or. *or.* 29.15; idem, *princ.* 2.10.6; idem, *hom. in Jer.* 19.15; ibid., 20.8; idem, *hom. in Ez.* 5.1. On the significance of this text for Origen's doctrine of eschatological punishment, see Crouzel, "L'exégèse origénienne de I Cor 3, 11-15," 273-83; Anrich, "Clemens und Origenes als Begründer der Lehre vom Fegfeuer," 97-120; and Gnilka, *Ist 1 Kor. 3,10-15 ein Schriftzeugnis für das Fegfeuer?*, 20-25.

[107]Or. *hom. in Ez.* 1.13; idem, *hom. in Jer.* 1.3; ibid., 2.3.

[108]Or. *princ.* 2.10.6.

[109]Or. *or.* 29.15; idem, *princ.* 2.10.6.

[110]Ibid.

[111]Ibid.

[112]Or. *or.* 29.15; idem, *princ.* 2.10.6.

[113]Or. *hom. in Ez.* 1.3.

[114]Or. *comm. in Rom.* 7.5 (FontChr 2,4:66; PG 14:1115); idem, *princ.* 2.10.4-6.

[115]On Origen's use of medical imagery and its significance for his soteriology, see D. Gerald Bostock, "Medical Theory and Theology in Origen," in *Origeniana Tertia: The Third International Colloquium for Origen Studies*, ed. Richard Hanson and Henri Crouzel (Rome: Edizioni dell'Ateneo, 1985), 191-99.

[116]Ibid., 2.10.6.

[117]Or. *hom. in Jer.* 20.3.

[118]Or. *or.* 29.15; idem, *princ.* 2.10.1.

[119]Ibid., 2.10.8.

[120]E.g., ibid., 2.10.1; ibid., 2.10.8.

[121]E.g., ibid., 2.10.1.

[122]Ibid.

[123]Ibid.

[124]*BibPatr* 3:336-37.

[125]Ibid., 3:348.

[126]Or. *princ.* 2.4.2.

[127]Or. *comm. in Mt.* 17.15; ibid., 17.16; 16; ibid, 17.19; idem, *comm. ser. in Mt.* 55.

[128]Or. *Jo.* 1.91.

[129]Cf. Harmon, "Critical Use of *Instrumenta*," 100.

[130]Or. *princ.* 2.3.5; cf. "ἀποκαταστάσεως πάντων" in Acts 3:21.

[131]Or. *hom. in Jer.* 14.18.

[132]*BibPatr* 3:362.

[133]Or. *comm. in Rom.* 5.1 (FontChr 2,3:36; PG 14:1006).

[134]Ibid.; ibid., 5.2 (FontChr 2,3:88; PG 14:1023); ibid., 5.5 (FontChr 2,3:108; PG 14:1029). Origen appealed to similar language in 1 Cor 15:22 as evidence for this interpretation of Rom 5:18-19. On Origen's universalistic exegesis of Rom 5:18-21, see Gorday, *Principles of Patristic Exegesis*, 65, 198, 200-2, 210.

[135]*BibPatr* 3:375-76.

[136]Gorday, *Principles of Patristic Exegesis*, 297, n. 151.

[137]Ibid., 94. See also Hans Bietenhard, *Caesarea, Origenes und die Juden* (Stuttgart: W. Kohlhammer, 1974), 73, n. 28, for a listing and classification of Origen's references to this text.

[138]Jer. *comm. in Is.* 18.66.24.

[139]*BibPatr* 3:376.

[140]Or. *comm. in Rom.* 8.13 (FontChr 2,4:308-10; PG 14:1198); ibid.(FontChr 2,4:312-14; PG 14:1200); ibid., 9.1 (FontChr 2,5:22-24; PG 14:1203).

[141]*BibPatr* 3:388-89.

[142]Gnilka, *Ist 1 Kor. 3,10-15 ein Schriftzeugnis für das Fegfeuer?*, 22.

[143]See also Crouzel, "L'exégèse origénienne de I Cor 3, 11-15," 273-83, and Anrich, "Clemens und Origenes als Begründer der Lehre vom Fegfeuer," 97-120.

[144]*BibPatr* 3:403-5.

[145]Peter Nemeshegyi, *La paternité de Dieu chez Origène*, Bibliothèque de Théologie, ser. 4, Histoire de la Thèologie, vol. 2 (Tournai: Desclée, 1960), 206: "Origène cite ce texte avec une fréquence extraordinaire. Toute son eschatologie se présente comme un commentaire des paroles de saint Paul."

[146]*BibPatr* 3:413.

[147] E.g., Or. *comm. in Rom.* 9.41 (FontChr 2,5:140-42; PG 14:1243-44).

[148]*BibPatr* 3:423.

[149]Or. *Eph. cat.* 5 (J. A. F. Gregg, "The Commentary of Origen upon the Epistle to the Ephesians," *JTS* 3 [1902]: 241).

[150]Ibid.

[151]Or. *hom. in Jos.* 7.5; idem, *hom. in Lev.* 3.5.

[152]*BibPatr* 3:433.

[153]*BibPatr* 3:437.

[154]See Gorday, *Principles of Patristic Exegesis*, 200-2.

[155]*BibPatr* 3:444.

[156]Or. *comm. ser. in Mt.* 2.

[157]Or. *hom. in Ex.* 8.6. The final biblical quotation is from Ps 88:32-33 (LXX).

[158]Or. *comm. in Rom.* 8.12 (FontChr 2,4:308; PG 14:1198).

[159]*BibPatr* 3:448.

[160]Or. *hom. in Jos.* 14.1.

[161]See the apparatus of Barbara Aland and others, eds., *Novum Testamentum Graece*, 27th rev. ed. (Stuttgart: Deutsche Bibelgesellschaft, 1994), 558.

[162]*BibPatr* 3:462.

[163]Or. *comm. ser. in Mt.* 37; idem, *comm. in Rom.* 2.3 (FontChr 2,1:172-74; PG 14:874-75).

[164]*BibPatr* 3:463.

[165]*BibPatr* 3:233.

[166]Or. *princ.* 4.3.3.

[167]Or. *Jo.* 20.149; idem, *comm. in Mt.* 13.24; ibid., 15.2; ibid., 25.3; idem, *hom. in Jos.* 7.6.

[168]Or. *hom. in Lev.* 9.7.

[169] *BibPatr* 3:238-39.

[170] *BibPatr* 3:242; ibid., 3:300.

[171] Or. *Jo.* 13.417; idem, *comm. in Rom.* 7.5 (FontChr 2,4:70; PG 14:1117).

[172] Or. *mart.* 34.

[173] Especially Or. *hom. in Ex.* 10.4; idem, *comm. ser. in Mt.* 57; ibid., 62; idem, *hom. in Num.* 18.4; ibid., 19.4.

[174] *BibPatr* 3:256; ibid., 3:283.

[175] Or. *comm. in Mt.* 13.22; ibid., 13.24 (seven references); ibid., 13.25 (two references); ibid.,15.2.

[176] Ibid., 13.7.

[177] *BibPatr* 3:272-73.

[178] E.g., Or. *princ.* 2.10.1, 5-6.

[179] *BibPatr* 3:303.

[180] Or. *hom. in Lc.* 35 is a homily on Luke 12:57-59, while the next homily in sequence in Jerome's translation treats Luke 17:20-21, 33.

[181] Ibid., frgs. 222-23.

[182] E.g., Or. *hom. in Lev.* 3.4; ibid., 9.4; idem, *hom. in Ex.* 8.6; idem, *or.* 29.6.

[183] E.g., Or. *Jo.* 32.265; idem, *hom. in Gen.* 11.3; ibid., 16.4.

[184] E.g., Or. *hom. in Ex.* 3.3; idem, *hom. in Lc.* 33; idem, *Jo.* 6.30.

[185] Or. *hom. in Lev.* 14.4.

[186] *BibPatr* 3:442.

[187] Or. *comm. ser. in Mt.* 50.

[188] Ibid., 3:468.

[189] Or. *hom. in Jud.* 9.1; idem, *comm. ser. in Mt.* 16.

Chapter 4

"Salvation Comes through Subjection": Gregory of Nyssa

Origen's literary legacy contributed much to the theological formation of the three great "Cappadocian Fathers."[1] Although it was Basil of Caesarea and his fellow student Gregory of Nazianzus whose admiration for Origen resulted in the compilation of the *Philocalia*, an anthology of extracts from Origen's works, among the Cappadocians it was Basil's younger brother Gregory of Nyssa who most thoroughly incorporated Origen's thought into his own. This was especially true in the case of Cappadocian interaction with Origen's individual eschatology. Basil clearly rejected Origen's concepts of universal salvation and an end to eschatological punishment.[2] Gregory of Nazianzus expressed a cautious ambivalence about such matters,[3] but Gregory of Nyssa repeatedly affirmed the basic features of Origen's concept of *apokatastasis*: all rational creatures will ultimately be restored to their pre-fall condition; some who have successfully purged themselves of evil in this life will experience this restoration immediately after death, while others will experience this restoration only after a period of remedial punishment.[4]

Gregory's version of the universal *apokatastasis* differed from that of Origen, however, in that Gregory's eschatology was rooted in a different protology. Origen had posited the preexistence of souls in a state of unembodied contemplation of God and a subsequent fall from this contemplation that resulted in their present corporeality, but Gregory rejected the preexistence of the soul and attributed the current bodily residence of the soul to God's work of creation.[5] The resurrection of the body consequently figured more prominently in Gregory's depiction of the state restored in the *apokatastasis* than in its portrayal by Origen.[6]

I. *Apokatastasis* in the Thought of Gregory of Nyssa

A. The Universal Restoration

Gregory's understanding of the *apokatastasis*[7] figures prominently in a number of passages of the *Dialogus de anima et resurrectione*, a treatise which recounted a dialogue between Gregory and his elder sister and teacher Macrina on her deathbed.[8] Early in the dialogue, after Macrina has dealt with the incorporeality of the soul after death, Gregory asks Macrina about the relationship of these things to the idea of Hades as a "place," citing a possible objection to incorporeality based on Phil 2:10:

> "What then," I said, "if the opponent should put forward the apostle, who says that in the restoration of all things, the whole rational creation will look to the one who governs everything? Regarding this (i.e., the rational creation) he mentions also some who are under the earth, saying in the epistle to the Philippians, "to him every knee should bow of those in heaven and those on the earth and those under the earth."[9]

Macrina does not object to the idea of "the restoration of all (τῇ τοῦ παντὸς ἀποκαταστάσει)" in her response to Gregory, but she does object to the hypothetical opponent's spatial interpretation of "those under the earth (καταχθονίων)," arguing that this refers not to people in a place under the earth but rather to the state of human beings after death when separated from their bodies. She alludes to Origen's position that "those under the earth" refers to demonic beings who when finally "nothing outside of the good will remain (οὐδὲν ἔξω τοῦ ἀγαθοῦ καταλειφθήσεται)" will also bend their knees to Christ, introducing it as a viable alternative that, though not her own interpretation of the text, would also rule out the conception of Hades as a place.[10] In this passage, Gregory via Macrina's part in the dialogue affirms the idea of the universal restoration of rational creatures but distinguishes it from Origen's exegetical rationale for the restoration of the demons.

Passages elsewhere in *Dialogus de anima et resurrectione* affirm the restoration of all rational creatures more explicitly. Near the end of the treatise, Macrina begins a summary response to opponents' arguments about the nature of the resurrection by defining the resurrection as "the restoration of our nature to the original state (ἡ εἰς τὸ ἀρχαῖον τῆς φύσεως ἡμῶν ἀποκατάστασις),"[11] a state in which there was no infancy or old age, no bodily degeneration of any kind, and no irrational passion, things which belong to the "irrational skins (τῶν ἀλόγων δερμάτων)" with which human beings were clothed after the Fall.[12] Although this passage is a description of the restored state, there is no necessary implication that all will share in it. Later in her discourse, however, Macrina develops these ideas in such a way as to leave no doubt that Macrina/Gregory understood resurrection as the restoration of the pre-Fall state to be an ultimately universal experience. In addressing the problem of the relationship of one's manner of conduct in this life to one's state in the next life, Macrina contends that the power and purpose of God diminish the problem:

> But when God restores[13] (human) nature to the first creation of humanity through the resurrection, it would be fruitless to speak of such things and to suppose that the power of God would be thwarted from the goal on account of such obstacles. He has one goal: after all the fullness of our nature has been perfected in each person—some immediately who have been purified from evil during this life, others later who have been healed through fire for the appropriate periods of time, and still others who are equally unaware of the experience of good and of evil—to set before everyone participation in the good things in him, which the Scripture says eye has not seen, nor ear has heard, nor has it become accessible to reasoning.[14]

This is essentially the same concept of the *apokatastasis* that appeared in the thought of Clement and Origen: all will ultimately experience God's salvation; those who have been sufficiently purified during their earthly lives will experience it immediately following death, while those who have not been sufficiently purified during their earthly lives will experience it only after an intermediate process of purification. Macrina repeats this concept at the end of her discourse in an application of the agricultural imagery in 1 Cor 15:42-44, which "is in agreement with our understanding of the resurrection and shows what our definition comprehends when we say that the resurrection is nothing other than the restoration of our nature to the original state."[15]   In the "sowing" and "raising" of the human nature, what grows from the seed is the same species as that which originally grew and produced the seed, but some seeds become deformed so that they fail to grow fully in this life and therefore must undergo harsh treatment by the farmer before they can fully ripen.[16]

Brief expressions of these ideas developed more fully in *Dialogus de anima et resurrectione* are scattered throughout Gregory's works. In *De vita Moysis* there is a passing reference to "the restoration of those condemned to Gehenna anticipated after these things in the kingdom of heaven."[17]   In the last sentence of the final homily on the Song of Solomon, Gregory envisions a time when "all become one, looking to the same goal of desire: no longer will there be any evil remaining in anyone, for God will be all in all, as all will be joined together through unity in fellowship with the good in Jesus Christ our Lord."[18]   The effects of the *apokatastasis* are described as the regaining of heaven in *De oratio dominica orationes* and *Orationes de beatitudinibus*[19] and as the restoration of the likeness of God in *De mortuis non esse dolendum.*[20]

In the *Oratio catechetica magna*, Gregory extends this understanding of the *apokatastasis* to include not only wicked human beings but also the suprahuman being who had enticed them to evil in the first place:

> In the same manner, after the evil of the (human) nature which is now mingled and united with it has been removed through long periods of time, when the restoration to the original state of those now lying dead[21] in evil has come to pass, there will be a harmonious thanksgiving from all creation, even from those who have been chastised through purification, as well as from those who needed no purification in the first place. The great mystery of the divine incarnation grants these and other such things. For through those things that were mingled with human nature when he came into being through all the properties of the nature—birth, rearing, growth, even to the extent of going through the experience of death—he accomplished all the aforementioned things, both freeing humanity from evil and healing even the originator of evil himself. For the purification of moral disease is the healing of illness, even if it is painful.[22]

Gregory clearly affirmed what Origen hinted at but explicitly denied: that even Satan will be restored in the *apokatastasis*.[23]   This passage suggests that in differing with Origen's identification of "καταχθονίων" in Phil 2:10 with demonic spirits in *Dialogus de anima et resurrectione*, it was not the possibility of the salvation of the demons to which Macrina/Gregory objected but rather Origen's specific exegetical support for this idea. Indeed, the language employed in that treatise in explaining Origen's position is strikingly similar to that used in this passage from the *Oratio catechetica magna*.[24]

The primary rationale Gregory offered in support of the universal *apokatastasis* is his view of evil as the "deprivation of the good (στέρησις ἀγαθοῦ)."[25] Only good—the fullness of which is the nature of God in which humanity participates via the *imago dei*[26]—has real, infinite existence; evil as a parasitic corruption of the good has no independent existence and is therefore finite.[27] Consequently there will ultimately be a time when there will be "no evil remaining in anyone (μηδεμίας ἐν μηδενὶ κακίας ὑπολειφθείσης)."[28] Gregory expressed this reasoning through the voice of Macrina in *Dialogus de anima et resurrectione*:

> For it is necessary that evil at some point be wholly and completely removed from existence, and . . . that what does not really exist should not exist at all. For since it does not belong to its nature for evil to exist outside of the will, when every will rests in God evil will depart into utter destruction, since there is no receptacle remaining for it.[29]

Gregory's conclusion that evil will ultimately meet with "utter destruction (παντελῆ ἀφανισμὸν)" thus rested on two assumptions: first, evil "exists" only through the improper exercise of the divinely bestowed human faculty of free moral choice (προαίρεσις); second, ultimately every exercise or exerciser of this faculty will come to be "ἐν τῷ θεῷ." The latter is an expression of Gregory's conviction of the universality of the *apokatastasis*, a conviction that in turn is based partly on Gregory's ideas about the nature of evil as a deprivation of the good and therefore ultimately finite.[30] The concepts are interdependent in Gregory's thought.

B. The Nature and Duration of Punishment after Death

Although Gregory occasionally hinted that he conceived of eternal punishment as everlasting torment,[31] the understanding of punishment after death as redemptive rather than retributive in purpose and limited in duration predominates in his writings. The necessity of the purification of the soul through remedial punishment before its restoration to the state of beatitude is a recurrent theme in the *Dialogus de anima et resurrectione*. Toward the end of a long discussion of the matter in the dialogue,[32] Gregory and Macrina arrive at a definitive summary of the subject:

> "Then," I said, "it seems to me in light of the foregoing discussion that the divine judgment does not bring punishment upon sinners but rather, as the discourse has demonstrated, it only effects the separation of the good from evil and direction toward the fellowship of blessedness; but the tearing in pieces of what has grown together brings about pain for the one being torn apart." "So," said the teacher, "that is also my reasoned opinion, and moreover that the measure of suffering is the quantity of evil in each person; for it is not likely that the one who has become involved to such an extent in forbidden evils and the one who has fallen into moderate evils will be distressed on an equal basis in the purification of bad habits, but rather that the painful flame will be kindled either to a greater or lesser degree according to the amount of matter, as long as its source of nourishment exists. Accordingly if one has a great load of this material, then the consuming flame will necessarily be great and longer-lasting for that one; but if one occasions the consumption of the fire to a lesser degree, then the punishment will diminish its actions of violence and ferocity in proportion to the lesser measure of evil which exists in that one. For it is necessary that evil at some point be wholly and completely removed out of existence, and . . . that what does not really exist should not exist at all. For since it does not belong to its nature for evil to exist outside of the will, when every will rests in God evil will depart into utter destruction, since there is no receptacle remaining for it.[33]

This passage sets forth the three main themes in Gregory's doctrine of *apokatastasis* and suggests the manner in which they are intertwined: first, every free will ultimately will rest in God; second, this requires that evil ultimately cease to exist, for evil "exists" only through the exercise of the will, and when every will chooses God, evil can no longer be chosen; and third, the means by which this will be accomplished is a process of purifying punishment that consumes the accretions of evil on the soul until only the good is left.

In the *Oratio catechetica magna* Gregory clearly portrays punishment after death as ultimately redemptive. Gregory echoes Clement and Origen in drawing heavily upon medical imagery for analogies to the healing character of punishment.[34] Later in the same work he combines medical imagery with the image of the refiner's fire in arguing for the beneficial nature of divine punishment, conceived as a long process which will heal and purify those in whom good has become mingled with evil during their earthly existence, including even the "originator of evil himself," until all creation is unified in giving thanks to God.[35] In the section on baptism later in the treatise, Gregory calls attention to the relationships between baptism and resurrection and then distinguishes between the destinies of those who have been sufficiently purified in this life and those who need further purification after death:

> For not everything that receives a restitution to exist again through the resurrection returns to the same life; rather, there is much difference between those who have been purified and those who are still in need of purification. For those who have experienced the purification of baptism[36] in this life, there is the departure to that which is of like kind. Now the state of passionlessness is associated with the pure, and no one disputes that there is blessedness in passionlessness. But for those in whom the passions have become habitual and to whom no purification of the defilement has been applied—no mystical water, no invocation of divine power, no correction by repentance—it is by all means necessary that they should come to be in the corresponding state. Now the smelting furnace is the corresponding thing for gold that has become adulterated, so that, after the evil that has become mingled with them has been removed through long succeeding ages, their nature might be preserved pure for God. Since then there is a certain cleansing power in the fire and the water, those who have washed away the filth of evil through the mystical water do not need another form of purification; but those who are uninitiated in purification must be purified by fire.[37]

Gregory concludes the *Oratio catechetica magna* with an exhortation to make every effort to rid oneself of evil in the present life, since the torment of the punishments revealed in the Scriptures is worse than anything experienced as pain in one's earthly existence. In doing so, however, he suggests that the biblical "fire" and "worm" ought to be conceived as something altogether different from their literal associations, since an earthly fire can be extinguished and an earthly worm dies, but what is referenced by these images can neither be extinguished nor die.[38] A superficial reading of this passage might lead to the conclusion that Gregory understood punishment after death as eternal torment. In light of Gregory's views to the contrary expressed in this treatise and elsewhere, however, it is probably the case that Gregory viewed the purifying effects of the fire and the worm as eternal but the painful experience of purification as temporal.

References to remedial punishment appear elsewhere in Gregory's works. In *De virginitate*, Gregory viewed cleansing discipline as something that could be voluntarily undertaken in this life through ascetical practices (including but not limited to celibacy) so that, in theory, punishment could be completely averted in the next life.[39] In *De infantibus praemature abreptis* Gregory debated whether infants who died before having an opportunity fully to live would be subject to purifying punishment, concluding that they would not.[40] He applied the recurrent images of the physician's painful cure and the refiner's fire to the corrective discipline that God may administer either in one's earthly life or after death in *De mortuis non esse dolendum*.[41]

Throughout Gregory's writings there is a consistent view of the nature and duration of punishment after death. God does not administer punishment to exact vengeance but rather to restore humanity to the state of union with God originally intended in creation; this punishment has the same purpose as painful curative measures in medicine or the melting away of dross from precious metal; such punishment will come to an end when evil has been completely separated from the good in each person; and the duration and degree of such punishment may be lessened, if not avoided entirely, by separating oneself from evil during one's earthly lifetime.

II. *Apokatastasis* and Exegesis

A. The Use of Scripture in the Articulation of Apokatastasis

1. The Universal Restoration. The interdependence of the concepts of an ultimate restoration of all to their original state and the finitude of evil becomes apparent when one examines the function of Scripture in the primary passages in which Gregory expresses these concepts. This is especially the case in Gregory's use of 1 Cor 15:28. Nevertheless, it is helpful to consider the exegetical rationales for each of these concepts separately.

(a) The Ultimate Restoration of All. Gregory found direct exegetical support for a universal outcome of salvation in two primary biblical texts: 1 Cor 15:28 and Phil 2:10-11. In addition to these, Gregory found in 1 Cor 15:42-44 and Exod 10:21-23 significant suggestions of this understanding of the *apokatastasis*.

In the *Dialogus de anima et resurrectione*, Macrina/Gregory voiced the conviction that humanity will ultimately leave evil behind "for the purpose (ἵνα)" of fulfilling the hope of the Apostle Paul in 1 Cor 15:28: "ὁ θεὸς τὰ πάντα ἐν πᾶσιν."[42] This text was full of eschatological significance for Gregory. It meant that God would become the fundamental reality in place of all other claimants to genuine being: "God will be (γενέσθαι τὸν θεὸν) instead of all other things (εἰς παντα)."[43] God will become "all things" needed for "happy (μακαριότης)" human existence, and God will be "in all things" (or "in all creatures"); this requires the "complete annihilation (τὸν παντελῆ ἀφανισμὸν)" of evil.[44] The word "all" precluded for Gregory the existence of any evil in the *apokatastasis*, for the existence of any evil would mar the "comprehensiveness (τὴν περίληψιν)" of the word "all."[45]

Gregory employed Phil 2:10-11 frequently in the course of anti-Anomoean polemic in *Contra Eunomium libri*, but the majority of these uses have reference to Christology rather than eschatology. In the *Refutatio confessionis Eunomii*,[46] however, he used it in conjunction with an echo of 1 Cor 15:28 as an explanation of what it means for God to be "all in all":

> But it is with reference to the subjection of all human beings to God—when we all, united with one another through faith, become one body of the Lord who exists in all things—that the apostle speaks of the subjection of the Son to the Father, when the adoration given to the Son by all with one accord, by those in heaven and those upon the earth and those under the earth, will be transferred to the glory of God the Father. Thus Paul says "to him every knee should bow of those in heaven and those on the earth and those under the earth, and every tongue should confess that Jesus Christ is Lord to the glory of God the Father." The great wisdom of Paul affirms that when this comes about the Son, who is in all, will himself be subjected to the Father through the subjection of all those in whom the Son is. Therefore whatever sort of once-for-all subjection Eunomius loudly proclaims for the Spirit is not taught by the phrase to which he attributes it, although it may have to do with the irrational or captives or servants or chastened children or those who are saved through subjection. For the subjection of people to God is salvation to those who are subjected, according to the voice of the prophet, who says that the soul is subject to God, since from him comes salvation through subjection; thus subjection is a protection against destruction. Just as medicine is zealously pursued by the sick, so also is subjection by those in need of salvation.[47]

In the course of refuting Eunomius's appeal to 1 Cor 15:27-28 as evidence for an eternal subordination within the Godhead, Gregory reveals his own understanding of the relationship between Phil 2:10-11 and his concept of the *apokatastasis*. All people ("οἱ πάντες"; "πάντων τῶν ἀνθρώπων") will become subject to God and so be united in the Lord, who is in all ("ἐν πᾶσιν"; cf. 1 Cor 15:27-28). The subjection of the Son is explained as the subjection of all those who will be "one body of the Lord (ἓν σῶμα τοῦ κυρίου)" rather than an eternal subjection of the Son himself to the Father. Gregory interprets Phil 2:10-11 as a reference to the same eventual subjection of all people in Christ to God. His use of this text as a witness to universal salvation hinges on two equations: the equivalence of the subjection of all to God in 1 Cor 15:28 with the worship and confession of Christ by all in Phil 2:10-11, and especially the equivalence of subjection with salvation. Gregory bases his equation of subjection and salvation on Scripture by adducing "the voice of the prophet," actually an allusion to Ps 61:2 (LXX): "Will my soul not be subjected to God? For from him is my salvation."[48] In comparing the salvation available in subjection to the healing sought by the sick, Gregory draws on the medicinal imagery so prominent in his predecessors Clement of Alexandria and Origen.

Gregory differed from Origen in a specific point of exegesis concerning a phrase in Phil 2:10 and its relationship to the objects of salvation through subjection in the *apokatastasis*. In the *Dialogus de anima et resurrectione*, Macrina identifies what she believes the apostle Paul "signified (ἀποσημαίνειν)" by the phrase "ἐπουρανίων καὶ ἐπιγείων καὶ καταχθονίων": these are not spatial references but rather "that which he calls 'in heaven' is the angelic and unembodied state, that which is 'on the earth' is what is entangled with the body, and that which is 'under the earth' is what is already separated from the body."[49] Then in mentioning an alternative interpretation she alludes to a position that is undoubtedly the one Origen advocated in *De principiis*:

> Or if in fact any other nature besides what we have said is thought to be among rational beings—which someone might wish to name as either demons or spirits or any other such thing—we will not differ. For it is believed on the basis of both common sense and the tradition of the Scriptures that there is some nature apart from such bodies, situated opposite the good and hurtful to human life. This nature has willingly fallen away from the better allotment; it is in revolt against the good and has given substance in itself to what is considered its opposite. It is said the apostle counts this nature among "those under the earth," signifying in that phrase that when evil has been extinguished through long periods of time, nothing

outside of the good will be left, but even from those the confession
of the lordship of Christ will be in unison.[50]

Macrina's point of contention is not over the suggestion that demonic
beings would share along with human beings in the restoration that
takes place when evil ceases to exist but rather with the identification
of "καταχθονίων" as demonic beings. Gregory's interpretation, mir-
rored by Macrina's part in the dialogue, was a different application of
Origen's interiorized eschatology: "ἐπιγείων" and "καταχθονίων"
refer respectively to things associated with the resurrection body and to
things that in the resurrection will no longer have bodily associations.
That Gregory's dissenting exegesis of this text did not rule out the ultimate salvation of the demons is confirmed by *or. catech.* 26, in which
Gregory taught that "even the originator of evil himself" will be healed
in the *apokatastasis*.

In the concluding discourse from the *Dialogus de anima et resurrectione*, Macrina finds in the agricultural imagery Paul employed in
his argument for the resurrection in 1 Cor 15:42-44 evidence for the
ultimate restoration of all to the state conceived by God in creation.[51]
Paul compares the resurrection of the body to the transformation of the
grain that is sown into the ear that is raised. This, says Macrina, "is in
agreement with our notion of the resurrection and shows what our definition comprehends when we say that the resurrection is nothing other
than the restoration of our nature to the original state."[52] She combines
this text with her observation of the order of creation in Gen 1:11-12:
God created seed-bearing plants, and then vegetation sprouted from the
earth, implying that what sprouted was identical to the plant that provided the seed from which it sprang. Macrina further develops this
resurrection analogy by equating the original species (Gen 1:11) or the
ear (1 Cor 15:42-44) with the state God originally intended for humanity. Evil dries up the full ear of this original state so that it dies, leaving
behind a seed, but in the resurrection it springs up to become what it
was before it fell to the earth. Some seeds, however, are so deformed
by evil that they must receive harsh treatment by the farmer before they
can grow to maturity. In this way, Macrina argues, all will eventually
"after long periods of time receive the common form that was placed
upon us by God from the beginning."[53]

In the second book of *De vita Moysis*, Gregory moved beyond the
literal sense (ἱστορία) of the narratives treated in the first book to their
"deeper meaning" (θεωρία).[54] The quest for the θεωρία of Exod 10:21-

23 led Gregory to find in that passage a suggestion of the *apokatasta-sis*:

> Now if after the three days in darkness it came about that the Egyp-tians also shared in the light, then perhaps one might come to per-ceive the restoration of those who have been condemned to Gehenna, which is expected after these things in the kingdom of heaven. For that "palpable darkness,"[55] as the bare narrative says, has a great kinship to the "outer darkness"[56] both in word and in concept. Each of these was dispelled when Moses, as we have al-ready perceived, stretched out his hands on behalf of those in the darkness.[57]

In Exod 10:21-23, Yahweh directed Moses to stretch out his hands to-ward heaven so that darkness might fall over the land of Egypt. Moses did so, and for three days the Egyptians experienced darkness. The temporality of the darkness followed once again by light, an experience shared even by the Egyptians, suggested to Gregory that those tor-mented in Gehenna would ultimately be restored. Gregory found fur-ther evidence that the deeper meaning of Exod 10:21-23 did in fact point to a universal restoration in the verbal and conceptual similarities between the "τὸ ψηλαφητὸν σκότος" of Exod 10:21 and the Matthean expression "τὸ ἐξώτερον σκότος." According to this reasoning, there must be an end to the torments of Gehenna if all are to share in the *apokatastasis*.

(b) The Finitude of Evil. In the *Dialogus de anima et resurrectione*, Gregory disclosed two assumptions upon which he based his view of the finitude of evil. First, evil owes its existence to the improper exer-cise of the divine gift of free moral agency. Second, all free rational creatures will ultimately exercise their freedom in choosing to rest in union with God; thus evil is no longer chosen and therefore will no longer exist. Initially the grounds for this view of the nature of evil might seem to be philosophical rather than exegetical.[58] There are par-allels to the Plotinian conceptions of the good and the nature of evil,[59] and frequently Gregory's direct discussions of the finitude of evil are devoid of explicit citations of Scripture. Nevertheless, an exegetical substructure may be found for both assumptions involving the Genesis creation narrative (Gen 1-3), Jas 1:13-15, and once again 1 Cor 15:28.

Gregory found in the appearance of humanity at the end of the order of creation an indication of the role of humanity as royal ruler of all the preceding creation, for "it is not reasonable that the ruler should appear prior to those who are ruled; rather, first the realm was prepared, and then the one who rules it was brought forth."[60] The regality of the human soul as created by God consisted in its complete freedom of will: "For the soul shows that it is both regal and well-fitted of its own accord, far removed from uncultivated baseness, in consequence of which it has no master and possesses free will, controlled with absolute authority of its own volition."[61]

Gregory understood the chief significance of the *imago dei* (Gen 1:27) as the creation of humanity for participation in the goodness of God ("ἐπὶ μετουσίᾳ τῶν ἰδίων ἀγαθῶν").[62] This included participation in "that most excellent and precious of good things," free moral agency:

> For the one who made humanity for participation in his own good things and placed in human nature inclinations toward all things excellent, so that this inclination might in each case be appropriately attracted to what is similar to it, would not have withheld the most excellent and precious of good things: I speak of course of the gift of having no master and possessing free will. For if any necessity were set over human life, the image would have been falsified in regard to that part, being estranged by its dissimilarity to the archetype. For how can that which is yoked and enslaved to any necessities be called the image of the one who rules by nature? Surely then that which in all things was made entirely similar to the divine in its foundation has in its nature the possession of free will and independence from mastery, so that it might have participation in the good things as the prize of virtue.[63]

Gregory found in the two trees of the garden (Gen 2:9, 16-17) a representation of the moral alternatives, the good and the corruption of the good, that called for the exercise of free choice.[64] The first man[65] willfully turned away from the good and so brought evil into "existence":

> Thus also "the first man from the earth," or rather the one who generated evil in humanity, by nature had that which is excellent and good lying around everywhere for free choice, but voluntarily inaugurated for himself things which were contrary to nature, creating the exercise of evil in turning away from virtue by his own deliberate choice. For apart from deliberate choice, evil has no force and cannot be observed as having its own substance in the manner of things that exist.[66]

Gregory's concept of the finitude of evil was therefore firmly rooted in his reading of the Genesis account of the origin of evil among humanity.

Gregory repeatedly stressed that God neither created nor willed evil; evil must therefore have an origin apart from God and God's intention for creation. In the *Oratio catechetica magna*, Gregory taught that evil originates within the human soul in its choice to turn away from that which is excellent ("ἀπὸ τοῦ καλοῦ"):

> No inception of evil had its beginning in the divine will. For evil would have been without blame if it were assigned to God as its maker and father. But evil somehow has its origin from within, coming into being by deliberate choice when there comes about a certain departure of the soul from that which is excellent.[67]

Although there is an absence of clear verbal parallels, it is probable that Gregory based this idea on Jas 1:13-15:[68]

> Let no one say when being tempted, "I am being tempted by God." For God is not capable of being tempted by evil, and he himself tempts no one. But each one is tempted when dragged down and baited by one's own desires; then desire, having conceived, gives birth to sin, and sin, having been accomplished, brings forth death.

Gregory understood the result of this choice of evil as a "deprivation (στέρησις)" of the natural (i.e., divinely intended) orientation of the soul toward virtue, so that vice is "the absence of virtue (ἀρετῆς ἀπουσίαν)" and is therefore inherently non-existent ("ἀνύπαρκτον").[69]

Gregory's conviction in the *Dialogus de anima et resurrectione* that every free human will one day will find eternal rest in God[70] was grounded in 1 Cor 15:28. Gregory believed this to be the natural outcome of human freedom. Although it is temporarily obscured by its misuse, freedom was given to humanity by God as a reflection of God, and "everything that is free will be in harmony (συναρμοσθήσεται) with whatever is similar (τῷ ὁμοίῳ) to itself."[71] This must come to pass, says Macrina, for Paul taught that God will be "all in all (τὰ πάντα ἐν πάσιν)" (1 Cor 15:28).[72] If God is truly to be all in all things, evil cannot have any existence in them. The Scriptures then appear ("δοκεῖ") to teach the finitude of evil.[73] Gregory's hope for God to become "all in all" and therefore to bring evil to an end is at the heart of his conviction of the universality of the *apokatastasis*. First Corinthians 15:28 is a key biblical text in his exegetical argument for this hope.

2. The Nature and Duration of Punishment after Death.

Gregory made use of several biblical texts in the expression of his concept of punishment after death as redemptive rather than retributive in nature. In Gregory's opinion, 1 Cor 3:10-15, Mal 3:2-3, Matt 9:12/Mark 2:17, Luke 15:8-10, and Matt 18:23-25 supported such an understanding.

The refiner's fire appeared frequently as an image of eternal punishment in Gregory's writings. Just as gold mixed with impurities must be purified by fire, so the human soul must undergo the purifying fire in order to melt away its accretions of evil.[74] Although Gregory did not explicitly cite 1 Cor 3:10-15 in this connection, close conceptual and verbal parallels suggest this text as the source of that image.[75]

In a passage from the *Oratio catechetica magna*, Gregory echoed Malachi's comparison of the coming of Yahweh in judgment to a refiner's fire that purifies gold and silver (Mal 3:2-3). Although painful, this judgment is ultimately redemptive: "by achieving the disappearance of that which is contrary to nature, the approach of the divine power in the manner of fire benefits the nature by purification, even if the separation is painful."[76]

Gregory drew upon the biblical image of Jesus as physician in his portrayal of the medicinal nature of punishment. Jesus' healing work is not directed towards those who are already well, but to the sick (Matt 9:12; Mark 2:17):

> For as those who use a knife or cautery to scrape off calluses and warts contrary to nature which have become attached to the body do not apply a painless cure to the one being treated—only they do not use the knife with the intent to do harm—so also whatever sort of material accretions have become calluses on our souls, which have become fleshly through fellowship with the passions, are cut away and scraped off at the time of judgment by that indescribable wisdom and power of the one who, just as the Gospel says, "heals those who are sick." For it says, "those who are healthy have no need of a physician, but rather those who are sick." [77]

Those whose souls have become sick in this life and remain unhealed at its end stand in need of the painful cure of "the knife, cauteries, and bitter medicines."[78] God therefore uses punishment after death as a remedy for the diseases of the soul.

Gregory used the parable of the lost coin to illustrate the purification of the soul both in this life and in the life to come. The ten drach-
mas are the virtues of the *imago dei*. If even one virtue is missing, the
others are useless. The missing virtue has been lost within one's own
house (the soul) and is likely hidden under dirt (accretions of evil). The
virtue may be recovered in this life by lighting a lamp (the illuminating
Word) and sweeping away the dirt ("the filth of the flesh") or in the
next through purifying punishment.[79]

The parable of the unforgiving servant (Matt 18:23-35) suggested
to Gregory four aspects of redemptive punishment. First, all will be
judged in some way. Some owe small debts, some owe large debts, but
all must settle their accounts. Second, the degree and duration of punishment necessary vary from person to person. Those whose debts are
larger through "participation in the troubles of life" face more severe
punishments. Third, the pains of punishment are redemptive: the
debtor is "delivered to the torturers until he has paid the last cent."
Fourth, punishment is not unending, for when the debtor has finally
paid the debt, he is free.[80]

B. Apokatastasis and the Interpretation of Other Selected Biblical Texts

1. Universalistic Texts. Of the biblical texts suggestive of a universal
outcome of God's work of salvation, Gregory did not cite or allude to
John 12:32, Rom 11:25-26a (unless one includes a single reference in
the doubtfully authentic *De occursu domini*[81]), Col 1:20, or 2 Pet 3:9.
His interaction with the remaining texts in this category does offer additional insight into the relationship between his universalism and his
biblical interpretation.

(a) Acts 3:21. While Acts 3:21 contains the sole New Testament occurrence of the noun ἀποκατάστασις, Gregory did not seem to make explicit use of that text in setting forth his idea of a universal restoration.
The compilers of *Biblia Patristica* identified citations of or allusions to
Acts 3:21 in *ascens.* (GNO 9:327); *mort.* (GNO 9:51); *hom. opif.* 17, 24,
26 (PG 44:188-189, 213, 224); *or. catech.* 26 (GNO 3,4:67); and *v. Mos.*
2.82 (SC 1:154.3).[82] Although all these passages do contain some form
of the noun ἀποκατάστασις, in no case does there appear to be an explicit reference, even at the level of allusion, to Acts 3:21, for the language is too dissimilar.[83] Gregory did express some element of his
doctrine of the universal *apokatastasis* in these passages, but he did not
refer to Acts 3:21 in doing so. It is nevertheless possible that Acts 3:21

influenced Gregory's use of the word ἀποκατάστασις or that when Gregory encountered the word in Acts 3:21 he read it with his own technical use of the word in mind, but this cannot be established apart from an explicit citation of Acts 3:21.

(b) Romans 5:18-21. Gregory alluded to portions of Rom 5:18-21 on eight occasions.[84] In seven of these instances, the allusions have no necessary connection with any expression of Gregory's eschatological universalism. An allusion to v. 18 appears in *Pss. titt.* 2.8 (GNO 5:96) with reference to the "second man" who reintroduces life and destroys death; a similar allusion to v. 18 appears in *sanct. sal. pasch.* (GNO 9:310) along with an echo of v. 21. In *Apoll.* (GNO 3,1:160-61) the reference to the death-destroying obedience of the "one man," Christ, is based upon the idea expressed in v. 19.[85] A brief verbal echo of a phrase from v. 19 ("διὰ τῆς παρακοῆς") occurs in *hom. in cant.* 2 (GNO 6:51) with reference to the entrance of sin into the world, but there is no allusion to life through obedience of Christ in the second part of the verse. Later in *hom. in cant.* 4 (GNO 6:123) there is another echo of the same phrase, this time with an allusion to the second part of the verse, in a restatement of the meaning of Cant 2:4-5. Verse 19 also underlies Gregory's mention of the healing of the disobedience of humanity through the obedience of Christ in *Ref. conf. Eun.* 134 (GNO 2:370). The *Oratio in diem natalem Christi* contains a close verbal parallel to a short phrase from v. 20, but again there is no explicit connection of the reference to Gregory's concept of the *apokatastasis*.[86] In the homily *In illud: Tunc et ipse filius*, Gregory's allusion to v. 21 with reference to the dominion of death through sin over all humanity is set in the context of a passage expressing confidence in a future universal restoration after all evil is destroyed, but he did not use the text directly to substantiate that conviction.[87] Although these references to Rom 5:18-21 are not exegetical arguments for universal salvation, it is not necessary to conclude that Gregory did not consider this passage consistent with the concept. It is nevertheless surprising that Gregory failed to make use of this text as exegetical evidence for his position.

(c) 1 Corinthians 3:12-15. Eight passages in Gregory's works contain brief references or allusions to 1 Cor 3:12-13; there are no references to vv. 14-15.[88] In the *In Canticum canticorum homiliae*, Gregory used Paul's mention of the "wood, hay, and stubble" that would ultimately be burned to illustrate the kind of building materials which the bride in Cant 2:4-5 did not choose as support for her house[89] and Solomon in

Cant 3:9-10 did not choose for the construction of his chariot.[90] In his attempt to discern the θεωρία underlying the ἱστορία of the biblical story of the life of Moses, Gregory equated the straw and chaff which Pharaoh commanded the Hebrews to mix in the brick with the material to be burned by fire mentioned by the "voice of the apostle."[91] The "gold, silver, precious stones, wood, hay, stubble" of v. 12 represented respectively the things to be built up and the things to be torn down (Eccl 3:3) in one's earthly life.[92] In a subsequent homily on Ecclesiastes in which Gregory discussed the spiritual significance of Sabbath legislation in the Old Testament, v. 12 indicated that the firewood that could not be gathered on the Sabbath signified the vain pursuits of life that would be consumed in the end.[93] Gregory countered an argument of Eunomius in *Eunom.* 3.2.101 (GNO 2:86) by pointing out that when Paul combined wood, hay, stubble, gold, silver, and precious stones in the same phrase in v. 12, he still considered these to be of different substances. In *Steph.* 2 (GNO 10,1:100) the stones with which the Jews stoned Stephen became for him "precious stones," and in *virg.* 18.1 (SC 119:464) Gregory praised virginity as a thing to be counted among "gold, silver, and precious stones."

Although some of these references to the "wood, hay, and stubble" of v. 12 are consistent with Gregory's theology of punishment after death, they were not employed in direct arguments for a purifying punishment after death by which all people would ultimately be restored to God. It may be asked, however, whether the criteria employed by the compilers of *Biblia Patristica* for identifying allusions to 1 Cor 3:12-15 were too narrow. Numerous passages in which Gregory used the image of the refiner's fire when explaining punishment after death as redemptive may also allude to 1 Cor 3:12-15.[94] Since the image of the refiner's fire often appears in passages in which Gregory did explicitly affirm remedial punishment, Gregory in all probability made more extensive use of 1 Cor 3:12-15 in his reflection on the nature and duration of punishment after death than a perusal of the citations and allusions identified in *Biblia Patristica* might initially suggest.[95]

(d) 1 Corinthians 15:22-28. According to *Biblia Patristica*, Gregory referred to some portion of 1 Cor 15:22-28 sixty-five times (or, if consecutive references are combined, forty-five times).[96] Since twenty-eight of these references (or thirteen if consecutive references are combined and the title is not counted) appear in *In illud: Tunc et ipse filius*, a homily on 1 Cor 15:28, this work merits special attention in examining Gregory's exegesis of this passage. In five of these instances,

Gregory quoted or alluded to the passage in mentioning or refuting his opponents' appeal to this text as evidence of an eternal subjection of the Son to the Father.[97] Twice Gregory quoted or echoed part of this text with no necessary overtones of eschatological universalism.[98] In six passages of *In illud: Tunc et ipse filius*, however, 1 Cor 15:22-28 served as a direct exegetical argument for the universal *apokatastasis*. After quoting v. 22 and alluding to v. 28, Gregory drew some conclusions from the text:

> What then is the goal of the word which the divine apostle teaches in that part of the text? That the nature of evil will pass over into non-being after being completely obliterated from existence, and the divine and pure goodness will contain in itself every rational nature, with nothing made by God failing to obtain the kingdom of God. This will come about when everything mixed with the things of evil adulterated matter has been consumed through refining by the purifying fire, which all had its origin from God and did not receive evil in the beginning. And this he said to be so: he said that the pure and undefiled divinity of the only-begotten one came to exist in the mortal and perishable nature of humanity. And on account of the whole human nature with which the divinity was mixed—which is a certain sort of first-fruits of the common dough—humanity exists according to Christ, through whom all humanity is joined to the divinity.[99]

Verses 22 and 28 therefore suggested to Gregory the finitude of evil, the ultimate universality of humanity's participation in the kingdom of God by virtue of God's creative purpose, purifying punishment as the means by which this universal participation would come to pass, and the final union of all of humanity with God. Gregory developed similar ideas from 1 Cor 15:22-28 in the remainder of the homily. In Gregory's estimation, the subjection of all things to God in Christ in v. 28 required the complete alienation of all evil.[100] After quoting 1 Cor 15:22-28 in its entirety, Gregory reaffirmed that the passage required the ultimate non-existence of evil if God were truly to be "all in all."[101] The reference to the handing over of the kingdom to the Father in v. 24 meant that the whole body of Christ will have access to God, since for Gregory the body of Christ is the entirety of human nature and is inclusive of all humankind.[102] Gregory understood the subjection referred to in v. 28 as union with God and the indwelling of Christ in every person,[103] and by linking vv. 24-28 with Rom 5:10 he concluded that subjection is equivalent to reconciliation, which is equivalent to salvation; accordingly, all will yield to and be united with God.[104] Finally, the reference to the "enemies" who will become subject to God in v. 25 meant that even those who have been opposed to God in their earthly lives will share in the divine nature in the restoration.[105]

The present context permits only a brief summary of the ways in which Gregory employed 1 Cor 15:22-28 apart from *In illud: Tunc et ipse filius*. On some occasions Gregory referred to portions of this passage in polemic against Eunomius or other forms of subordinationism, but without any connection to the concept of *apokatastasis*.[106] In many other passages Gregory quoted or alluded to part of 1 Cor 15:22-28 with no necessary implication of universal salvation.[107] In seven additional passages from Gregory's works, however, 1 Cor 15:22-28 functioned as a direct exegetical argument for his conviction of the restoration of all rational creatures to the original state.[108]

(e) 2 Corinthians 5:19. Gregory quoted or alluded to 2 Cor 5:19 on six occasions.[109] A trio of references to that text in *Antirrheticus adversus Apollinarium* has no universalistic overtones,[110] as is also true of an allusion in a homily on the Song of Songs.[111] Gregory does take 2 Cor 5:19 to mean that even God's enemies are reconciled to God in the restoration in another homily from *In Canticum canticorum homiliae* and in a passage in *De perfectione christiana ad Olympium monachum*.[112]

(f) Ephesians 1:10. Twice Gregory made brief reference to Eph 1:10.[113] In *hom. in cant.* 3 (GNO 6:97) he mentioned "τὸ πλήρωμα τῶν καιρῶν"[114] but did not refer to "the summing up of all things in Christ (ἀνακεφαλαιώσασθαι τὰ πάντα ἐν τῷ Χριστῷ)." The latter phrase is quoted in *ascens.* (GNO 9:327) in a doxological passage at the conclusion of the homily, but with no elaboration. This text therefore appears not to have played a role in Gregory's exegetical rationale for the *apokatastasis*.

(g) Philippians 2:9-11. Gregory quoted or alluded to Phil 2:9-11 (or some portion thereof) forty-five times (or forty times if consecutive references are combined).[115] Eighteen of these references involve only v. 9, which in isolation is not conceivably suggestive of eschatological universalism; these have little relevance for the role of Phil 2:9-11 in Gregory's universalism.[116] A number of references to vv. 10-11 also have no necessary connection to Gregory's thoughts about the universal restoration.[117]

Elsewhere the passage figured prominently in explicit exegetical support for the idea. In addition to references to Phil 2:10-11 in the

Dialogus de anima et resurrectione in which Macrina/Gregory refuted appeals to the passage as evidence for a spatial conception of Hades,[118] alluded to Origen's alternative identification of "καταχθονίων" in v. 10 as demonic spirits,[119] and hinted at a universalistic interpretation of the text, a quotation of vv. 10-11 later in the dialogue is interpreted to mean that "those who are now outside on account of evil will at some time come to be within the sanctuary of divine blessedness";[120] this will result in "the harmony of everything in the good (τὴν τοῦ παντὸς πρὸς τὸ ἀγαθὸν συμφωνίαν)."[121] In commenting on a phrase from Ps 150:5, "Praise him with euphonious cymbals (αἰνεῖτε αὐτὸν ἐν κυμβάλοις εὐήχοις)," in *In inscriptiones psalmorum*, Gregory linked this praise with the confession of Phil 2:10-11: one cymbal is the supernatural angelic nature and the other cymbal is the rational human nature restored to its original state, so that both angelic and human natures become united in the praise of God and confession of Christ as Lord.[122] The interpretive key to Gregory's use of this text as a witness to the universal restoration lies in his equation of the subjection involved in the bending of the knee in worship and the confession that Jesus Christ is Lord with salvation.[123]

(h) 1 Timothy 2:4. Quotations or allusions to 1 Tim 2:4 appear in fourteen passages in Gregory's works.[124] In three of these passages Gregory quoted the text against his opponents as evidence that the Father and Son are united in will (i.e., both desire the salvation of all),[125] and in others there are references to the text with other applications but also without any explanation suggestive of an ultimately universal accomplishment of God's salvific will.[126] Only in two passages is there a clear suggestion by Gregory that God's intention to save all as attested by 1 Tim 2:4 will assuredly lead to the salvation of all people. In *Eunom.* 3.10.38 (GNO 2:304) Gregory affirmed his conviction that the Son will in fact accomplish the divine will, and in *hom. in cant.* 4 (GNO 6:130-31) he interpreted this expression of God's will as an oath which God is bound to fulfill. The latter two passages suggest that this confidence in the ultimate accomplishment of God's intention to save all may be implicit in the other passages as well.

(i) Titus 2:11. Gregory cited or alluded to Tit 2:11 five times.[127] In four of these passages Gregory echoed the first part of the verse, "For the grace of God has appeared (Ἐπεφάνη γὰρ ἡ χάρις τοῦ θεοῦ)," with no reference to rest of the verse, "for salvation to all people (σωτήριος πᾶσιν ἀνθρώποις)," and no suggestion of a connection between this

text and the concept of universal restoration.[128] Only in *or. catech.* 18 (GNO 3,4:51) did Gregory quote the latter portion of v. 11, but here also he did not employ the text as a biblical testimony to the *apokatastasis*. Titus 2:11 therefore played no role in the written expression of Gregory's thought on this theme.

(j) 1 John 2:2. Gregory alluded to 1 John 2:2 only once.[129] A verbal parallel to v. 2a appears in *Contra Eunomium libri*,[130] but there is neither any allusion to the potentially universalistic phrase in v. 12b nor any hint of a universalistic application of the text.

2. Texts Suggesting Eternal Punishment. Gregory seems not to have made written use of Rev 20:14-15 or 21:8, but there are references to other texts that traditionally supported a double outcome of eternal judgment.

(a) Matthew 5:29-30. Gregory referred to Matt 5:29-30 in two passages in his works.[131] There are allusions to vv. 28-30 in *v. Mos.* 2.304 (GNO 7,1:138) and *Eunom.* 1.545 (GNO 1:184), but no references to the possibility of being cast "εἰς γέενναν."

(b) Matthew 8:12. Gregory cited or alluded to Matt 8:12 ten times.[132] In some of these passages the text is referenced without any comment or elaboration which might indicate Gregory's understanding of the nature of the "outer darkness" into which some will be cast or of the "weeping and gnashing of teeth" experienced there.[133] Other passages supply the text with some commentary but seemingly reveal a degree of ambivalence about its meaning. In *beat.* 3 (GNO 7,2:100) Gregory portrayed the function of the "outer darkness" in medicinal terms: the warning of this punishment serves as a "bitterly astringent medicine" that turns sinners from the error of their way and thus heals them. In *beat.* 5 (GNO 7,2:136), however, he seems to have viewed the "outer darkness" simply as retribution for the evil done in one's earthly life. A similar ambivalence is evident in a pair of passages from *In inscriptiones psalmorum*. On the one hand, Gregory explained the "weeping and gnashing of teeth" along with the "pangs of death" and the "perils of Hades" (Ps 114:3 [LXX]) as referring to "the end unto which the nature of sin comes,"[134] implying that it is the sin rather than the sinner that is thus condemned. On the other hand, he wrote that those condemned to the "outer darkness" have "no means (ἐφόδιον) of salvation."[135]

Still other passages confirm that Gregory did not understand Matt 8:12 as teaching unending, retributive torment. In *pasch.* (GNO 9:268) the "darkness" is viewed as a penalty imposed only on the body, which has caused the soul to choose evil; it cannot harm the soul, which has no inherent evil; therefore God will accomplish the resurrection (which elsewhere Gregory equated with *apokatastasis*). A trio of passages from *De vita Moysis* substantiates this as Gregory's understanding of the significance of Matt 8:12: the "outer darkness" is expelled when the restoration of those condemned to Gehenna takes place;[136] deliverance is available for those being so punished;[137] and those who have managed to live without sin in their earthly lives will not have to undergo the "outer darkness."[138]

(c) Matthew 10:28/Luke 12:5. According to *Biblia Patristica*, Gregory referred twice to Matt 10:28 and once to the parallel passage in Luke 12:5.[139] An allusion to Matt 10:28 is listed for the *Dialogus de anima et resurrectione*,[140] but this reference to fear as an aid in the development of virtue is probably not an intentional echo of that text. Gregory did not elaborate on an allusion to Matt 10:28 in *Pulch.* (GNO 9:466) or a quotation of Luke 12:5 in *hom. in cant.* 15 (GNO 6:462) in such a way as to clarify his understanding of these texts.

(d) Matthew 18:8-9/Mark 9:42-48. Gregory quoted or echoed Matt 18:8-9 or its parallel in Mark 9:42-48 on nine occasions.[141] An allusion to Matt 18:8 in *Eunom.* 1.545 (GNO 1:184) makes no reference to the possibility of being cast into "eternal fire" at the end of the verse and thus sheds no light on Gregory's understanding of it. The other passages indicate that although Gregory did not conceive of the "fire" and "worm" of Matt 18:8-9 and Mark 9:42-48 in literal terms,[142] he nonetheless considered them to be real threats. Gregory found anticipations of this threatened punishment in the θεωρία of the story of the life of Moses. Just as the furnace ashes caused the Egyptians to become afflicted with boils (Exod 9:8-12), so the threat of punishment in Gehenna applies to all those who follow the Egyptians in their way of life.[143] Just as the manna which the Israelites hoarded for the next day turned to worms (Exod 16:20), so the objects of covetousness in the present life become the "undying worm" in the future life.[144] One may avoid the fire, worm, and Gehenna by avoiding sin in the present life.[145] In the *Orationes de beatitudinibus*, Gregory portrayed the threat of this punishment as a medicine that heals by warning sinners to repent in the present life,[146] but in the future life this punishment is in some sense

retributive.[147] In the homily *In sextum psalmum* he equated the "undying worm" with the torments of the conscience, which causes shame and pain through the remembrance of evil deeds.[148] Only in *pasch.* (GNO 9:268) does Gregory seem to have thought of these punishments as ultimately coming to an end: the fact that the fire and worm are inflicted only on the flesh without harming the soul means that eventually the soul will experience the resurrection.

(e) Matthew 25:31-46. References to all or part of Matt 25:31-46 occur thirty times in Gregory's corpus.[149] Eighteen of these references are to v. 31 alone or focus on portions of the passage that refer only to the reward of the righteous and therefore have little relevance for the issue at hand.[150] Nine additional references mention the division of humanity into the "sheep" and the "goats" and/or the respective reward or retribution for each group, but elaboration that might clarify Gregory's understanding of this text and its relationship to his views on eschatological punishment is absent or insignificant in these passages.[151] The remaining four references are supplied with more suggestive commentary; three of them emphasize the retributive aspect of eschatological punishment. In *De beneficentia*, Gregory referred to vv. 31-46 and described the judgment of evil, misanthropic persons as "fiery eternal punishment."[152] Two passages from the *Orationes de beatitudinibus* in which Gregory employed phrases from vv. 31-34, 40, 41, and 45 highlight the division between the two groups of people and portray the punishment meted out to the wicked as retribution, but Gregory offered no clarification of the duration either of the division of the faithful from the wicked or of the punishment of the wicked. An allusion to v. 41 in *pasch.* (GNO 9:268), however, suggests the possibility of an end to the torment of the "goats": because the "just punishment" of "fire" ("δίκαιαι τιμωρίαι πῦρ") is imposed only on the body and does not harm the soul, the soul will be raised. The predominant emphasis on retribution in Gregory's use of this passage is attributable to Gregory's homiletical agenda: the majority of the references appear in the course of discussions of the reward of the faithful, and biblical texts that warn of the judgment of the wicked underscore the consequences of the hearer's or reader's decisions and deeds. Gregory's rhetorical purposes thus minimize any ostensive influence of his concept of *apokatastasis* upon his exegesis of this text.

(f) Luke 16:19-31. Gregory interacted with portions of Luke 16:19-31 in twenty-seven passages in his works.[153] His exegesis of this passage

in various contexts initially appears contradictory. Three instances in which Gregory appealed to the text in discussions of the nature of the intermediate state[154] and two passages in which he existentialized the "chasm" of v. 26 to emphasize the theological and spiritual distance between his opponents and himself[155] pose little difficulty. An interpretive "chasm" seems to exist, however, between a group of passages in which Gregory made rather literal ethical-eschatological applications of Luke 16:19-31 and a less literal treatment of that text in the *Dialogus de anima et resurrectione*. The majority of Gregory's references to Luke 16:19-31 emphasized the eschatological reward of Lazarus and/or the retributive punishment of the rich man for the manner in which they lived during their earthly existence and the "great chasm" that separated them after death.[156] A reading of these passages in isolation might suggest that Gregory interpreted Luke 16:19-31 with a more traditional understanding of eternal punishment in mind. This classical proof-text for the traditional view of eternal punishment, however, actually pointed to something entirely different according to his reading of the parable in the *Dialogus de anima et resurrectione*. The illogic of a literal reading of this text, Macrina contended, "summons the one who listens with diligent inquiry to a more subtle understanding (θε- ωρίαν)."[157] The rich man has left his physical body in the tomb. How, then, does he "lift up eyes," "feel the flame," or "cool his tongue" without his body? The meaning of the text, Macrina said, must be sought in its θεωρία rather than the "ordinary sense (τὸ προχείρως νοου- ΄μενον)."[158] The "great gulf" is not a physical chasm but rather that which separates those souls who choose the good, focusing not on this life but on the life to come, from those souls who choose evil, focusing not on the life to come but on this present life.[159] The rich man is unable to cross the gulf because he is still too much focused on earthly life, as evidenced by his fixation on the welfare of his wealthy family.[160] The implication is that he may eventually cross the abyss when he has ceased clinging to the fleshly existence he has left behind.

The apparent conflict between these two major lines of interpretation in Gregory's use of Luke 16:19-31 may be resolved if one takes into account their respective contexts and purposes.[161] The focus on eternal reward and punishment appears mainly in homiletical literature and has as its purpose motivation for ethical conduct in the present life. The suggestion that the rich man may ultimately be restored after his torment is complete is limited to the *Dialogus de anima et resurrectione*, in which Gregory engaged in pure theological and philosophical reflection apart from homiletical considerations. As Monique Alexan-

dre noted, "le public est autre" as well.[162] The homiletical literature is
directed toward the catechumenate or the ordinary faithful and tends to
focus on the literal meaning of the texts expounded (although not exclusively); the *Dialogus de anima et resurrectione* has a more philosophically inclined audience in mind and exhibits a greater affinity for the
deeper meaning of Scripture. In should be noted that even in the passages in which Gregory emphasized the torment of Lazarus, he never
specified the duration of this torment. This leaves open the possibility
that Gregory believed it important to warn his audience of the painful
aspects of divine punishment but thought it unwise to mention its purifying function in certain contexts, lest people lose their motivation to
lead righteous lives in the present.

(g) 2 Thessalonians 1:7-9. Gregory made use of 2 Thess 1:7-9 in only
one passage.[163] He quoted this text in *Ar. et Sab.* (GNO 3,1:77) to emphasize the role of the Son in executing judgment, but he did not elaborate on the nature of "ὄλεθρον αἰώνιον" (v. 9).

III. Conclusions

An examination of Gregory's interaction with Scripture in written
expressions of his hope for universal salvation demonstrates clear connections between biblical exegesis and the interrelated concepts of the
ultimate restoration of all rational creatures to the state intended for
them in creation, the finitude of evil, and the redemptive purpose and
limited duration of punishment after death. Gregory believed the universal *apokatastasis* to be explicitly taught by a pair of Pauline passages linked closely together in his development of the idea. Gregory
repeatedly interpreted 1 Cor 15:22-28 as teaching the salvific subjection of all creatures to God, including the enemies of God. In his opinion, this required the ultimate finitude of evil, for when all are subject
to God and God is "all in all," evil can no longer exist, since it has no
existence apart from the choice not to be subject to God. Gregory interpreted Phil 2:10-11 similarly, often in connection with 1 Cor 15:22-
28: if all will worship and confess Christ as Lord, all will be subject to
God and therefore will experience God's salvation. The equation of
subjection and salvation in 1 Cor 15:22-28 and Phil 2:10 was in turn
based on Ps 61:2 (LXX). Two additional texts functioned as more indirect biblical arguments for Gregory's understanding of the *apokatastasis.* Gregory considered Paul's agricultural analogy to the resurrection
in 1 Cor 15:42-44 consistent with the concept, and he suggested that the

discerning interpreter might find the idea in the Egyptians' experience of light following the darkness in Exod 10:21-23.

The same texts to which Gregory appealed for biblical support for the universal restoration also meant for him that evil must eventually cease to exist. He explicitly related 1 Cor 15:22-28 to the finitude of evil; the concept is implicitly connected to Phil 2:10-11 in the frequent interweaving of Phil 2:10-11 with 1 Cor 15:22-28. The conclusion that evil must come to an end is additionally rooted in Gregory's understanding of the origin of evil in free human choice. Gregory also tied this understanding to biblical texts, directly to Genesis 1-3 and indirectly to Jas 1:13-15.

Gregory employed Scripture in his explanations of the redemptive nature and limited duration of punishment after death in various ways. He drew upon the imagery of Mal 3:2-3 and 1 Cor 3:10-15 in portraying the purifying function of punishment and used the image of Jesus as physician in Matt 9:12 and Mark 2:17 in explaining the medicinal purpose of punishment. Although Gregory made use of these texts in writing about the nature and duration of punishment after death, they did not function as direct exegetical proofs. The parable of the unforgiving servant in Matt 18:23-25 as interpreted by Gregory, however, taught a number of aspects of his understanding of punishment after death, *viz.*, the universality of judgment, the correlation of the severity and duration of punishment with the seriousness of a person's sins, the redemptive purpose of punishment, and the eventual end of punishment. The parable of the lost coin in Luke 15:8-10 similarly taught (in allegorical fashion) the necessity of purification for the removal of the soul's accretions of evil, either through penance and asceticism in one's earthly life or through purifying punishment after death.

Gregory's universalism had a significant impact upon his exegesis of both the selected biblical texts that could conceivably receive a universalistic interpretation and those passages that are more suggestive of the traditional understanding of eternal punishment. Although Gregory surprisingly did not refer to John 12:32, Rom 11:25-26a, Rom 11:32, Col 1:20, or 2 Pet 3:9 and did not employ Acts 3:21, Rom 5:18-21, Eph 1:10, Tit 2:11, or 1 John 2:2 with reference to the universal *apokatastasis*, he found the concept to be either supported by or consistent with 1 Cor 3:12-15, 1 Cor 15:22-28, 2 Cor 5:19, Phil 2:10-11, and 1 Tim 2:4. Gregory's convictions about individual eschatology also led him to reinterpret certain passages in which punishment after death is depicted as unending torment. Gregory did not cite Rev 20:14-15 or Rev 21:8, offered no revealing explanations of Matt 5:29-30, Matt 10:28/Luke

12:5, or 1 Thess 1:7-9, and only hinted at an understanding of Matt 25:31-46 in other than traditional terms, but his treatment of Matt 8:12, Matt 18:8-9/Mark 9:42-48, and especially Luke 16:19-31 may be explained as an attempt to reconcile his eschatological universalism with biblical warnings about punishment after death.

Gregory's biblical exegesis in the service of his concept of *apokatastsis* drew upon both literal (λέξις) and non-literal (ἀλληγορία, θεωρία) levels of meaning in the text. His most direct exegetical arguments for the universality of the restoration to the original state appealed to a rather literal understanding of πᾶς in 1 Cor 15:22-28, Phil 2:10-11, and 1 Tim 2:4, of κόσμος in 2 Cor 5:19, and of the temporality of ἕως in Matt 18:34. The use of similar language in one passage of Scripture to explain its meaning in another passage, as in the equation of subjection and salvation (1 Cor 15:22-28, Phil 2:10-11) on the basis of the psalmist's equation of the two in Ps 61:2 (LXX), is an early Christian hermeneutical procedure ultimately traceable to earlier Jewish and Christian midrashic exegesis. The perception of a universal restoration following a period of redemptive punishment in Exod 10:21-23 is based on the θεωρία or "deeper insight" of the text, as is the rejection of the "ordinary sense (τὸ προχείρως νοούμενον)" of Luke 16:19-31 in favor of a non-spatial, non-physical reading of the parable that admits the possibility of an end to the "great chasm" that separates Lazarus and the rich man. The non-literal explanation of the threats of Gehenna and the "outer darkness" (Matt 8:12, Matt 18:8-9/Mark 9:42-48) is similarly rooted in the θεωρία of the text.

Did Gregory read the Scriptures in light of his theological and philosophical convictions about the nature of punishment and the ultimate extent of God's salvation, or did he derive these convictions primarily from the reading of Scripture? That the former may have been the case is suggested by the basic pattern that emerges in his interaction with the relevant biblical texts: passages that are more consistent with Gregory's view of the universality of the *apokatastasis* are interpreted literally; passages that seem to contradict Gregory's position when taken literally tend to be interpreted more allegorically. In all likelihood Gregory, the admirer of Origen, found in Origen's concept of a restoration of all to the original state accomplished partly through purifying punishment a hermeneutical key that enabled him to find coherence in the biblical witness to the divine economy of salvation. From Origen Gregory would have inherited a basic exegetical substructure for this concept; he would not have needed to rediscover these arguments from Scripture independently.

Notes

[1]See, e.g., Brooks Otis, "Cappadocian Thought as a Coherent System," *DOP* 12 (1958): 95-124; James Herbert Srawley, "Cappadocian Theology," in *ERE* 3:212-17.

[2]Bas. *moral.* 8 (PG 31:672); idem, *reg. br.* 267 (PG 31:1265). For a survey of Basil's perspective on eternal punishment, see Daley, *Hope of the Early Church*, 81-83.

[3]Gr. Naz. *or.* 3.7; ibid., 30.6; ibid., 39.19; ibid., 40.36. See Daley, *Hope of the Early Church*, 83-85, and Sachs, "Apocatastasis in Patristic Theology," 629-32, and the literature cited therein.

[4]Cf. Hans Urs von Balthasar, *Présence et pensée: Essai sur la philosophie religieuse de Grégoire de Nysse* (Paris: Gabriel Beauchesne, 1942), 58: "Cette idée chère à Origène, discrètement énoncée par Grégoire de Nazianze, trouve chez Grégoire de Nysse un fondement ontologique." *Contra* Jean Daniélou, *L'Être et le temps chez Grégoire de Nysse* (Leiden: E. J. Brill, 1970), 224, who contended that Gregory did not actually affirm universal salvation but rather held to a more nuanced position similar to that later articulated by Maximus the Confessor: "il pose la possibilité d'une distinction entre une éternité heureuse et une éternité malheureuse, et d'une restauration de l'humanité à sa condition première qui n'entraîne pas la béatitude de tous les hommes" (Jean Daniélou, "L'apocatastase chez Saint Grégoire de Nysse," *Recherches de Science Religieuse* 30 [1940]: 346-47). On Maximus the Confessor's modification of the Origenian and Gregorian *apokatastasis* in which both the divine goal of the salvation of all humanity and the freedom of humanity to choose eternal, retributive punishment are affirmed, see Brian E. Daley, "Apokatastasis and 'Honorable Silence' in the Eschatology of Maximus the Confessor," in *Maximus Confessor: Actes du Symposion sur Maxime le Confesseur*, ed. Felix Heinzer and Christoph Schönborn, Paradosis, no. 27 (Fribourg: Éditions Universitaires Fribourg Suisse, 1982), 309-39. For critique of Daniélou's conclusions about Gregory and eschatological universalism, see Constantine N. Tsirpanlis, "The Concept of Universal Salvation in Saint Gregory of Nyssa," in *StudPat*, vol. 17, pt. 3, ed. Elizabeth A. Livingstone (Oxford: Pergamon Press, 1982), 1138-41, and Sachs, "Apocatastasis in Patristic Theology," 635, n. 111. Sachs, however, apparently misread Daniélou's French and so wrote that Daniélou "does admit that Gregory's doctrine included the beatitude of all humanity" (ibid.); he seems to have missed the "n' . . . pas" construction in Daniélou's sentence. In addition to Daniélou, Georges Barrois, "The Alleged Origenism of St. Gregory of Nyssa," *SVTQ* 30, no. 1 (1986): 7-16, attempted to prove that Gregory did not embrace an Origenist eschatological universalism, but apologetic motives appear to underlie this attempt: "All things considered, the teaching of our saint, as I have tried to show, seems unimpeachable, and we must conclude that his orthodoxy is not to be questioned" (ibid., 16). This chapter should demonstrate that Gregory did in fact affirm this position and that his affirmation of a universal *apokatastasis* was based, at least in part, upon his understanding of biblical texts.

[5]Gr. Nyss. *hom. opif.* 28.4; idem, *anim. et res.* (Oehler, *Gespräch über Seele und Auferstehung,* 114-16, 128-30; PG 46:113, 125).

[6]E.g., Gr. Nyss. *hom. opif.* 27.5.2; idem, *anim. et res.* (Oehler, *Gespräch über Seele und Auferstehung,* 16-18, 40, 72-74, 84, 106-10, 130-38; PG 46:28-29, 48, 76-77, 85, 108-9, 128-32). On the relationship between protology and eschatology in Gregory, see Monique Alexandre, "Protologie et eschatologie chez Grégoire de Nysse," in *Arche é Telos: l'antropologia di Origene e di Gregorio di Nissa,* ed. Ugo Bianchi, SPM, no. 12 (Milan: Vita E Pensiero, 1981), 122-59. On the resurrection of the body in Gregory's eschatological thought, see Jean Daniélou, "La résurrection des corps chez Grégoire de Nysse," *VC* 7, no. 3 (1953): 154-70; Bruno Salmona, "Origene e Gregorio di Nissa sulla resurrezione dei corpi e l'apocatastasi," *Aug* 18 (1978): 383-88; T. J. Dennis, "Gregory on the Resurrection of the Body," in *The Easter Sermons of Gregory of Nyssa, Translation and Commentary: Proceedings of the Fourth International Colloquium on Gregory of Nyssa,* ed. Andreas Spira and Christoph Klock, PMS, no. 9 (Philadelphia: Philadelphia Patristic Foundation, 1981), 55-80.

[7]In Gregory the word ἀποκατάστασις came to have the technical theological meaning of an eschatological restoration of an original state and sometimes was equated with ἀνάστασις; only occasionally did he employ it in non-theological connections, e.g. the return of a constellation to a previous position in the sky. For an extensive analysis of Gregory's uses of ἀποκατάστασις, see Friedhelm Mann, ed., *Lexicon Gregorianum: Wörterbuch zu den Schriften Gregors von Nyssa* (Leiden: Brill, 1999-), vol. 1, s.v. "ἀποκατάστασις, εως, ἡ," which offers the basic definitions "Zurückversetzen, Wiederherstellung, Rückkehr in den ursprünglichen (früheren, vorigen) Stand." The verb ἀποκαθίστημι frequently had similar connotations; see ibid., s.v. "ἀποκαθίστημι."

[8]Patricia Wilson-Kastner, "Macrina: Virgin and Teacher," *AUSS* 17 (1979): 110, *inter alios,* has noted the similarities between this dialogue and that between Socrates and his friends in Plato's *Phaedo.* This apparently self-conscious use of the Platonic dialogue form led Catharine P. Roth, *St. Gregory of Nyssa: The Soul and the Resurrection* (Crestwood, N.Y.: St. Vladimir's Seminary Press, 1993), 10-11, to suggest that in doing so "Gregory wanted to be recognized as a successor to the tradition of Plato." Since Macrina's explanation of the significance of the *apokatastasis* in this dialogue is conceptually identical to treatments of the concept in Gregory's other works, it must be asked whether Gregory reported Macrina's part of the dialogue exactly as it occurred or, as Johannes Quasten concluded (*Patrology,* 3:261), Gregory used it to mirror his own thought on the nature of the soul and the resurrection. The latter is probably the case, and for the purposes of this study Macrina's thought as portrayed by Gregory will be regarded as a source for the interpretation of Gregory's thought. This recognition, however, should not detract from the significance of Macrina as a theologian in her own right who could have shared or even influenced Gregory's understanding of the *apokatastasis.* See Jaroslav Pelikan, *Christianity and Classical Culture: The Metamorphosis of Natural Theology in the Christian Encounter with Hellenism* (New Haven, Conn.: Yale

University Press, 1993), 8-9, who called Macrina the "Fourth Cappadocian" and throughout his Gifford Lectures took seriously her contribution to fourth-century patristic theology.

[9]Gr. Nyss. *anim. et res.* (Oehler, *Gespräch über Seele und Auferstehung,* 66; PG 46:69).

[10]Ibid. (Oehler, *Gespräch über Seele und Auferstehung,* 66-68; PG 46:69-72).

[11]Ibid. (Oehler, *Gespräch über Seele und Auferstehung,* 154; PG 46:148). The same definition also appears in Gr. Nyss. *hom. opif.* 17.2: "Now the grace of the resurrection promises to us nothing other than the restoration to the original state of those who have fallen; for the grace which is awaited is a restitution to the first life, restoring again to Paradise the one who was cast out from it. Cf. also idem, *hom. in Eccl.* 1 (GNO 5:296); idem, *Pulch.* (GNO 9:472); idem, *mort.* (GNO 9:51).

[12]Gr. Nyss. *anim. et res.* (Oehler, *Gespräch über Seele und Auferstehung,* 156; PG 46:148). David L. Balás, "Plenitudo Humanitatis: The Unity of Human Nature in the Theology of Gregory of Nyssa," in *Disciplina Nostra: Essays in Memory of Robert F. Evans,* ed. Donald F. Winslow, PMS, no. 6 (Cambridge, Mass.: Philadelphia Patristic Foundation, 1979), 127, noted that for Gregory "the 'original state' that is 'restored' at the end is *not* that of the first individuals (Adam and Eve) in paradise, but that of the fullness of humanity as conceived in God's eternity, of which the historical existence of Adam and Even [*sic*] was but an inchoate anticipation (soon lost by sin)" (emphasis is that of Balás). This qualification should be kept in mind in connection with all of Gregory's references to the restoration of an original state.

[13]The reading "ἐπανάγῃ," which appears in two manuscripts and the margin of another according to the annotations of Krabinger, *De anima et resurrectione,* 347, is preferable to the reading "ἐπαναγάγῃ" retained in the text by Krabinger, Oehler, and Migne. The latter reading may be accounted for by supposing a scribal confusion with the stem of the noun ἐπαναγωγή, which connotes a similar concept.

[14]Gr. Nyss. *anim. et res.* (Oehler, *Gespräch über Seele und Auferstehung,* 158; PG 46:149-52).

[15]Ibid. (Oehler, *Gespräch über Seele und Auferstehung,* 164; PG 46:156).

[16]Ibid. (Oehler, *Gespräch über Seele und Auferstehung,* 164-70; PG 46:156-60). The same concept appears without mention of 1 Cor 15:42-44 in Gr. Nyss. *mort.* (GNO 9:50-51).

[17]Gr. Nyss. *v. Mos.* 2.82 (GNO 7,2:57): "τὴν ἀποκατάστασιν τὴν μετὰ ταῦτα ἐν τῇ βασιλείᾳ τῶν οὐρανῶν προσδοκωμένην τῶν ἐν τῇ γεέννῃ καταδεδικασμένων." In the MSS upon which the edition reproduced in Migne depended, this passage was replaced with "τὴν ἀπὸ κακίας πρὸς ἀρετὴν δι' ἐπιγνώσεως τοῦ σταυρωθέντος καὶ μετανοίας μετάστασιν τῶν πρὶν κατὰ τὸν βίον Αἰγυπτιαζόντων" (PG 44:349), thus eliminating any reference to a universal restoration that would include those tormented in Gehenna. The reading printed in the text of GNO that includes the reference to ἀποκατάστασις (so codex Venetus Marcianus 67, eleventh century) was apparently known in

the eighth century to Germanus of Constantinople (fl. ca. 770). According to Phot. *bibl. cod.* (PG 103:1105), Germanus believed passages in a work called Περὶ τελείου βίου which affirmed a universal *apokatastasis* to be Origenist interpolations. Daniélou, "Apocatastase chez Grégoire de Nysse," 329-30, identified the work mentioned by Germanus with book 2 of *De vita Moysis*: "La seconde partie de la *Vie de Moïse*, en effet, consacrée à une exégèse spirituelle du texte du Pentateuque, porte souvent dès l'antiquité le sous-titre de Περὶ τελειότητος, dont le Περὶ τελείου βίου n'est sans doute qu'une variante." Rather than an Origenist interpolation, the reading of codex Venetus Marcianus 67 "est préférable et que c'est le texte qui contient l'apocatastase qui a le plus de chance d'être eclui de Grégoire" (ibid., 332-33). The origin of the reading printed in Migne may be attributed to the "uneasiness of later scribes on Gregory's espousal of the *apokatastasis* theory" (Daley, *Hope of the Early Church*, 241, n. 23), and the context seems to require the reading from codex Venetus Marcianus 67: "Moreover, section 84 demands this passage" (Abraham J. Malherbe and Everett Ferguson, *Gregory of Nyssa: The Life of Moses*, CWS, ed. Richard J. Payne [New York: Paulist Press, 1978], 168, n. 102).

[18]Gr. Nyss. *hom. in Cant.* 15 (GNO 6:469).

[19]Gr. Nyss. *or. dom.* 4 (GNO 7,2:49), "τῇ ἀποκαταστάσει τῶν πάντων εἰς τὸν οὐράνιον χῶρον"; idem, *beat.* 8 (GNO 7,2:162), "τὴν εἰς τοὺς οὐρανοὺς ἔχει τῶν εἰς δουλείαν μὲν ἐκπεσόντων."

[20]Gr. Nyss. *mort.* (GNO 9:51).

[21]"Κεῖμαι," which has the basic meaning "lie," can when used with reference to persons mean "*be* in an attitude or position" (*PGL*, s.v. "κεῖμαι," 2.a.) or more specifically "*lie dead*" (LSJ, s.v. "κεῖμαι," I.4.). The latter meaning seems to fit the present context best.

[22]Gr. Nyss. *or. catech.* 26 (GNO 3,4:67).

[23]In a preceding passage in *or. catech.* 26, Gregory had already mentioned the ultimate conferral of salvation upon "him who had brought about our ruin."

[24]Cf. Gr. Nyss. *anim. et res.* (Oehler, *Gespräch über Seele und Auferstehung*, 68; PG 46:72), "ἀλλὰ καὶ παρ' ἐκείνων ὁμόφωνος ἡ ὁμολογία τῆς Χριστοῦ κυριότης ἔσται," with idem, *or. catech.* 26, "ὁμόφωνος ἡ εὐχαριστία παρὰ πάσης ἔσται τῆς κτίσεως."

[25]So Tsirpanlis, "Concept of Universal Salvation," 1134-35, and Daley, *Hope of the Early Church*, 87. Extensive treatments of the relationship of Gregory's understanding of the nature of evil to his eschatology are provided by Wilhelm Vollert, *Die Lehre Gregors von Nyssa vom Guten und Bösen und von der schließlichen Überwindung des Bösen* (Leipzig: Deichert, 1897); Jean Daniélou, "Le comble du mal et eschatologie chez Grégoire de Nysse," in *Festgabe Joseph Lortz*, ed. Erwin Iserloh and P. Mann (Baden-Baden: Bruno Grimm, 1958), 27-45; and Mariette Canévet, "Nature du mal et économie du salut chez Grégoire de Nysse," *RSR* 56, no. 1 (1968): 87-95. On Gregory's understanding of evil in general, see Angelos J. Philippou, "The Doctrine of Evil in St. Gregory of Nyssa," in *StudPat*, vol. 9, ed. F. L. Cross, TU, no. 94 (Berlin: Akademie-Verlag, 1966), 251-56; Lucas Francisco Mateo-Seco, "La

teologia de la muerte en la 'Oratio Catechetica Magna' de San Gregorio de Nissa," *ScrTh* 1 (1969): 453-73; Georges Leroy "La présence du mal et de la mort dans la création," *Contacts* 38 (1986): 180-94; Constantine Scouteris, *"Malum Privatio Est*: St. Gregory of Nyssa and Pseudo-Dionysius on the Existence of Evil (Some Further Comments)," in *StudPat*, vol. 18, pt. 3, ed. Elizabeth A. Livingstone (Kalamazoo, Mich.: Cistercian Publishers, 1989), 539-50.

[26]Gr. Nyss. *hom. opif.* 16.10 (PG 44:184A15-B7): "For this reason the Word declares all these things, drawing them together in a comprehensive phrase, in saying that humanity was created in the image of God. For this is the same as saying that he made human nature a participant in all good; for if deity is the fullness of good—and this is his image—then the image has the likeness in being in the fullness of all good." On the participation of humanity in the goodness of God in Gregory's thought, see David L. Balás, Μετουσία Θεοῦ: *Man's Participation in God's Perfections according to Saint Gregory of Nyssa*, StudAnselm, no. 55 (Rome: Pontificium Institutum S. Anselmi, 1966), 54-75.

[27]Gr. Nyss. *anim. et res.* (Oehler, *Gespräch über Seele und Auferstehung*, 92; PG 46:93): "But outside it (the divine nature) there is only evil, which (although it is a paradox) has existence in not existing. For the origin of evil is nothing other than the deprivation of being. That which really exists is the nature of the good. Therefore, that which does not exist in being exists entirely in non-being."

[28]Gr. Nyss. *hom. in Cant.* 15 (GNO 6:469).

[29]Gr. Nyss. *anim. et res.* (Oehler, *Gespräch über Seele und Auferstehung*, 100; PG 46:101).

[30]Gregory's view of the nature of evil is grounded in Neoplatonic thought. Although Gregory (as well as Basil and Gregory of Nazianzus) cited neither Plotinus (ca. 205-70) nor his successors Porphyry (ca. 232-ca. 305) and Iamblichus (ca. 245-330), there are clear connections between their thought (Anthony Meredith, "Gregory of Nyssa and Plotinus," in Livingstone, ed., *StudPat*, vol. 17, pt. 3 [Oxford: Pergamon Press, 1982], 1120-30). Cf. Gregory's understanding of evil and its relationship to the good with that of Plotinus: "The Good is that on which all else depends, towards which all Existences aspire as to their source and their need, . . . If such be the Nature of Beings and of That which transcends all the realm of Being, Evil cannot have place among Beings or in the Beyond-Being; these are good. There remains only, if Evil exist at all, that it be situate in the realm of Non-Being, that it be some mode, as it were, of the Non-Being, that it have its seat in something in touch with Non-Being or to a certain degree communicate in Non-Being" (Plotinus *Enneades* 1.8.2-3 [Stephen MacKenna, trans. *The Enneads*, 2d ed., rev. B. S. Page (London: Faber and Faber, 1956)]. Meredith did not note this parallel. On the influence of Neoplatonism in general upon Gregory, see Heinrich Dörrie, "Gregors Theologie auf dem Hintergrunde der neuplatonischen Metaphysik," in *Gregor von Nyssa und die Philosophie: Zweites internationales Kolloquium über Gregor von Nyssa*, ed. Heinrich Dörrie, Margarete Altenburger, and Uta Schramm (Leiden: E. J. Brill, 1976), 21-42.

[31]E.g., Gr. Nyss. *or. catech.* 40 (GNO 3,4:105-6); idem, *infant.* (GNO 3,2:87).

[32]Gr. Nyss. *anim. et res.* (Oehler, *Gespräch über Seele und Auferstehung,* 96-102; PG 46:97-101). See also Oehler, *Gespräch über Seele und Auferstehung,* 158-60, 166-68; PG 46:152, 157.

[33]Ibid. (Oehler, *Gespräch über Seele und Auferstehung,* 98-100; PG 46:100-101).

[34]Gr. Nyss. *or. catech.* 8 (GNO 3,4:32-33).

[35]Ibid., 26 (GNO 3,4:67).

[36]Gregory made it clear in ibid., 40 (GNO 3,4:102-4) that, in his understanding, baptism in and of itself effects no purification, but rather the purification of baptism is efficacious only for those who subsequently lead a purified life. On Gregory's doctrine of baptism, see Jean Daniélou, "Onction et baptême chez Grégoire de Nysse," *EL* 90 (1976): 440-45.

[37]Gr. Nyss. *or. catech.* 35 (GNO 3,4:91-92).

[38]Ibid., 40 (GNO 3,4:104-6).

[39]Gr. Nyss. *virg.* 12.2-4 (SC 119:398-420).

[40]Gr. Nyss. *infant.* (GNO 3,2:73-74).

[41]Gr. Nyss. *mort.* (GNO 9:54).

[42]Gr. Nyss. *anim. et res.* (Oehler, *Gespräch über Seele und Auferstehung,* 102; PG 46:104). Cf. also the echo of 1 Cor 15:28 in *hom. in Cant.* 15.6.9 (GNO 6:469): " . . . all will become one, looking to the same goal of desire; no longer will there be any evil remaining in anyone; God will be all in all, being joined together through unity in fellowship with the good in Jesus Christ our Lord."

[43]Gr. Nyss. *anim. et res.* (Oehler, *Gespräch über Seele und Auferstehung,* 102; PG 46:104). The reading "εἰς πάντα," which appears in some MSS as cited in the annotations of Krabinger, *De anima et resurrectione,* 281, is more likely to be the original reading than "ἐν πᾶσι," which appears in other MSS and is printed in the text in the editions of Krabinger, Oehler, and Migne. Two factors favor the priority of "εἰς πάντα." First, the context provides internal evidence for the reading. This appears not to be a repetition of the preceding echo of 1 Cor 15:28 but rather a restatement which functions as an exposition of its meaning. Second, intrinsic probabilities suggest that a scribe would be likely to assimilate this text to the wording of 1 Cor 15:28 as in the previous echo of that passage, a likelihood which would account for the origin of the reading "ἐν πᾶσι."

[44]Gr. Nyss. *anim. et res.* (Oehler, *Gespräch über Seele und Auferstehung,* 102-4; PG 46:104-5).

[45]Gr. Nyss. *anim. et res.* (Oehler, *Gespräch über Seele und Auferstehung,* 104; PG 46:105). If the finitude of evil is Gregory's exegetical conclusion from 1 Cor 15:28, it may be necessary to qualify the assertion of Tsirpanlis, "Universal Salvation," 1134-35, and Daley, *Hope of the Early Church,* 87, that the finitude of evil as the deprivation of the good is Gregory's primary rationale for the concept of *apokatastasis.* This passage seems to suggest the opposite: that

the *apokatastasis* promised in 1 Cor 15:28 is the primary rationale for the idea of the finitude of evil.

[46]Although included in the Migne edition of Gregory's works as book 2 of *Contra Eunomii libri*, the *Refutatio confessionis Eunomii* is actually a separate work occasioned by a synod held in Constantinople in 383. See Werner Jaeger, *Contra Eunomium Libri: Pars Altera*, GNO, ed. Werner Jaeger, vol. 2 (Leiden: E. J. Brill, 1960), xi-xii; Jean Daniélou, "La chronologie des oeuvres de Grégoire de Nysse," in *StudPat*, vol. 7, ed. F. L. Cross, TU, no. 92 (Berlin: Akademie-Verlag, 1966), 346-72.

[47]Gr. Nyss. *ref. conf. Eun.* (GNO 2:396-97).

[48]Ps 61:2 (LXX).

[49]Gr. Nyss. *anim. et res.* (Oehler, *Gespräch über Seele und Auferstehung,* 66; PG 46:72).

[50]Ibid. (Oehler, *Gespräch über Seele und Auferstehung,* 66-68; PG 46:72).

[51]Ibid. (Oehler, *Gespräch über Seele und Auferstehung,* 164-70; PG 46:156-60).

[52]Ibid. (Oehler, *Gespräch über Seele und Auferstehung,* 164; PG 46:156).

[53]Ibid. (Oehler, *Gespräch über Seele und Auferstehung,* 168; PG 46:157).

[54]On the relationship between ἱστορία and θεωρία in Gregory's exegesis, see Malherbe and Ferguson, trans., *Life of Moses*, 5-9.

[55]Exod 10:21 (LXX).

[56]Cf. Matt 8:12: "οἱ δὲ υἱοὶ τῆς βασιλείας ἐκβληθήσονται εἰς τὸ σκότος τὸ ἐξώτερον."

[57]Gr. Nyss. *v. Mos.* 2.82 (GNO 7,1:57-58).

[58]So Tsirpanlis, "Universal Salvation," 1131, who classified as biblical arguments for universal salvation in Gregory of Nyssa the concepts of the creation of humanity in the image of God, the superiority of God's love and power over Satan's hatred and death, the subjection of all things to Christ, and Christ's resurrection as the restoration of the fullness of human nature but classified as a philosophical argument the concept of the finitude of evil.

[59]E.g., Plotinus *Enneades* 1.8.2-3. See Anthony Meredith, "The Good and the Beautiful in Gregory of Nyssa," in *EPMHNEYMATA: Festschrift für Hadwig Hörner zum sechszigsten Geburtstag*, ed. Herbert Eisenberger, BKAW, n.s., vol. 79. (Heidelberg: Carl Winter Universitätsverlag, 1990), 133-45, for a focused investigation of philosophical influences on this aspect of Gregory's thought.

[60]Gr. Nyss. *hom. opif.* 2.1 (PG 44:132). Gregory's exegesis often found much significance in the "enchaînement logique d'un texte" (Canévet, *Grégoire de Nysse et l'herméneutique biblique*, 268-73).

[61]Gr. Nyss. *hom. opif.* 4.1 (PG 44:136). In the context of this section of *De opificio hominis*, this had reference to the condition of the human soul prior to the fall.

[62]Gr. Nyss. *or. catech.* 5 (GNO 3,4:19).

[63]Ibid. (GNO 3,4:19-20). According to Balás, *Μετουσία Θεοῦ*, 54, in Gregory's thought goodness is the most important of the divine perfections in

which humanity participates. This goodness also "includes all perfections with a special emphasis on virtue" (ibid., 75).

[64]Gr. Nyss. *hom. opif.* 19.2-20.4 (PG 44:196-201).

[65]A gender-specific translation of ἄνθρωπος is frequently required in the following passage from *De virginitate*, as the quotation from 1 Cor 15:47 makes it clear that Gregory had in mind Adam in particular rather than humanity in general.

[66]Gr. Nyss. *virg.* 12 (SC 119:404). Cf. idem, *or. catech.* 5. The reference to "the first man on earth (ὁ πρῶτος ἐκ γῆς ἄνθρωπος)" is a close verbal echo of 1 Cor 15:47: "ὁ πρῶτος ἄνθρωπος ἐκ γῆς." Cf. Gen 2:7 (LXX): "καὶ ἔπλασεν ὁ θεὸς τὸν ἄνθρωπον χοῦν ἀπὸ τῆς γῆς."

[67]Gr. Nyss. *or. catech.* 5 (GNO 3,4:20).

[68]So William Moore, "The Great Catechism," in NPNF² 5:479. *Contra* Hubertus R. Drobner, *Bibelindex zu den Werken Gregors von Nyssa* (Paderborn: Self-published, 1988), 120, *BibPatr* 5:405, and GNO 3,4:20, which list no allusions to Jas 1:13-15 in *or. catech.* 5 or elsewhere in Gregory's works.

[69]Gr. Nyss. *or. catech.* 5 (GNO 3,4:20).

[70]Gr. Nyss. *anim. et res.* (Oehler, *Gespräch über Seele und Auferstehung,* 100; PG 46:101).

[71]Ibid. (Oehler, *Gespräch über Seele und Auferstehung,* 102; PG 46:101).

[72]Ibid. (Oehler, *Gespräch über Seele und Auferstehung,* 102; PG 46:104).

[73]Ibid. (Oehler, *Gespräch über Seele und Auferstehung,* 104; PG 46:105).

[74]See, e.g., ibid. (Oehler, *Gespräch über Seele und Auferstehung,* 98; PG 46:100); ibid. (Oehler, *Gespräch über Seele und Auferstehung,* 168; PG 46:160); idem, *or. catech.* 26 (GNO 3,4:67); ibid., 35 (GNO 3,4:91-92).

[75]So Gnilka, *Ist 1 Kor. 3,10-15 ein Schriftzeugnis für das Fegfeuer?*, 25: "Gregor bezieht sich—allerdings nur im entfernten Sinn—auf die Korintherstelle. Er zitiert sie nicht und will sie auch nicht erklären. Unbedenklich greift er das vom Apostel Gesagte auf, um seine eigenen zu veranschaulichen und zu stützen."

[76]Gr. Nyss. *or. catech.* 26 (GNO 3,4:66); cf. Mal 3:2-3 (LXX).

[77]Gr. Nyss. *or. catech.* 8 (GNO 3,4:32-33).

[78]Ibid (GNO 3,4:32).

[79]Gr. Nyss. *virg.* 12 (SC 119:412-20).

[80]Gr. Nyss. *anim. et res.* (Oehler, *Gespräch über Seele und Auferstehung,* 102; PG 46:101).

[81]On the question of the authenticity of *De occursu domini*, see Roberto Caro, *La Homilética Mariana Griega en el siglo V*, MLS, no. 5 (Dayton, Ohio: Dayton University, 1972), 3:600-3, who attributed the homily to an unknown fifth- or sixth-century author from Jerusalem. Jerome's mention of Rom 11:25-26a as a text which some had cited in support of the idea of a limited duration for eschatological punishment seems therefore not to have been directed toward Gregory (Jer. *com. in Is.* 18.66.24).

[82]Ibid., 5:330.

[83]Cf. Harmon, "Critical Use of *Instrumenta*," 100.

[84]Ibid., 5:337-38.

[85]Although Gregory did not utilize Rom 5:19 as an exegetical argument for the universal *apokatastasis* here, there are conceivably implicit connections with the concept. The reference to Rom 5:19 is part of an extended commentary on the Christ-hymn of Phil 2:5-11, a passage used explicitly by Gregory in the articulation of his universalism, and the explanation of the destruction of death effected by Christ's obedience as "the resurrection of humanity (ἀφανισ- μὸς γάρ ἐστι θανάτου ἡ ἐκ θανάτου τοῦ ἀνθρώπου ἀνάστασις)" may be related to the concept in light of Gregory's frequent equation of ἀποκατάστασις and ἀνάστασις. On the connection between Phil 2:5-11 and Rom 5:12 and 19 in Gregory's eschatology, see Luca Francisco Mateo-Seco, "Kenosis, exaltación de Cristo y apocatástasis en la exégesis a Filipenses 2,5-11 de S. Gregorio de Nisa," *ScrTh* 3 (1971): 319-24.

[86]Gr. Nyss. *nativ.* (GNO 10,2:242); cf. Rom 5:20.

[87] Gr. Nyss. *hom. in 1 Cor. 15:28* (GNO 3,2:16).

[88]*BibPatr* 5:350.

[89]Gr. Nyss. *hom. in cant.* 4 (GNO 6:124).

[90]Ibid., 7 (GNO 6:207-8).

[91]Gr. Nyss. *v. Mos.* 2.62 (GNO 7,1:51).

[92]Gr. Nyss. *hom. in Eccl.* 6 (GNO 5:385).

[93]Ibid., 7 (GNO 5:396).

[94]E.g., Gr. Nyss. *hom. in 1 Cor. 15:28* (GNO 3,2:3); idem, *anim. et res.* (Oehler, *Gespräch über Seele und Auferstehung,* 98; PG 46:100); ibid. (Oehler, *Gespräch über Seele und Auferstehung,* 168; PG 46:160); idem, *or. catech.* 26 (GNO 3,4:67); ibid., 35 (GNO 3,4:91-92).

[95]See Gnilka, *Ist 1 Kor. 3,10-15 ein Schriftzeugnis für das Fegfeuer?*, 25-26.

[96]*BibPatr* 5:359.

[97]Gr. Nyss. *hom. in 1 Cor. 15:28* (GNO 3,2:4); ibid. (GNO 3,2:5); ibid. (GNO 3,2:6); ibid. (GNO 3,2:9); ibid. (GNO 3,2:10).

[98]Ibid. (GNO 3,2:15); ibid. (GNO 3,2:20).

[99]Ibid. (GNO 3,2:13-14).

[100]Ibid. (GNO 3,2:16).

[101]Ibid. (GNO 3,2:17-18).

[102]Ibid. (GNO 3,2:21). On the significance of Gregory's concept of a universal human nature for his eschatological universalism, see Johannes Zachhuber, *Human Nature in Gregory of Nyssa: Philosophical Background and Theological Significance*, SVC, vol. 46 (Leiden: Brill, 2000), 200-237, and Morwenna Ludlow, *Universal Salvation: Eschatology in the Thought of Gregory of Nyssa and Karl Rahner*, OTM (Oxford: Oxford University Press, 2000), 89-95, who is partially dependent on Zachhuber's work in this section. Both monographs are revisions of Oxford D.Phil. theses supervised in part by Mark Edwards in the late 1990s.

[103]Gr. Nyss. *hom. in 1 Cor 15:28* (GNO 3,2:25).

[104]Ibid. (GNO 3,2:26-28).

[105]Ibid.

[106]Gr. Nyss. *Ar. et Sab.* (GNO 3,1:72); ibid. (GNO 3,1:77); ibid. (GNO 3,1:78); ibid. (GNO 3,1:79); idem, *Eunom.* 1.193 (GNO 1:83). The authenticity of *Adversus Arium et Sabellium de patre et filio* was questioned by Karl Holl, "Über die Gregor von Nyssa zugeschriebene Schrift 'Adversus Arium et Sabellium,'" *ZKG* 25 (1904): 380-98, but was later affirmed by Jean Daniélou, "L'Adversus Arium et Sabellium de Grégoire de Nysse et l'origénisme cappadocien," *RSR* 54 (1966): 61-66.

[107]Gr. Nyss. *Apoll.* (GNO 3,1:226); idem, *or. dom.* 5 (GNO 7,2:66); idem, *hom. in cant.* 4 (GNO 6:124); ibid., 14 (GNO 6:421); ibid., 15 (GNO 6:459); idem, *perf.* (GNO 8,1:206); idem, *ref. conf. Eun.* 81 (GNO 2:346); ibid., 124 (GNO 2:365); idem, *tres dii* (GNO 3,1:49); idem, *ep.* 5.9 (GNO 8,2:33-34); idem, *trid.* (GNO 9:283); ibid. (GNO 9:285); ibid. (GNO 9:303); idem, *ascens.* (GNO 9:326); idem, *infant.* (GNO 3,2:85); idem, *Pulch.* (GNO 9:469).

[108]Gr. Nyss. *Pss. titt.* (GNO 5:97); idem, *hom. in cant.* 15 (GNO 6:469); idem, *ref. conf. Eun.* 200 (GNO 2:396); idem, *mort.* (GNO 9:65); idem, *anim. et res.* (Oehler, *Gespräch über Seele und Auferstehung*, 104; PG 46:105); ibid. (Oehler, *Gespräch über Seele und Auferstehung*, 136; PG 46:132); idem, *or. catech.* 36 (GNO 3,4:92).

[109]*BibPatr* 5:364.

[110]Gr. Nyss. *Apoll.* (GNO 3,1:154); ibid. (GNO 3,1:186); ibid. (GNO 3,1:202).

[111]Gr. Nyss. *hom. in cant.* 14 (GNO 6:407).

[112]Ibid., 7 (GNO 6:201); idem, *perf.* (GNO 8,1:205).

[113]*BibPatr* 5:372.

[114]Cf. Eph 1:10, "τοῦ πληρώματος τῶν καιρῶν."

[115]*BibPatr* 5:381-82.

[116]Gr. Nyss. *tres dii* (GNO 3,1:52); idem, *Apoll.* (GNO 3,1:161); ibid. (GNO 3,1:165); ibid. (GNO 3,1:166); idem, *hom. in cant.* 2 (GNO 6:61); ibid., 6 (GNO 6:182); idem, *hom. in Eccl.* 7 (GNO 5:406); ibid. (GNO 5:411); idem, *Eunom.* 1.683 (GNO 1:222); ibid., 2.587 (GNO 1:397); ibid., 3.3.44 (GNO 2:123); ibid., 3.3.60 (GNO 2:129); ibid., 3.4.55 (GNO 2:155); ibid., 3.4.63 (GNO 2:158); ibid., 3.8.10 (GNO 2:242); ibid., 3.9.41 (GNO 2:279); idem, *ref. conf. Eun.* 15 (GNO 2:318); ibid., 85 (GNO 2:347).

[117]Gr. Nyss. *Apoll.* (GNO 3,1:161-62); ibid. (GNO 3,1:203); idem, *nativ.* (GNO 10,2:269); idem, *Eunom.* 3.2.48 (GNO 2:68); ibid., 3.2.160 (GNO 2:104); ibid., 3.3.40 (2:122); ibid., 3.3.66 (2:131); ibid., 3.4.64 (GNO 2:159); idem, *ref. conf. Eunom.* 30 (GNO 2:324); ibid., 85 (2:347); idem, *or. catech.* 32 (GNO 3,4:81); idem, *perf.* (GNO 8,1:174); idem, *v. Mos.* 2.182 (SC 1:226); idem, *hom. in Eccl.* 6 (GNO 5:382).

[118]Gr. Nyss. *anim. et res.* (Oehler, *Gespräch über Seele und Auferstehung*, 66; PG 46:69).

[119]Ibid. (Oehler, *Gespräch über Seele und Auferstehung*, 66-68; PG 46:72).

[120]Ibid. (Oehler, *Gespräch über Seele und Auferstehung*, 140; PG 46:133).

[121]Ibid. (Oehler, *Gespräch über Seele und Auferstehung*, 140; PG 46:136).

[122]Gr. Nyss. *Pss. titt.* 1.9 (GNO 2:159). This identification of the "cymbals" as angelic and human natures in connection with Phil 2:10-11 is rooted Gregory's interpretation of "ἐπουρανίων" as a reference to angelic beings and "ἐπιγείων καὶ καταχθονίων" as a reference to human beings in *anim. et res.* (Oehler, *Gespräch über Seele und Auferstehung*, 66-68; PG 46:72).

[123]Gr. Nyss. *ref. conf. Eun.* 128 (GNO 2:367); ibid., 199 (GNO 2:396); idem, *hom. in 1 Cor. 15:28* (GNO 3,2:20). The latter two passages link Phil 2:10-11 and 1 Cor 15:22-28 together in equating subjection with salvation.

[124]Ibid., 5:391.

[125]Gr. Nyss. *Apoll.* (GNO 3,1:176); ibid. (GNO 3,1:181); idem, *beat.* 4 (GNO 7,2:117).

[126]Gr. Nyss. *hom. in cant.* 1 (GNO 6:15); ibid. (GNO 6:33); ibid., 4 (GNO 6:130-31); ibid., 7 (GNO 6:215); ibid., 10 (GNO 6:304); idem, *ep.* 17.3 (GNO 8,2:52); idem, *Eunom.* 2.249 (GNO 1:299); idem, *ref. conf. Eun.* 16 (GNO 2:319); idem, *pent.* (GNO 10,2:287); idem, *v. Gr. Thaum.* (GNO 10,1:54).

[127]*BibPatr* 5:397.

[128]Gr. Nyss. *Apoll.* (GNO 3,1:189); idem, *hom. in cant.* 7 (GNO 6:205); ibid., 15 (GNO 6:448); idem, *nativ.* (GNO 10,2:242).

[129]*BibPatr* 5:408.

[130]Gr. Nyss. *Eunom.* 3.4.18 (GNO 2:140); cf. I John 2:2a.

[131]*BibPatr* 5:259.

[132]Ibid., 5:263.

[133]Gr. Nyss. *hom. in cant.* 15 (GNO 6:464); idem, *ordin.* (GNO 9:338).

[134]Gr. Nyss. *Pss. titt.* 1.8 (GNO 5:62), "τὸ πέρας εἰς ὃ τελευτᾷ τῆς ἁμαρτίας ἡ φύσις."

[135]Ibid., 2.16 (GNO 5:172). The translation is that of Ronald E. Heine, *Gregory of Nyssa's Treatise on the Inscriptions of the Psalms: Introduction, Translation, and Notes*, OECS (Oxford: Clarendon Press, 1995), 117. A different translation of "ἐφόδιον," however, may resolve the apparent contradiction. In its most basic meaning and most common usage, ἐφόδιον referred to supplies, provisions, or resources for traveling (LSJ, s.v. "ἐφόδιον, τό"; *PGL*, s.v. "ἐφόδιον, τό"). On the basis of this understanding of "ἐφόδιον," it is conceivable that Gregory did not mean that those condemned to the "outer darkness" have no possible means of salvation, but rather that they have not taken along for this journey the salvific provisions which would have enabled them to escape the "outer darkness."

[136]Gr. Nyss. *v. Mos.* 2.82 (GNO 7,1:57-58).

[137]Ibid., 2.84 (GNO 7,1:58).

[138]Ibid., 2.88 (GNO 7,1:59).

[139]*BibPatr* 5:266, 295.

[140]Gr. Nyss. *anim. et res.* (Oehler, *Gespräch über Seele und Auferstehung*, 50-52; PG 46:57).

[141]*BibPatr* 5:273, 286-87.

[142]Gr. Nyss. *or. catech.* 40 (GNO 3,4:105-6).

[143]Gr. Nyss. *v. Mos.* 2.83 (GNO 7,1:58).

[144]Ibid., 2.143 (GNO 7,1:79).

[145]Ibid., 2.88 (GNO 7,1:58).

[146]Gr. Nyss. *beat.* 3 (GNO 7,2:100).

[147]Ibid., 5 (GNO 7,2:136).

[148]Gr. Nyss. *Ps. 6* (GNO 5:190).

[149]*BibPatr* 5:279-80. Although the compilers of *BibPatr* listed 62 references, two of these are from a fragment of dubious authenticity and the possibly spurious *De instituto christiano.* Of the remaining sixty, thirty may be combined in some fashion as consecutive references to parts of Matt 25:31-46 within single passages in Gregory, leaving thirty occasions on which the passage is quoted, alluded to, or discussed. On the much-debated question of the authenticity of *De instituto christiano* and the document's relationship to the *Epistula magna* of Pseudo-Macarius of Egypt, see Joseph Stiglmayr, "Makarius der Große und Gregor von Nyssa," *ThGl* 2 (1910): 571; George Leicester Marriott, "The *De instituto Christiano* Attributed to Gregory of Nyssa," *JTS* 19 (1918): 328-30; André Wilmart, "La tradition de l'hypotypose ou traité sur l'ascèse attribué à saint Grégoire de Nysse," *ROC* 21 (1919): 412-21; Werner Jaeger, *Two Rediscovered Works of Ancient Christian Literature: Gregory of Nyssa and Macarius* (Leiden: E. J. Brill, 1954), 37-47; A. Wenger, "Grégoire de Nysse et le Pseudo-Macaire," *REByz* 13 (1955): 145-50; Jean Gribomont, "Le *De instituto christiano* et le messalianisme de Grégoire de Nysse," in *StudPat*, vol. 5, ed. F. L. Cross, TU, no. 80 (Berlin: Akademie-Verlag, 1962), 312-22; Aelred Baker, "The Great Letter of Pseudo-Macarius and Gregory of Nyssa," *StMon* 6 (1964): 381-87; idem, "Pseudo-Macarius and Gregory of Nyssa," *VC* 20 (1966): 227-234; Mariette Canévet, "Le 'De instituto christiano': est-il de Grégoire de Nysse? Problèmes de critique interne," *REG* 82 (1969): 404-23; Reinhart Staats, "Der Traktat des Gregor von Nyssa 'De instituto christiano' und der Große Brief Symeons," *STL* 17 (1963): 120-28; idem, "Der Traktat des Gregor von Nyssa 'De instituto christiano': Beweis seiner Abhängigkeit vom Großen Brief des Symeon von Mesopotaien" (D.Theol. diss., Universität Göttingen, 1964); idem, *Makarios-Symeon Epistola Magna: Eine messalianische Mönchsregel und ihre Umschrift in Gregors von Nyssa "De instituto christiano,"* AAWG, Philologisch-Historische Klasse, 3d ser., no. 134 (Göttingen: Vandenhoeck & Ruprecht, 1984), 28-42;

[150]Gr. Nyss. *benef.* (GNO 9:101); idem, *hom. in cant.* 2 (GNO 6:69); ibid., 10 (GNO 6:307); ibid., 15 (GNO 6:464); idem, *Quat.* (GNO 9:111); ibid. (GNO 9:112); ibid. (GNO 9:113); ibid. (GNO 9:121); ibid. (GNO 9:125); idem, *Eunom.* 2.328 (GNO 1:322); ibid., 3.2.47 (GNO 2:68); ibid., 3.3.36 (GNO 2:120); idem, *ref. conf. Eun.* 42 (GNO 2:329); idem, *Flacill.* (GNO 9:487); idem, *bapt. diff.* (GNO 10,2:370); idem, *hom. in Eccl.* 8 (GNO 5:441); idem, *ep.* 2.3 (GNO 8,2:110); idem, *Pss. titt.* 2.5 (GNO 5:83).

[151]Gr. Nyss. *hom. in cant.* 2 (GNO 6:65); ibid. (GNO 6:66); ibid., 9 (GNO 6:265); ibid., 15 (GNO 6:462-63); idem, *infant.* (GNO 3,2:73); ibid.

(GNO 3,2:74); idem, *beat.* (GNO 7,2:162); idem, *Eunom.* 2.328 (GNO 1:322); idem, *nativ.* (GNO 10,2:245).

[152]Gr. Nyss. *benef.* (GNO 9:99-100): "τοῖς δὲ μισανθρώποις καὶ πον- ηροῖς τιμωρία πυρὸς καὶ αὕτη διαιωνίζουσι."

[153]*BibPatr* 5:298-99 lists fifty-three references, but when consecutive references are combined, there are twenty-seven instances in which Gregory quoted, alluded to, and/or discussed portions of this text.

[154]Gr. Nyss. *hom. opif.* 27 (PG 44:225); idem, *Apoll.* (GNO 3,1:178); ibid. (GNO 3,1:211).

[155]Gr. Nyss. *Eunom.* 2.84 (GNO 1:251); idem, *ep.* 25.16 (GNO 8,2:83).

[156]Gr. Nyss. *pasch.* (GNO 9:265); idem, *bapt. diff.* (GNO 10,2:364); idem, *beat.* (GNO 7,2:108); ibid. (GNO 7,2:113); ibid. (GNO 7,2:135-36); idem, *v. Mos.* 2.247 (GNO 7,1:119); ibid. (GNO 7,1:131); idem, *hom. in Eccl.* 6 (GNO 5:389); idem, *benef.* (GNO 9:106); idem, *Flacill.* (GNO 9:489); idem, *Pss. titt.* 2.6 (GNO 5:87); ibid., 2.16 (GNO 5:173); idem, *Melet.* (GNO 9:451-52); idem, *Quat.* (GNO 9:123); idem, *python.* (GNO 3,2:102-3).

[157]Gr. Nyss. *anim. et res.* (Oehler, *Gespräch über Seele und Auferstehung,* 78; PG 46:80).

[158]Ibid. According to Monique Alexandre, "La théorie de l'exégèse dans le *De hominis opificio* et l' *In Hexaemeron,*" 104, in Gregory's exegetical theory the presence in a text of certain indicators required the rejection of the literal sense: "inconvenance théologique, impossibilité matérielle et logique, inutilité, immoralité de la lettre." Since it is a physical and logical impossibility for the disembodied soul of the rich man to lift his eyes, feel the flame, or cool his tongue, the parable requires a "more subtle understanding" than the literal interpretation.

[159]Gr. Nyss. *anim. et res.* (Oehler, *Gespräch über Seele und Auferstehung,* 80; PG 46:81).

[160]Ibid. (Oehler, *Gespräch über Seele und Auferstehung,* 84-86; PG 46:85-88).

[161]So Monique Alexandre, "L'interprétation de *Luc* 16 19-31, chez Grégoire de Nysse," in *Epektasis: mélanges patristiques offerts au Cardinal Jean Daniélou,* ed. Jacques Fontaine and Charles Kannengiesser (Paris: Éditions Beauchesne, 1972), 425-41, who examined the problem at length in her article. "Cette diversification des interprétations, selon le contexte différent— sermons ou traités philosophiques—est un aspect important de l'usage exégetique de Grégoire, en particulier pour les textes sur l'au-delà. . . . Grégoire en est conscient lui aussi et sa prédication sur l'au-delà sait utiliser le registre de la métaphore opératoire. Sa réflexion sur le langage lui permet de percevoir l'unité entre ce registre et le registre de référence qui apparaît dans le *De Anima*" (ibid., 441).

[162]Ibid.

[163]*BibPatr* 5:390.

Chapter 5

"A More Subtle Understanding": Conclusions

Clement of Alexandria, Origen, and Gregory of Nyssa shared in common the hopeful belief that God would ultimately reconcile all rational creatures to God. At the core of their distinctively crafted arguments for this conviction is a common trio of rationales. First, each maintained that evil in inherently finite and, owing to its parasitic relationship to the good, will ultimately pass into nonexistence. Second, each posited a period of remedial punishment that will remove the parasitic accretions of evil from God's creatures so that only the good remains. Third, each believed that the Scriptures taught these things. As thinkers whose minds were shaped first and foremost through their reading of the Bible, this third rationale was the most significant. The "more subtle understanding"[1] of the Scriptures that led Clement, Origen, and Gregory to discern in the biblical story a universal restoration as the story's most fitting conclusion is both a common feature of their understanding of the *apokatastasis* and the aspect of it that most clearly highlights the distinctiveness of each theologian's arguments for the concept.

The only texts that unquestionably provided Clement of Alexandria with an explicit exegetical rationale for the universal *apokatastasis* are 1 John 2:2 and Phil 2:10. He did not cite other texts that are conceivable candidates for use as prooftexts for universal salvation (John 12:32, Acts 3:21, Rom 5:18-21, Rom 11:25-26, Rom 11:32, 1 Cor 15:28, 2 Cor 5:19, Eph 1:10, Col. 1:20, 1 Tim 2:4, Tit 2:11-13, 2 Pet 3:9) in a manner which would indicate that he regarded them as such. He made no direct biblical arguments for his understanding of punishment after death as redemptive in nature and limited in duration. His interaction with texts suggestive of a more traditional perspective on punishment after death reveals little of his own understanding of those passages. Nevertheless, he frequently quoted or alluded to biblical texts in conjunction with the auxiliary concepts of the universality of God's offer of salvation (Deut 9:19; Ps 33:9, 12-13; Ps 109:3 [LXX]; Matt 3:3, 17; Matt 18:3; Matt 25:41; Luke 2:49; John 3:5; John 15:26; Rom 8:29; Eph 4:17-19; Eph 5:14; Phil 4:5; Col 1:15, 18; 1 Tim 1:14; 1 Tim 2:4; 1 Tim 4:8, 10; 2 Tim 3:7, 13-17; Heb 1:6; Heb 3:7-8, 10-11; Heb 12:5, 21-23; 1 John 1:9), the results of restoration (Matt 5:8, 1 Cor 3:12, 1 Thess 4:17), the pedagogical nature of punishment in the present life or in the life to come (Exod 20:20; Deut 32:23-25; Ps 103:4 [LXX]; Hos 5:2; Sir 1:21-22; Sir 22:6; Sir 34:13; John 15:1-8), the generally medicinal nature of punishment (Luke 5:31), the accomplishment of punishment by the "wise fire" (Gen 19, Isa 43:12, Matt 3:11-12, Luke 3:16-17, 1 Cor 3:13, Heb 4:12), and punishment as an expression of the goodness of God (Sir 16:11-12; Wis 11:23-12:2; Matt 5:45; Mark 10:18; Luke 6:28, 36; Luke 18:19; Rom 7:12; Rom 12:17). Although these references did not function as direct exegetical arguments for the universal restoration, their occurrence in connection with closely related concepts suggests a more thoroughgoing reading of Scripture in light of the *apokatastasis* than might initially appear to be the case.

In contrast to Clement, Origen related the idea of a universal restoration directly and frequently to biblical texts (1 Cor 15:22-28, Ps 109:1 [LXX], Isa 45:23, Rom 14:11, Zeph 3:7-13, Phil 2:10-11, Ps 61:2 [LXX], John 1:29, John 11:50, Rom 11:25-26, 2 Cor 5:19, Col 1:20, 1 Tim 4:10, Heb 2:9, Heb 9:28, and 1 John 2:2, with pride of place going to 1 Cor 15:22-28). Likewise his understanding of punishment after death as essentially remedial in nature was firmly rooted in several biblical texts (1 Cor 3:10-15, Deut 28:22, Isa 4:4 [LXX], Isa 10:16-17, Isa 47:14-15, Isa 66:16-17, Ezek 1:27, Mal 3:2-3, Matt 3:1, Luke 3:16, Luke 12:49, and Heb 12:29, with 1 Cor 3:10-15 as the most significant text). This remedial interpretation of eschatological punishment led him to find a deeper meaning in biblical images usually associated with everlasting, retributive punishment (Matt 5:25-26, Matt 8:12, Matt 13:42, Matt 25:41, 1 Pet 3:19, 2 Pet 3:10).

Gregory of Nyssa followed Origen in his appeals to 1 Cor 15:22-28, Phil 2:10-11, and Ps 61:2 (LXX) as the core texts that supported the notion of a universal salvation. Gregory did not, however, relate the idea as comprehensively to Scripture as did Origen: in addition to the trio of core texts, Gregory mentioned only Exod 10:21-23 and 1 Cor 15:42-44 as passages in which the universal restoration might be discerned. As was the case with Clement, a more extensive relationship between his eschatological universalism and biblical exegesis may be found in his use of Scripture in connection with related concepts. An important corollary of the *apokatastasis* for Gregory was the finitude of evil, a conclusion he believed to be required by 1 Cor 15:22-28 and Phil 2:10-11, and supported by Jas 1:13-15 and the account of the origin of evil in Genesis 1-3. His portrayal of the nature of punishment as purificatory drew upon 1 Cor 3:10-15 and Mal 3:2-3. He associated Matt 9:12 and Mark 2:17 with the medicinal nature of punishment, and he found several indications of the redemptive nature and limited duration of punishment in Matt 18:23-25 and Luke 15:8-10. Although Gregory did not match the expansiveness of Origen's biblical rationale for the universal restoration, he surpassed Origen in the creativity with which he reinterpreted such traditional prooftexts for eternal punishment as Matt 8:12, Matt 18:8-9/Mark 9:42-48, and especially Luke 16:19-31.

Our inquiry highlights a number of trajectories in the relationship between *apokatastasis* and exegesis in Clement, Origen, and Gregory. While Clement first interpreted 1 John 2:2 as teaching the salvation of all people and Origen after him appealed to that text in his arguments for universal salvation, Gregory made no use of 1 John 2:2 in connection with the concept. First Corinthians 15:22-28 was the key text for both Origen and Gregory in the development of their biblical rationales for eschatological universalism, but it was completely absent from Clement's earlier universalistic affirmations. The one text common to all three authors in the articulation of their universalism was Phil 2:10. Among the many biblical references associated with the several dimensions of remedial punishment, some references were shared by Clement and Origen but not Gregory, and other references were shared by Origen and Gregory but not Clement. Two texts, however, were common to all three: Luke 3:16 (the coming of Christ to baptize with fire) and 1 Cor 3:12-15 (the refiner's fire). It is important also to note the texts to which these authors did not appeal as universalistic texts. Neither

Clement nor Origen nor Gregory referred to John 12:32, Eph 1:10, Tit 2:11, or 2 Pet 3:9 as biblical testimonies to the ultimate universality of the experience of salvation. The absence of appeal to 2 Pet 3:9, with its assertion of the divine wish for "all to come to repentance," is especially surprising. The references to Acts 3:21 may also fall into this category. Clement and Gregory clearly did not refer to that text as evidence for a universal restoration despite the presence of the word ἀπο- κατάστασις in the verse, and Origen only made use of it to clarify his intended meaning in using the word with reference to a return to an earlier state (but not necessarily with reference to the return of the soul to its pre-fall condition in that context).

Origen gave no indication of exegetical dependence on Clement in his biblical arguments for universal salvation. Gregory, on the other hand, seems to have been directly dependent upon Origen for the use of 1 Cor 15:22-28, Phil 2:10-11, and Ps 61:2 (LXX) in his attempt to demonstrate the equivalence of subjection to God with salvation. All three texts are used to develop the same argument in the same way by Origen in *princ.* 1.6.1 and *hom. in Ez.* 1.15 and by Gregory in *ref. conf. Eun.* (GNO 2:396-97). Although it is possible that Gregory was familiar with Origen's *In Ezechielem homiliae*, it is likely that *De principiis* was the specific source of this exegetical pattern for Gregory, since Gregory betrays specific knowledge of that treatise at several points in the *Dialogus de anima et resurrectione* without mentioning Origen or his work by name.

Although all three authors are now remembered as allegorical exegetes, their direct appeals to biblical texts as support for their eschatological universalism were rooted in a very literal reading of these texts. Their exegesis became more allegorical when they dealt with passages which, when read literally, seemed to contravene the understanding of eschatological punishment they were advocating. Origen frequently reinterpreted such texts as references to psychological torment rather than physical torment and freely redefined the meaning of "eternal" with reference to punishment. It was Gregory, however, who developed the allegorical approach to these texts more fully, finding in the θεωρία of these passages a different nature and purpose of punishment than that which the "letter" of the texts expressed. It should be remembered that all three authors frequently assigned both literal and non-literal meanings to the same passages in different contexts and found the truth of the text in both levels of meaning.

Clement, Origen, and Gregory were each influenced by Greek philosophy as well as by the sacred Scriptures in the development of their understandings of the *apokatastasis*. Clement was heavily influenced by Stoicism and Middle Platonism, Origen's thought was shaped by Middle and early Neoplatonism, and Gregory was significantly impacted by Plotinian Neoplatonism. Clement unabashedly pointed to the parallels between his understanding of the pedagogical nature of punishment and that of Plato. Origen seems to have been influenced by a Platonic philosophy of history in his emphasis on the correspondence between beginning and end. Gregory exhibited several parallels to Plotinus in his discussions of the finitude of evil. More research needs to be done in the area of these philosophical influences on the concept of the *apokatastasis* in all three early Christian theologians. At present, it is sufficient to note the probability that these influences formed part of the hermeneutical pre-understanding they brought to the biblical text and had some impact upon their exegetical conclusions, while not determining them.

Whatever the other sources for the development of their concepts of universal salvation may have been, it is certain that Clement, Origen, and Gregory believed their ideas to be firmly rooted in the Scriptures. Evaluation of whether they were right in this reading of the biblical text is more appropriately the task of a study in biblical or systematic theology than of this inquiry in historical theology.[2] Those who undertake this important task will need to consider whether these interpretations are consistent with the intentions of the biblical authors;[3] whether the hermeneutical methods by which these interpretations were drawn may be utilized by those who interpret the Bible today;[4] whether the philosophical systems with which some aspects of the universal *apokatastasis* were associated may still make a contribution to theology's interaction with philosophy;[5] and whether the concept coheres with the Bible as a canonical whole, the shared wisdom of the community of faith across the ages,[6] reason in the service of Christian thought, and the experience of Christian faith and mission.[7] In the end even the historical theologian may place these biblical rationales within the larger Christian theological tradition and join Jean Daniélou in observing that however grand the "great theological symphony" of the universal *apokatastasis* as orchestrated by Clement, Origen, and Gregory may be, it nonetheless "is contrary to another element in Christian dogma, viz., the doctrine that the choice made in this life is decisive in character."[8]

Notes

[1]This is Macrina's characterization of this manner of narrating the biblical story in Gr. Nyss. *anim. et res.* (Oehler, *Gespräch über Seele und Auferstehung*, 78; PG 46:80), where she argues that the illogic of the traditional literal interpretation of Luke 16:19-31 "summons the one who listens with diligent inquiry to a more subtle understanding (θεωρίαν)."

[2]Although a theological evaluation of these early Christian biblical rationales for universal salvation has not been the goal of this inquiry, as a teacher of systematic theology within a tradition (Baptist) that has historically emphasized the urgency of personal response to God's offer of salvation in light of the eternal implications of that response, I cannot take leave of the subject without giving some attention to the questions raised in this final paragraph. Pure historical reconstruction is a tempting refuge where controversial proposals in Christian theology are concerned, but this study is also intended to provide a point of historical departure for contemporary systematic theological reflection by others. The following notes merely suggest some systematic routes that might be taken from this historical starting place.

[3]Unless one begins with the presupposition that the modern reader of the biblical text is better equipped to discern the *divinum mysterium* than were the writers and communities responsible for the production and canonization of the Scriptures (as one of my colleagues has aptly summarized this perspective in order to critique it, "Yes, the text says that, but we know better now!"), the question of whether an exegetical conclusion of universal salvation does violence to the intentions of those who produced the Scriptures is crucially important. (I do not intend to suggest a hermeneutic that merely reconstructs authorial intent and moves immediately to contemporary application. One of the most helpful contributions of recent synchronic interpretive methodologies is the insight that meaning resides on both "sides" of the text—in both the production and the reading of a text. Indeed, within certain limits the recognition of the polyvalence of texts is more consistent with the manner in which the early church read Scripture than is a purely historical-critical approach. Nevertheless, the effort to determine the authorial agenda of a text serves as a necessary check against the excesses of allegorical fancy or reader-oriented subjectivity.)

Jürgen Moltmann has recently given attention to the tension in Scripture between the texts that hint of universalism in the outcome of God's work of salvation and the texts that point to a "double outcome of judgment," concluding that "universal salvation *and* a double outcome of judgment are therefore both well attested biblically," while the tension between them is not easily resolved via biblical exegesis alone (*Coming of God*, 241). This tension is attributable in part to the fact that the New Testament addresses a different soteriological concern than does the later patristic controversy over *apokatastasis*. In historical context, the universalistic New Testament texts are extensions to the Gentiles of Israel's eschatological hopes—the atoning work of Christ is "not only for our sins"—i.e., for Jewish Christians—but also for "the sins of the whole world"—i.e., for Gentiles as well (1 John 2:2). The Pauline expressions of universalism in particular make sense against the backdrop of the identity crisis occasioned by the encounter of primitive Jewish Christianity with the positive response of the Gentiles to God's work of redemption. The universalistic language of the New Testament does not necessarily preclude the kind of universal salvation envisioned by Clement, Origen, and Gregory, but neither does it advocate such an understanding.

A much greater difficulty is posed by the texts that speak of eschatological punishment. It is difficult to read the New Testament and escape noticing the "double outcome of judgment" as a recurrent theme. At the very least, it means "the irrevocability of the decision for faith or unbelief," as Moltmann notes en route to making the case for a universal salvation that does not simply dismiss this key biblical teaching (ibid., 243). It is possible for a theologian to read the biblical story as culminating in the salvation of all creation and be true to the normativity of Scripture, so long as this reading of the story also has a place for the reality of judgment and its eternal implications. Without the sub-plot of judgment, an eschatology of universal salvation becomes an altogether different story from the one told by the church's Scriptures. The patristic universalists considered in this book avoided this pitfall through their emphasis on the "refiner's fire" as the key biblical image communicating the purpose of eternal punishment.

[4]David C. Steinmetz answers this question with a cogently-argued "yes" in "The Superiority of Pre-Critical Exegesis," *ThTo* 37 (April 1980): 27-38, reprinted in idem, *Memory and Mission: Theological Reflections on the Christian Past* (Nashville: Abingdon Press, 1988), 143-63. For a construal of patristic biblical interpretation that renders allegorical exegesis intelligible to post-critical biblical interpreters and theologians, see Frances M. Young, *Biblical Exegesis and the Formation of Christian Culture* (Cambridge: Cambridge University Press, 1997).

[5]The rejection of philosophical foundationalism in postmodern theology need not lead one to dismiss the fathers' use of Hellenistic philosophy, for these were *ad hoc* appeals to Plato, Plotinus *et al.* in contrast to the Aristotelian foundationalism of late Scholastic theology. For an example of how contemporary Christian thought might make constructive, nonfoundationalist use of the "participatory philosophy" of Plato, see John Milbank, Catherine Pickstock, and Graham Ward, eds., *Radical Orthodoxy: A New Theology* (London: Routledge, 1999).

[6]In its efforts to clarify this not insignificant ambiguity in the plot of the biblical story of God's salvation, early Christian theology offered three major readings of the manner in which the story concludes for those who have not responded positively to the divine work of salvation during their earthly lives (cf. E. Earle Ellis, *Christ and the Future in New Testament History*, NovTSup, vol. 97 [Leiden: Brill, 2000], 179-84). The majority reading, represented by Tertullian and Augustine, understands the eschatological punishment of such persons as *eternal in duration*—the everlasting torment of separation from God. Some of the second- and third-century apologists, represented by Justin

Martyr and Arnobius, offered what was ultimately a minority reading in which punishment it *eternal in effect* rather than duration—following the resurrection, the wicked are destroyed, evil therefore ceases to exist, and God is "all in all." The other minority reading is represented by Clement, Origen, and Gregory—punishment is eternal in effect rather than duration, but its *effect is not destruction but transformation*. It is possible that these three early Christian readings of the biblical portrayal of the destiny of the impenitent might not be mutually exclusive. If we may theorize that it is possible for God to save Adolf Hitler, Eugene "Bull" Connor, or Osama Bin Ladin (or any other fallen human being) in the eschaton—and "for God all things are possible" (Matt 19:26)—such a salvation would require the destruction of the evil persons they had become in their earthly lives (cf. Justin Martyr and Arnobius), the painful transformation of who they had willingly become into what God intended them to be (cf. Clement, Origen, and Gregory), and the torment of knowing for eternity the tragedy of what was irrevocably lost in their refusal to participate in God's salvation during their earthly lives (cf. Tertullian and Augustine). For similar proposals in contemporary constructive theology, see Moltmann, *Coming of God*, 325-55, and (cautiously) Miroslav Volf, *Exclusion and Embrace: A Theological Exploration of Identity, Otherness, and Reconciliation* (Nashville: Abingdon Press, 1996), 295-301, esp. 299, nn.7-8.

Is belief in an ultimately universal salvation heresy from the perspective of the tradition of the community of faith across the ages? One certainly cannot claim with J. W. Hanson, a nineteenth-century Universalist (of the American denominational variety), that universal salvation was the consensus position of the patristic church (J. W. Hanson, *Universalism, the Prevailing Doctrine of the Christian Church During Its First Five Centuries* [Boston: Universalist Publishing House, 1899]). While it remained a minority viewpoint throughout the patristic period, one may argue that in its basic outlines universalism contradicted neither creed nor council. It affirmed belief in the coming of Christ "to judge the living and the dead," "the resurrection of the body" (the speculations of Origen excepted), and "the life everlasting." Even in the anathemas against Origen associated (in some manner) with the Fifth Ecumenical Council, the objection seems not to have been with a universal *apokatastasis* per se but rather with the protology presupposed by the Origenist version of the *apokatastasis*, as Anathema I suggests: "If anyone asserts the fabulous pre-existence of souls, and shall assert the monstrous restoration (ἀποκατάστασις) which follows from it: let him be anathema" (Henry B. Percival, ed. and trans., "The Fifth Ecumenical Council—The Second Council of Constantinople, A.D. 553," in NPNF[2] 14:318). It is significant that Gregory of Nyssa, who developed a concept of *apokatastasis* virtually identical to that of Origen sans Origen's protology, was never condemned by council or synod, was revered by the later church as a staunch defender of Nicene orthodoxy, and was canonized as a saint with a feast day on March 9 (although doubts of later copyists of Gregory's works about the orthodoxy of his eschatology are reflected in their emendations of a number of passages in which these ideas are expressed [Daley, *Hope of the Early Church*, 241, n. 23]).

Implicit in this traditional criterion of a proper protology is a healthy aversion to deterministic theologies that negate divine and human freedom, for "the monstrous restoration which follows from" a doctrine of the pre-existence of souls is deterministic in its requirement of a cyclical return to the beginning. This additional criterion of a heretical universalism is the rationale behind Karl Barth's denial of dogmatic universalism (even though the logic of his doctrine of election points in that direction): if God must save humanity and humanity must be saved, then neither God nor humanity would be free (*CD* II/2, e.g. 417-23). Cf. Ludlow, *Universal Salvation*, 265: " . . . although [Karl] Rahner and Gregory express a belief with which not all Christians would agree, there are good grounds for thinking theirs is a Christian belief—particularly if it is expressed as a hope rather than as a certain prediction."

Those who find themselves attracted to this hopeful eschatology must also consider Origen's own reservations about making it the customary public teaching of the church (*Cels.* 6.26). There is much wisdom in the words of the nineteenth-century German pietist Christian Gottlieb Barth: "Anyone who does not believe in the universal restoration is an ox, but anyone who teaches it is an ass" (Jaroslav Pelikan, *The Melody of Theology: A Philosophical Dictionary* [Cambridge: Harvard University Press, 1988], 5).

[7]The church is right to guard against a dogmatic universalism in light of its experience. Universal salvation as a foregone conclusion can lead, and has led, to indifference toward evangelistic endeavors and easy cultural accommodation rather than transformative engagement with culture. On the other hand, a hypothetical outcome of universal salvation ought not detract from the urgency of the mission of the church. In such a case, failure to experience God's salvation in one's earthly existence would be an eternal tragedy both for that person and for all those to whom that person relates, a tragedy that the church should be urgently concerned about preventing. As I sometimes tell my students, "I will not be surprised if I discover in the resurrection that the God revealed in Jesus Christ has saved all people, but in the meantime I cannot count on that."

In the meantime, God does wish to save all people (1 Tim 2:4). Whether all will be saved must remain a mystery of divine and human freedom.

[8]Jean Daniélou, *Origen*, trans. Walter Mitchell (New York: Sheed &Ward, 1955), 288.

Selected Bibliography

I. Primary Texts

A.1. Clement of Alexandria: Editions

Eclogae propheticae. In *Clemens Alexandrinus*, vol. 3, *Stromata Buch VII und VIII, Excerpta ex Theodoto, Eclogae propheticae, Quis dives salvetur, Fragmente*, ed. Otto Stählin, 137-55, 235. GCS, vol. 17, pt. 2. Leipzig: Hinrichs'sche Buchhandlung, 1909.

Excerpta e Theodoto. In *Clemens Alexandrinus*, vol. 3, *Stromata Buch VII und VIII, Excerpta ex Theodoto, Eclogae propheticae, Quis dives salvetur, Fragmente*, ed. Otto Stählin, 105-33. GCS, vol. 17, pt. 2. Leipzig: Hinrichs'sche Buchhandlung, 1909.

_____. Robert Pierce Casey, ed. and trans. *The Excerpta ex Theodoto of Clement of Alexandria*. SD, no. 1. London: Christophers, 1934.

_____. In PG 9:697-728. Paris: Garnier, 1857-66.

Hypotyposes. In *Clemens Alexandrinus*, vol. 3, *Stromata Buch VII und VIII, Excerpta ex Theodoto, Eclogae propheticae, Quis dives salvetur, Fragmente*, ed. Otto Stählin, 195-215. GCS, vol. 17, pt. 2. Leipzig: Hinrichs'sche Buchhandlung, 1909.

Paedagogus. In *Clemens Alexandrinus*, vol. 1, *Protrepticus and Paedagogus*, 3d rev. ed., ed. Otto Stählin and Ursula Treu, 89-292, 359-65. GCS, vol. 12. Berlin: Akademie-Verlag, 1972.

_____. Claude Mondésert, Chantal Matry, and Henri-Irénée Marrou, eds. *Clément d'Alexandrie: Le Pédagogue, Livre III*. SC, no. 158. Paris: Éditions du Cerf, 1970.

_____. Claude Mondésert and Henri-Irénée Marrou, eds. *Clément d'Alexandrie: Le Pédagogue, Livre II.* SC, no. 108. Paris: Éditions du Cerf, 1965.

_____. Henri-Irénée Marrou and Marguerite Harl, eds. *Clément d'Alexandrie: Le Pédagogue, Livre I.* SC, no. 70. Paris: Éditions du Cerf, 1960.

_____. In PG 8:249-684. Paris: Garnier, 1857-66.

Protrepticus. Claude Mondésert, ed. *Clément d'Alexandria: Le Protreptique.* 3d ed. SC, no. 2. Paris: Éditions du Cerf, 1976.

_____. In *Clement of Alexandria*, ed. G. W. Butterworth, 2-262. LCL, no. 92. Cambridge: Harvard University Press, 1979.

_____. In *Clemens Alexandrinus*, vol. 1, *Protrepticus and Paedagogus*, 3d rev. ed., ed. Otto Stählin and Ursula Treu, 1-86, 353-59. GCS, vol. 12. Berlin: Akademie-Verlag, 1972.

_____. In PG 8:49-246. Paris: Garnier, 1857-66.

Quis dives salvetur. In *Clement of Alexandria*, ed. G. W. Butterworth, 270-366. LCL, no. 92. Cambridge: Harvard University Press, 1979.

_____. In *Clemens Alexandrinus*, vol. 3, *Stromata Buch VII und VIII, Excerpta ex Theodoto, Eclogae propheticae, Quis dives salvetur, Fragmente*, ed. Otto Stählin, 159-91, 236. GCS, vol. 17, pt. 2. Leipzig: Hinrichs'sche Buchhandlung, 1909.

_____. P[ercy] Mordaunt Barnard, ed. *Clement of Alexandria: Quis Dives Salvetur.* Texts and Studies: Contributions to Biblical and Patristic Literature, vol. 5, no. 2. Cambridge: Cambridge University Press, 1897.

_____. In PG 9:603-52. Paris: Garnier, 1857-66.

Stromata. In *Clemens Alexandrinus*, vol. 2, *Stromata Buch I-VI*, 4th ed., ed. Otto Stählin, Ludwig Früchtel, and Ursula Treu. GCS, vol. 52 (15). Berlin: Akademie-Verlag, 1985.

_____. In *Clemens Alexandrinus*, vol. 3, *Stromata Buch VII und VIII, Excerpta ex Theodoto, Eclogae propheticae, Quis dives salvetur, Fragmente*, ed. Otto Stählin, 3-102, 231-34. GCS, vol. 17, pt. 2. Leipzig: Hinrichs'sche Buchhandlung, 1909.

_____. Fenton John Anthony Hort and Joseph B. Mayor, eds. *Clement of Alexandria Miscellanies Book VII: The Greek Test with Introduction, Translation, Notes, Dissertations and Indices.* London: Macmillan & Co., 1902.

_____. In PG 8:685-9:602. Paris: Garnier, 1857-66.

A.2. Clement of Alexandria: English Translations

Paedagogus. Simon P. Wood, trans. *Clement of Alexandria: Christ the Educator.* FC, vol. 23. New York: Fathers of the Church, 1954.

_____. Translated by William Wilson. In ANF 2:209-96. Buffalo, N.Y.: Christian Literature Publishing Co., 1885-96; reprint, Peabody, Mass.: Hendrickson Publishers, 1994.

Protrepticus. Translated by William Wilson. In ANF 2:171-206. Buffalo, N.Y.: Christian Literature Publishing Co., 1885-96; reprint, Peabody, Mass.: Hendrickson Publishers, 1994.

Quis dives salvetur. Translated by William Wilson. In ANF 2:591-604. Buffalo, N.Y.: Christian Literature Publishing Co., 1885-96; reprint, Peabody, Mass.: Hendrickson Publishers, 1994.

Stromata. John Ferguson, trans. *Clement of Alexandria: Stromateis, Books One to Three.* FC, vol. 85. Washington, D.C.: The Catholic University of America Press, 1991.

_____. Otto Stählin, trans. *Des Clemens von Alexandreia ausgewählte Schriften*, vol. 5. BKV, 2d ser., vol. 20. Munich: Kösel-Pustet, 1938.

_____. Translated by William Wilson. In ANF 2:299-567. Buffalo, N.Y.: Christian Literature Publishing Co., 1885-96; reprint, Peabody, Mass.: Hendrickson Publishers, 1994.

B.1. Origen: Editions

Commentarii in Ephesios (fragmenta e catenis). J. A. F. Gregg, ed. "The Commentary of Origen upon the Epistle to the Ephesians." *JTS* 3 (1902): 233-44, 398-420, 554-76.

Commentarii in Epistulam ad Romanos. Theresia Heither, ed. *Origenes: Commentarii in Epistulam ad Romanos, Römerbriefkommentar.* FontChr, vol. 2. Freiburg: Herder, 1990-96.

_____. In PG 14:833-1292. Paris: Garnier, 1857-66.

Commentarii in Iohannem. Cécile Blanc, ed. *Origène: Commentaire sur Saint Jean.* 5 vols. SC, nos. 120, 157, 222, 290, 385. Paris: Éditions du Cerf, 1966-92.

_____. In *Origenes Werke*, vol. 4, *Der Johanneskommentar*, ed. E. Preuschen, 3-480. GCS, vol. 10. Leipzig: Hinrichs'sche Buchhandlung, 1903.

_____. A. E. Brooke, ed. *The Commentary of Origen on S. John's Gospel.* 2 vols. Cambridge: Cambridge University Press, 1896.

_____. In PG 14:21-830. Paris: Garnier, 1857-66.

Commentarii in Matthaeum. E. Klostermann and E. Benz, eds. *Origines Werke.* Vol. 10, *Origenes Matthäuserklärung.* Pt. 1, *Die griechisch erhaltenen Tomoi.* GCS, vol. 40. Berlin: Akademie-Verlag, 1955.

_____. In PG 13:836-1600. Paris: Garnier, 1857-66.

Commentarii in Matthaeum (Commentariorum series). E. Klostermann and E. Benz, eds. *Origines Werke.* Vol. 11, *Origenes Matthäuserklärung.* Pt. 2, *Die lateinisch Übersetzung der Commentariorum Series.* 2d ed., ed. Ursula Treu. GCS, vol. 38. Berlin: Akademie-Verlag, 1976.

_____. In PG 13:1599-1800. Paris: Garnier, 1857-66.

Contra Celsum. Marcel Borret, ed. *Origène: Contre Celse.* 5 vols. SC, nos. 132, 136, 147, 150, 227. Paris: Éditions du Cerf, 1967-1976.

_____. In PG 11:641-1632. Paris: Garnier, 1857-66.

Disputatio cum Heracleida. Jean Scherer, ed., *Entretien d'Origène avec Héra-clide.* SC, no. 67. Paris: Éditions du Cerf, 1960.

Epistula ad quosdam caros suos Alexandriam. Henri Courzel. "A Letter from Origen 'To Friends in Alexandria.'" Translated by Joseph D. Gauthier. In *The Heritage of the Early Church: Essays in Honor of the Very Reverend Georges Vasilievich Florovsky,* ed. David Neiman and Margaret Schatkin, 135-50. OCA, no. 195. Rome: Pontificium Intstitutum Studiorum Oriental-ium, 1973.

_____. In PG 17:624-26. Paris: Garnier, 1857-66.

In Exodum homiliae xiii. In *Origenes Werke,* vol. 6, *Homilien zum Hexateuch in Rufins Übersetzung,* pt. 1, *Die Homilien zu Genesis, Exodus und Leviti-cus,* ed. W. A. Baehrens, 145-279. GCS, vol. 29. Leipzig: Hinrichs'sche Buchhandlung, 1920.

_____. In PG 12:297-396. Paris: Garnier, 1857-66.

Exhortatio ad Martyrium. In *Origenes Werke,* vol. 1, *Die Schrift vom Mar-tyrium, Buch I-IV gegen Celsus,* ed. P. Koetschau, 3-47. GCS, vol. 2. Leip-zig: Hinrichs'sche Buchhandlung, 1899.

_____. In PG 11:564-637. Paris: Garnier, 1857-66.

In Ezechielem homiliae xiv. Marcel Borret, ed. *Origène: Homélies sur Ézéchiel.* SC, no. 352. Paris: Éditions du Cerf, 1989.

_____. In PG 13:665-768. Paris: Garnier, 1857-66.

Fragmenta in Proverbia (Fragmenta duo in Pamphili Apologia pro Origene). In PG 17:613-16. Paris: Garnier, 1857-66.

In Genesim homiliae. Henri de Lubac and Louis Doutreleau, eds. *Origène: Homélies sur la Genèse.* 2d ed. SC, no. 7. Paris: Éditions du Cerf, 1996.

_____. In PG 12:145-253. Paris: Garnier, 1857-66.

Homiliae in 1 Regnorum. Pierre and Marie-Thérèse Nautin, eds. *Origène: Homélies sur Samuel.* SC, no. 328. Paris: Éditions du Cerf, 1986.

_____. In PG 12:995-1028. Paris: Garnier, 1857-66.

Homiliae in Ieremiam. Pierre Nautin, ed. *Origène: Homélies sur Jéréme.* 2 vols. SC, nos. 232, 238. Paris: Éditions du Cerf, 1976-77.

_____. In *Origenes Werke,* vol. 3, *Jeremiahomilien, Klageliederkommen-tar, Erklärung der Samuel- und Königsbücher,* 2d ed., ed. Erich Kloster-mann and Pierre Nautin, 1-232. GCS, vol. 6. Berlin: Akademie-Verlag, 1983.

_____. In PG 13:256-525. Paris: Garnier, 1857-66.

In Iesu Nave homiliae xxvi. In *Origène: Homilies sur Josué,* ed. Annie Jaubert, 90-500. SC, no. 71. Paris: Éditions du Cerf, 1960.

_____. In PG 12:825-948. Paris: Garnier, 1857-66.

In Leviticum homiliae xxviii. Marcel Borret, ed. *Origène: Homélies sur le Lévitique.* 2 vols. SC, nos 286 and 287. Paris: Éditions du Cerf, 1981.

_____. In PG 12:405-574. Paris: Garnier, 1857-66.

Libri x in Canticum canticorum. Luc Brésard and Henri Crouzel, eds. *Origène: Commentaire sur le Cantique des Cantiques.* 2 vols. SC, nos. 375 and 376. Paris: Éditions du Cerf, 1991-92.

_____. In PG 13:61-198. Paris: Garnier, 1857-66.

In librum Iudicum homiliae. Pierre Messié, Louis Neyrand, and Marcel Borret, eds. *Origène: Homélies sur les Juges.* SC, no. 389. Paris: Éditions du Cerf, 1993.

_____. In PG 13:951-900. Paris: Garnier, 1857-66.

In Lucam homiliae xxxix. Henri Crouzel, François Fournier, and Pierre Périchon, eds. *Origène: Homélies sur S. Luc.* SC, no. 87. Paris: Éditions du Cerf, 1962.

_____. In *Origenes Werke*, vol. 9, *Die Homilien zu Lukas in der Übersetzung des Hieronymus und die griechischen Reste der Homilien und des Lukas-Kommentars*, 2d ed., ed. Max Rauer, 1-222. GCS, vol. 49 (35). Berlin: Akademie-Verlag, 1959.

_____. In PG 13:1799-1902. Paris: Garnier, 1857-66.

In Numeros homiliae xxviii. Louis Dourtreleau, ed. *Origène: Homélies sur les Nombres.* Vol. 1. SC, no. 415. Paris: Éditions du Cerf, 1996.

_____. In PG 12:585-806. Paris: Garnier, 1857-66.

De oratione. In *Origenes Werke*, vol. 2, *Buch V-VIII gegen Celsus, die Schrift vom Gebet*, ed. P. Koetschau, 297-403. GCS, vol. 3. Leipzig: Hinrichs'sche Buchhandlung, 1899.

_____. In PG 11:416-562. Paris: Garnier, 1857-66.

De Principiis. Henri Crouzel and Manlio Simonetti, eds. *Origène: Traité des Principes.* 5 vols. SC, nos. 252, 253, 268, 269, 312. Paris: Éditions du Cerf, 1978-1984.

_____. In PG 11:115-414. Paris: Garnier, 1857-66.

B.2. Origen: English Translations

Commentarii in Iohannem. Ronald E. Heine, trans. *Origen: Commentary on the Gospel According to John, Books 1-10.* FC, vol. 80. Washington, D.C.: The Catholic University of America Press, 1989.

_____. Ronald E. Heine, trans. *Origen: Commentary on the Gospel According to John, Books 13-32.* FC, vol. 89. Washington, D.C.: The Catholic University of America Press, 1993.

_____. Translated by Allan Menzies. In ANF 9:297-408. Buffalo, N.Y.: Christian Literature Publishing Co., 1885-96; reprint, Peabody, Mass.: Hendrickson Publishers, 1994.

Commentarii in Matthaeum. Translated by John Patrick. In ANF 9:413-512. Buffalo, N.Y.: Christian Literature Publishing Co., 1885-96; reprint, Peabody, Mass.: Hendrickson Publishers, 1994.

Contra Celsum. Henry Chadwick, trans. *Origen: Contra Celsum.* Cambridge: Cambridge University Press, 1953.

_____. Translated by Frederick Crombie. In ANF 4:395-669. Buffalo, N.Y.: Christian Literature Publishing Co., 1885-96; reprint, Peabody, Mass.: Hendrickson Publishers, 1994.

Disputatio cum Heracleida. Robert J. Daly, trans. *Origen: Treatise on the Passover and Dialogue of Origen with Heraclides and His Fellow Bishops on the Father, the Son, and the Soul.* ACW, no. 54. New York: Paulist Press, 1992.

Epistula ad quosdam caros suos Alexandriam. Henri Crouzel. "A Letter from Origen 'To Friends in Alexandria.'" Translated by Joseph D. Gauthier. In *The Heritage of the Early Church: Essays in Honor of the Very Reverend Georges Vasilievich Florovsky,* ed. David Neiman and Margaret Schatkin, 135-50. OCA, no. 195. Rome: Pontificium Intstitutum Studiorum Orientalium, 1973.

In Exodum homiliae. In *Origen: Homilies on Genesis and Exodus,* trans. Ronald E. Heine, 227-387. FC, vol. 71. Washington, D.C.: The Catholic University of America Press, 1982.

Exhortatio in Martyrium. John J. O'Meara, trans. *Origen: Prayer, Exhortation to Martyrdom.* ACW, no. 19. New York: Newman Press, 1954.

In Genesim homiliae. In *Origen: Homilies on Genesis and Exodus,* trans. Ronald E. Heine, 47-224. FC, vol. 71. Washington, D.C.: The Catholic University of America Press, 1982.

In Leviticum homiliae xxviii. Gary Wayne Barkley, trans. *Origen: Homilies on Leviticus 1-16.* FC, vol. 83. Washington, D.C.: The Catholic University of America Press, 1990.

Libri x in Canticum canticorum. R. P. Lawson, trans. *Origen: The Song of Songs Commentary and Homilies.* ACW, no. 26. Westminster, Md.: Newman Press, 1957; London: Longmans, Green & Co., 1957.

In Lucam homiliae. Joseph T. Lienhard, trans. *Origen: Homilies on Luke, Fragments on Luke.* FC, vol. 94. Washington, D.C.: The Catholic University of America Press, 1996.

De oratione. John J. O'Meara, trans. *Origen: Prayer, Exhortation to Martyrdom.* ACW, no. 19. New York: Newman Press, 1954.

De principiis. G. W. Butterworth, trans. *Origen: On First Principles.* Gloucester, Mass.: Peter Smith, 1973.

_____. Translated by Frederick Crombie. In ANF 4:239-382. Buffalo, N.Y.: Christian Literature Publishing Co., 1885-96; reprint, Peabody, Mass.: Hendrickson Publishers, 1994.

C.1. Gregory of Nyssa: Editions

Ad Ablabium quod non sint tres dei. In *Gregorii Nysseni: Opera Dogmatica Minora,* ed. Friedrich Mueller, 37-57. GNO, vol. 3, pt. 1. Leiden: E. J. Brill, 1958.

_____. In PG 45:116-36. Paris: Garnier, 1857-66.

Adversus Arium et Sabellium de patre et filio. In *Gregorii Nysseni: Opera Dogmatica Minora,* ed. Friedrich Mueller, 71-85. GNO, vol. 3, pt. 1. Leiden: E. J. Brill, 1958.

_____. In PG 45:1281-1301. Paris: Garnier, 1857-66.

Antirrheticus adversus Apollinarium. In *Gregorii Nysseni: Opera Dogmatica Minora,* ed. Friedrich Mueller, 131-233. GNO, vol. 3, pt. 1. Leiden: E. J. Brill, 1958.

_____. In PG 45:1124-1269. Paris: Garnier, 1857-66.

Apologia in Hexaemeron. In PG 44:61-124. Paris: Garnier, 1857-66.

In ascensionem Christi. In *Gregorii Nysseni: Sermones*, pt. 1, ed. Gunther Heil, Adrian van Heck, Ernest Gebhardt, and Andrea Spira, 323-27. GNO, vol. 9. Leiden: E. J. Brill, 1967.

De beneficentia. In *Gregorii Nysseni: Sermones*, pt. 1, ed. Gunther Heil, Adrian van Heck, Ernest Gebhardt, and Andrea Spira, 93-108. GNO, vol. 9. Leiden: E. J. Brill, 1967.

In Canticum canticorum homiliae xv. In *Gregorii Nysseni: In Canticum Canticorum*, ed. Hermann Langerbeck, 3-467. GNO, vol. 6. Leiden: E. J. Brill, 1960.

_____. In PG 44:756-1120. Paris: Garnier, 1857-66.

Dialogus de anima et resurrectione. In *Gregor von Nyssa*, ed. Franz Oehler, vol. 1, *Gregor's Bischof's von Nyssa Gespräch mit seiner Schwester Makrina über Seele und Auferstehung und Lebensbeschreibung seiner Schwester Makrina an den Mönch Olympius*, 2-171. BKV, vol. 1. Leipzig: Wilhelm Engelmann, 1858.

_____. Georg Krabinger, ed. *S. Gregorii Episcopi Nysseni: De anima et resurrectione cum sonore sua Macrina.* Leipzig: Libraria Gustavi Wuttigii, 1837.

_____. In PG 46:11-160. Paris: Garnier, 1857-66.

Contra Eunomium libri. Werner Jaeger, ed. *Contra Eunomium Libri.* 2 vols. GNO, vols. 1-2. Leiden: E. J. Brill, 1960.

_____. In PG 45:248-464, 572-1121. Paris: Garnier, 1857-66.

In Ecclesiasten homiliae viii. In *Gregorii Nysseni: In Inscriptiones Psalmorum, In Sextum Psalmum, In Ecclesiasten Homiliae*, ed. Jacob McDonough and Paul Alexander, 277-442. GNO, vol. 5. Leiden: E. J. Brill, 1962.

_____. In PG 44:616-753. Paris: Garnier, 1857-66.

Encomium in s. Stephanum protomartyrem ii. Otto Lendle, ed. In *Gregorii Nysseni : Sermones*, pt. 2, ed. Friedhelm Mann, 97-106. GNO, vol. 10, pt. 1. Leiden: E. J. Brill, 1990.

_____. In PG 46:721-36. Paris: Garnier, 1857-66.

Epistulae. George Pasqual, ed. *Gregorii Nysseni: Epistulae.* GNO, vol. 8, pt. 2. Leiden: E. J. Brill, 1959.

_____. In PG 45:237-40; 46:1000-1100. Paris: Garnier, 1857-66.

De iis qui baptismum differunt. Hilda Polack, ed. In *Gregorii Nysseni: Sermones*, pt. 3, ed. Friedhelm Mann, 355-70. GNO, vol. 10, pt. 2. Leiden: E. J. Brill, 1996.

In illud: Quatenus uni ex his fecistis mihi fecistis. In *Gregorii Nysseni: Sermones*, pt. 1, ed. Gunther Heil, Adrian van Heck, Ernest Gebhardt, and Andrea Spira, 111-27. GNO, vol. 9. Leiden: E. J. Brill, 1967.

In illud: Tunc et ipse filius. In *Gregorii Nysseni: Opera Dogmatica Minora*, pt. 2, ed. J. Kenneth Downing, Jacob A. McDonough, and Hadwiga Hörner, 3-28. GNO, vol. 3, pt. 2. Leiden: E. J. Brill, 1987.

De infantibus praemature abreptis. In *Gregorii Nysseni: Opera Dogmatica Minora*, pt. 2, ed. J. Kenneth Downing, Jacob A. McDonough, and Hadwiga Hörner, 67-97. GNO, vol. 3, pt. 2. Leiden: E. J. Brill, 1987.
_____. In PG 46:161-92. Paris: Garnier, 1857-66.

In inscriptiones psalmorum. In *Gregorii Nysseni: In Inscriptiones Psalmorum, In Sextum Psalmum, In Ecclesiasten Homiliae*, ed. Jacob McDonough and Paul Alexander, 24-175. GNO, vol. 5. Leiden: E. J. Brill, 1962.
_____. In PG 44:432-608. Paris: Garnier, 1857-66.

De mortuis non esse dolendum. In *Gregorii Nysseni: Sermones*, pt. 1, ed. Gunther Heil, Adrian van Heck, Ernest Gebhardt, and Andrea Spira, 28-68. GNO, vol. 9. Leiden: E. J. Brill, 1967.
_____. In PG 46:497-537. Paris: Garnier, 1857-66.

De opificio hominis. In PG 44:124-256. Paris: Garnier, 1857-66.

Oratio catechetica magna. Ekkehard Mühlenberg, ed. *Gregorii Nysseni Oratio Catechetica: Opera Dogmatica Minora*, pt. 4. GNO, vol. 3, pt. 4. Leiden: E. J. Brill, 1996.
_____. James Herbert Srawley, ed. *The Catechetical Oration of Gregory of Nyssa.* CPT. Cambridge: Cambridge University Press, 1903. Reprint, Cambridge: Cambridge University Press, 1956.
_____. In PG 45:11-105. Paris: Garnier, 1857-66.

Oratio consolatoria in Pulcheriam. In *Gregorii Nysseni: Sermones*, pt. 1, ed. Gunther Heil, Adrian van Heck, Ernest Gebhardt, and Andrea Spira, 461-72. GNO, vol. 9. Leiden: E. J. Brill, 1967.
_____. In PG46:864-77. Paris: Garnier, 1857-66.

De oratio dominica orationes v. In *Gregorii Nysseni: De Oratione Dominica, De Beatitudinibus*, ed. John F. Callahan, 5-74. GNO, vol. 7, pt. 2. Leiden: E. J. Brill, 1992.
_____. In PG 44:1120-1193. Paris: Garnier, 1857-66.

Oratio in diem natalem Christi. Friedhelm Mann, ed. In *Gregorii Nysseni: Sermones*, pt. 3, ed. Friedhelm Mann, 235-69. GNO, vol. 10, pt. 2. Leiden: E. J. Brill, 1996.

Oratio funebris in Flacillam imperatricem. In *Gregorii Nysseni: Sermones*, pt. 1, ed. Gunther Heil, Adrian van Heck, Ernest Gebhardt, and Andrea Spira, 475-90. GNO, vol. 9. Leiden: E. J. Brill, 1967.

Oratio funebris in Meletium episcopum. In *Gregorii Nysseni: Sermones*, pt. 1, ed. Gunther Heil, Adrian van Heck, Ernest Gebhardt, and Andrea Spira, 441-57. GNO, vol. 9. Leiden: E. J. Brill, 1967.

Orationes viii de beatitudinibus. In *Gregorii Nysseni: De Oratione Dominica, De Beatitudinibus*, ed. John F. Callahan, 77-170. GNO, vol. 7, pt. 2. Leiden: E. J. Brill, 1992.
_____. In PG 46:1193-1301. Paris: Garnier, 1857-66.

De perfectione christiana ad Olympium monachum. In *Gregorii Nysseni: Opera Ascetica*, ed. Wener Jaeger, Johannes P. Cavarnos, and Virginia Woods Callahan, 173-214. GNO, vol. 8, pt. 1. Leiden: E. J. Brill, 1952.
_____. In PG 46:252-85. Paris: Garnier, 1857-66.

De pythonissa ad Theodosium episcopum. In *Gregorii Nysseni: Opera Dogmatica Minora*, pt. 2, ed. J. Kenneth Downing, Jacob A. McDonough, and Hadwiga Hörner, 101-8. GNO, vol. 3, pt. 2. Leiden: E. J. Brill, 1987.

Refutatio confessionis Eunomii. In *Contra Eunomium Libri: Pars Altera*, ed. Werner Jaeger, 312-410. GNO, vol. 2. Leiden: E. J. Brill, 1960.

In sanctum et salutare pascha. In *Gregorii Nysseni: Sermones*, pt. 1, ed. Gunther Heil, Adrian van Heck, Ernest Gebhardt, and Andrea Spira, 309-11. GNO, vol. 9. Leiden: E. J. Brill, 1967.

In sanctam pascha. In *Gregorii Nysseni: Sermones*, pt. 1, ed. Gunther Heil, Adrian van Heck, Ernest Gebhardt, and Andrea Spira, 245-70. GNO, vol. 9. Leiden: E. J. Brill, 1967.

In sanctam Pentecosten. Ed. Dörte Teske. In *Gregorii Nysseni: Sermones*, pt. 3, ed. Friedhelm Mann, 285-92. GNO, vol. 10, pt. 2. Leiden: E. J. Brill, 1996.

In suam ordinationem. In *Gregorii Nysseni: Sermones*, pt. 1, ed. Gunther Heil, Adrian van Heck, Ernest Gebhardt, and Andrea Spira, 331-41. GNO, vol. 9. Leiden: E. J. Brill, 1967.

De tridui inter mortem et resurrectionem domini nostri Iesu Christi spatio. In *Gregorii Nysseni: Sermones*, pt. 1, ed. Gunther Heil, Adrian van Heck, Ernest Gebhardt, and Andrea Spira, 273-306. GNO, vol. 9. Leiden: E. J. Brill, 1967.

_____. In PG 46:600-28. Paris: Garnier, 1857-66.

De virginitate. Michael Aubineau, ed. *Grégoire de Nysse: Traité de la Virginité.* SC, no. 119. Paris: Éditions du Cerf, 1966.

_____. In *Gregorii Nysseni: Opera Ascetica*, ed. Wener Jaeger, Johannes P. Cavarnos, and Virginia Woods Callahan, 247-343. GCS, vol. 8, pt. 1. Leiden: E. J. Brill, 1952.

_____. In PG 46:317-416. Paris: Garnier, 1857-66.

De vita Gregorii Thaumaturgi. Gunter Heil, ed. In *Gregorii Nysseni : Sermones*, pt. 2, ed. Friedhelm Mann, 3-58. GNO, vol. 10, pt. 1. Leiden: E. J. Brill, 1990.

De vita Moysis. Herbert Musurillo, ed. *Gregorii Nysseni: De Vita Moysis.* GNO, vol. 7, pt. 1. Leiden: E. J. Brill, 1964.

_____. In PG 44:297-430. Paris: Garnier, 1857-66.

C.2. Gregory of Nyssa: English Translations

Ad Ablabium quod non sint tres dei. Translated by Cyril C. Richardson. In *Christology of the Later Fathers*, ed. Edward Rochie Hardy, 256-67. LCL. Philadelphia: Westminster Press, 1954.

_____. Translated by Henry Austin Williams. In NPNF[2] 5:331-36. New York: Christian Literature Publishing Co., 1887-94; reprint, Peabody, Mass.: Hendrickson Publishers, 1994.

In Canticum canticorum homiliae xv. Casimir McCambley, trans. *Saint Gregory of Nyssa: Commentary on the Song of Songs.* AILEHS, no. 12. Brookline, Mass.: Hellenic College Press, 1987.

_____. (Prologue). Translated by Joseph W. Trigg. Chap. in *Biblical Interpretation*. MFC, vol. 9. Wilmington, Del.: Michael Glazier, 1988.

Dialogus de anima et resurrectione. Jean Terrieux, trans. *Sur l'âme et la résurrection*. Sagesses Chrétiennes. Paris: Éditions du Cerf, 1995.

_____. Catharine P. Roth, trans. *St. Gregory of Nyssa: The Soul and the Resurrection*. Crestwood, N.Y.: St. Vladimir's Seminary Press, 1993.

_____. In *Gregorio di Nissa Opere*, trans. Claudio Moreschini, 389-486. CdR: Sezione Quarta, La religione cattolica, ed. Piero Rossano. Torino: Unione Tipografico-Editrice Torinese, 1992.

_____. Salvatore Lilla, trans. *Gregorio di Nissa: L'anima e la risurrezione*. CTePa, no. 26. Rome: Città Nuova Editrice, 1981.

_____. In *Saint Gregory of Nyssa: Ascetical Works*, trans. Virginia Woods Callahan, 198-272. FC, vol. 58. Washington, D.C.: The Catholic University of America Press, 1967.

_____. Luis M. de Cadiz, trans. *San Gregorio Niseno: Dialogo sobre el alma y la resurreccion*. COCG. Buenos Aires: Editorial Atlantida, 1952.

_____. In *Des Heiligen Bischofs Gregor von Nyssa Schriften: Grosse Kateches, Über das Gebet des Herrn, Über die acht Seligkeiten, Dialog über di Seele, Leben der seligen Makrina*, trans. Karl Weiß and Eugen Stolz, 243-334. BKV, vol. 56. Munich: Josef Kösel & Friedrich Pustet, 1927.

_____. Translated by William Moore. In NPNF[2] 5:430-68. New York: Christian Literature Publishing Co., 1887-94; reprint, Peabody, Mass.: Hendrickson Publishers, 1994.

Contra Eunomium libri. Translated by William Moore, H. C. Ogle, and Henry Austin Williams. In NPNF[2] 5:33-248. New York: Christian Literature Publishing Co., 1887-94; reprint, Peabody, Mass.: Hendrickson Publishers, 1994.

In illud: Tunc et ipse filius. Casimir McCambley, trans. "When (the Father) Will Subject All Things to (the Son), Then (the Son) Himself Will Be Subjected to Him (the Father) Who Subjects All Things to Him (the Son)--A Treatise on First Corinthians 15:28 by Saint Gregory of Nyssa." *GOTR* 28, no. 1 (Spring 1983): 1-25.

De infantibus praemature abreptis. Translated by William Moore. In NPNF[2] 5:372-81. New York: Christian Literature Publishing Co., 1887-94; reprint, Peabody, Mass.: Hendrickson Publishers, 1994.

In inscriptiones psalmorum. Ronald E. Heine, trans. *Gregory of Nyssa's Treatise on the Inscriptions of the Psalms: Introduction, Translation, and Notes*. OECS. Oxford: Clarendon Press, 1995.

_____. Casimir McCambley, trans. *Saint Gregory of Nyssa: Commentary on the Inscriptions of the Psalms*. AILEHS, no. 17. Brookline, Mass.: Hellenic College Press, 1987.

De opificio hominis. Translated by Henry Austin Williams. In NPNF[2] 5:387-427. New York: Christian Literature Publishing Co., 1887-94; reprint, Peabody, Mass.: Hendrickson Publishers, 1994.

Oratio catechetica magna. Translated by William Moore. In NPNF² 5:473-509. New York: Christian Literature Publishing Co., 1887-94; reprint, Peabody, Mass.: Hendrickson Publishers, 1994.

De oratione dominica orationes v. Translated by Hilda C. Graef. In *St. Gregory of Nyssa: The Lord's Prayer, The Beatitudes*, 21-84. ACW, no. 18. Westminster, Md.: Newman Press, 1954.

Orationes viii de beatitudinibus. Translated by Hilda C. Graef. In *St. Gregory of Nyssa: The Lord's Prayer, The Beatitudes,* 85-175. ACW, no. 18. Westminster, Md.: Newman Press, 1954.

_____. Translated by William Moore and Henry Austin Wilson. In NPNF² 5:428-68. New York: Christian Literature Publishing Co., 1887-94; reprint, Peabody, Mass.: Hendrickson Publishers, 1994.

Refutatio confessionis Eunomii. Translated by William Moore, H. C. Ogle, and Henry Austin Williams. In NPNF² 5:101-34. New York: Christian Literature Publishing Co., 1887-94; reprint, Peabody, Mass.: Hendrickson Publishers, 1994.

In sanctum et salutare pascha. Translated by Stuart G. Hall. In *The Easter Sermons of Gregory of Nyssa: Translation and Commentary. Proceedings of the Fourth International Colloquium on Gregory of Nyssa*, ed. Andreas Spira and Christoph Klock, 51-53. PMS, no. 9. Philadelphia: Philadelphia Patristic Foundation, 1981.

In sanctam pascha. Translated by Stuart G. Hall. In *The Easter Sermons of Gregory of Nyssa: Translation and Commentary. Proceedings of the Fourth International Colloquium on Gregory of Nyssa*, ed. Andreas Spira and Christoph Klock, 5-23. PMS, no. 9. Philadelphia: Philadelphia Patristic Foundation, 1981.

De tridui inter mortem et resurrectionem domini nostri Iesu Christi spatio. Translated by Stuart G. Hall. In *The Easter Sermons of Gregory of Nyssa: Translation and Commentary. Proceedings of the Fourth International Colloquium on Gregory of Nyssa*, ed. Andreas Spira and Christoph Klock, 31-50. PMS, no. 9. Philadelphia: Philadelphia Patristic Foundation, 1981.

De virginitate. Translated by William Moore. In NPNF² 5:343-71. New York: Christian Literature Publishing Co., 1887-94; reprint, Peabody, Mass.: Hendrickson Publishers, 1994.

De vita Moysis. Abraham J. Malherbe and Everett Ferguson, trans. *Gregory of Nyssa: The Life of Moses.* CWS. New York: Paulist Press, 1978.

D. Other Early Christian Literature

Didymus the Blind. *Commentarii in Zachariam.* Louis Doutreleau, ed. *Didyme l'Aveugle: Sur Zacharie.* 3 vols. SC, nos. 83-85. Paris: Éditions du Cerf, 1962.

_____. *In epistulas catholicas brevis enarratio.* Friedrich Zoepfl, ed. *Didymi Alexandrini in epistolas canonicas brevis enarratio.* NTA, vol. 4, no. 1. Münster: Aschendorffsche Verlagsbuchhandlung, 1914.

_____. *Fragmenta in psalmos.* In PG 39:1156-1622. Paris: Garnier, 1857-66.

_____. *Contra Manichaeos.* In PG 39:1085-1110. Paris: Garnier, 1857-66.

_____. *De Trinitate.* In PG 39:269-992. Paris: Garnier, 1857-66.

Evagrius of Pontus. *Epistulae lxii.* In *Evagrius Ponticus,* ed. W. Frankenberg, 564-611. AAWG, n.s., vol. 8, pt. 2. Berlin: Garnier, 1912.

_____. *Kephalaia gnostica.* A. Guillaumont, ed. *Les six Centuries des "Kephalaia Gnostica" d'Évagre le Pontique.* PO, no. 28, pt. 1. Paris: Firmin-Didot, 1958.

Gregory of Nazianzus. *Orationes xlv.* Jean Bernardi, ed. *Grégoire de Nazianze: Discours 1-3.* SC, no. 247. Paris: Éditions du Cerf, 1978.

_____. Paul Gallay and Maurice Jourjon, eds. *Grégoire de Nazianze: Discours 27-31 (Discours Théologiques).* SC, no. 250. Paris: Éditions du Cerf, 1978.

_____. Claudio Moreschini, ed. *Grégoire de Nazianze: Discours 38-41.* SC, no. 358. Paris: Éditions du Cerf, 1990.

Jerome. *Commentarii in Esaiam.* Marci Adriaen, ed. In *S. Hieronymi Presbyteri Opera,* pt. 1, *Opera Exegetica,* vol. 2a, *Commentariorum in Esaiam libri xii-xviii, In Esaia parvula adbreviatio,* 466-799. CCSL, vol. 73a. Turnhout: Brepols, 1963.

Schwartz, Edward, ed. *Acta Conciliorum Oecumenicorum.* Bk. 4, *Concilium Universale Constantinopolitanum sub Iustiniano Habitum,* ed. Johannes Straub, vol. 1. Berolini: Walter de Gruyter, 1971.

E. Other Primary Texts

Philo of Alexandria. *Quaestiones in Genesim.* Ralph Marcus, ed. and trans. *Philo.* Supplement I, *Questions and Answers on Genesis.* LCL. Cambridge: Harvard University Press, 1961.

Plotinus. *Enneades.* Stephen MacKenna, trans. *The Enneads.* 2d ed. Revised by B. S. Page. London: Faber and Faber, 1956.

II. Secondary Literature

Aland, Kurt, ed. *Vollständige Konkordanz zum griechischen Neuen Testament.* 2 vols. Berlin: Walter de Gruyter, 1983.

Alexandre, Monique. "L'interprétation de Lc 16.19-31 chez Grégoire de Nysse." In *Epektasis: mélanges patristiques offerts au Cardinal Jean Daniélou,* ed. Jacques Fontaine and Charles Kannengiesser, 425-41. Paris: Éditions Beauchesne, 1972.

_____. "Protologie et eschatologie chez Grégoire de Nysse." In *Arche é Telos: l'antropologia di Origene e di Gregorio di Nissa,* ed. Ugo Bianchi, 122-59. SPM, no. 12. Milan: Vita E Pensiero, 1981.

_____. "La théorie de l'exégèse dans le *De hominis opificio* et l'*In Hexaemeron.*" In *Écriture et culture philosophique dans la pensée de Grégoire de Nysse: Actes du Colloque de Chevetogne*, ed. Marguerite Harl, 87-110. Leiden: E. J. Brill, 1971.

Altaner, Berthold, and Alfred Stuiber. *Patrologie: Leben, Schriften und Lehre der Kirchenväter.* Freiburg: Herder, 1978.

Altenburger, Margarete, and Friedhelm Mann. *Bibliographie zu Gregor von Nyssa: Editionene—Übersetzungen—Literatur.* Leiden: E. J. Brill, 1988.

Anrich, G. "Clemens und Origenes als Begründer der Lehre vom Fegfeuer." In *Theologische Abhandlungen: Eine Festgabe für Heinrich Julius Holtzmann*, 97-120. Tübingen and Leipzig: J. C. B. Mohr, 1902.

Armantage, James Walter. *Will the Body Be Raised? Origen and the Origenist Controversies.* Ph.D. diss., Yale University, 1970.

Babcock, Harold E. "Origen's Anti-Gnostic Polemic and the Doctrine of Universalism." *UUC* 38, no. 3-4 (Fall-Winter 1983): 53-59.

Baker, Aelred. "The Great Letter of Pseudo-Macarius and Gregory of Nyssa." *StMon* 6 (1964): 381-87.

_____. "Pseudo-Macarius and Gregory of Nyssa." *VC* 20 (1966): 227-234.

Balás, David L. "Apokatastasis." In *Encyclopedia of Early Christianity*, ed. Everett Ferguson, 62-63. GRLH, vol. 846. New York: Garland Publishing, 1990.

_____. Μετουσία Θεοῦ: *Man's Participation in God's Perfections According to Saint Gregory of Nyssa.* StudAnselm, no. 55. Rome: Pontificium Institutum S. Anselmi, 1966.

_____. "Plenitudo Humanitatis: The Unity of Human Nature in the Theology of Gregory of Nyssa." In *Disciplina Nostra: Essays in Memory of Robert F. Evans*, ed. Donald F. Winslow, 115-31. PMS, no. 6. Cambridge, Mass.: Philadelphia Patristic Foundation, 1979.

Balthasar, Hans Urs von. "Le mystérion d'Origène." *RSR* 26 (1936): 513-62; 27 (1937): 38-64.

_____. *Origen, Spirit and Fire: A Thematic Anthology of His Writings.* Translated by Robert J. Daly. Washington, D. C.: The Catholic University of America Press, 1984.

_____. *Origenes Geist und Feuer: Ein Aufbau aus seinen Schriften.* Salzburg: Otto Müller Verlag, 1938.

_____. *Parole et mystère chez Origène.* Paris: Éditions du Cerf, 1957.

_____. *Présence et pensée: Essai sur la philosophie religieuse de Grégoire de Nysse.* Paris: Gabriel Beauchesne, 1942.

Bardenhewer, Otto. *Geschichte der altkirchlichen Literatur.* 2d ed. 5 vols. Freiburg: Herder, 1923; reprint, Darmstadt: Wissenschaftliche Buchgesellschaft, 1962.

Barrois, Georges. "The Alleged Origenism of St. Gregory of Nyssa." *SVTQ* 30, no. 1 (1986): 7-16.

Barth, Karl. *CD.* Vol. II, *The Doctrine of God*, pt. 2. Translated and edited by Geoffrey W. Bromiley and others. Edinburgh: T. &. T. Clark, 1957.

Bauer, Walter, ed. *A Greek-English Lexicon of the New Testament and Other Early Christian Literature.* 5th ed. 2d English ed. Translated, adapted, revised, and augmented by William F. Arndt, F. Wilbur Gingrich, and Frederick W. Danker. Chicago: University of Chicago Press, 1979.

Bienert, Wolfgang, ed., *Origeniana Septima: Origenes in den Auseinandersetzung des 4. Jahrhunderts*, BETL, vol. 137. Leuven: Leuven University Press, 1999.

Bietenhard, Hans. *Caesarea, Origenes und die Juden*. Stuttgart: W. Kohlhammer, 1974.

Bigg, Charles. *The Christian Platonists of Alexandria*. Oxford: n.p., 1886; reprint, New York: AMS Press, 1970.

Bonsirven, Joseph. "Exégèse Allegorique chez les Rabbis Tannaites" *RSR* 24 (1934): 35-46.

_____. *Exégèse Rabbinique et Exégèse Paulinienne*. BTH. Paris: Beauchesne, 1938.

Bostock, D. Gerald. "Medical Theory and Theology in Origen." In *Origeniana Tertia: The Third International Colloquium for Origen Studies*, ed. Richard Hanson and Henri Crouzel, 191-99. Rome: Edizioni dell'Ateneo, 1985.

_____. "The Sources of Origen's Doctrine of Pre-existence." In *Origeniana Quarta: Die Referate des 4. Internationalen Origeneskongress*, ed. Lothar Lies, 259-64. ITS, no. 19. Innsbruck: Tyrolia-Verlag, 1987.

Brambillasca, G. "Citations de l'Ecriture Sainte et des auteurs classiques dans le Προτρεπτικὸς πρὸς "Ελληνας de Clément d'Alexandrie." In *Studia Patristica*, vol. 11, pt. 2, ed. F. L. Cross, 8-12. TU, no. 108. Berlin: Akademie-Verlag, 1972.

Canévet, Mariette. *Grégoire de Nysse et l'herméneutique biblique: Études des rapports entre le langage et la connaissance de Dieu*. Paris: Études Augustiniennes, 1983.

_____. "Le 'De instituto christiano': est-il de Grégoire de Nysse? Problèmes de critique interne." *REG* 82 (1969): 404-23.

_____. "Nature du mal et économie du salut chez Grégoire de Nysse." *RSR* 56, no. 1 (1968): 87-95.

Caro, Roberto. *La Homilética Mariana Griega en el siglo V*. 3 vols. MLS, nos. 3-5. Dayton, Ohio: Dayton University, 1971-1973.

Centre d'Analyse et de Documentation Patristiques. *Biblia Patristica: Index des citations et allusions bibliques dans la littérature patristique*. 5 vols. Paris: Éditions du Centre National de la Recherche Scientifique, 1975-.

Cheek, James Edward. "Eschatology and Redemption in the Theology of Origen: Israelite-Jewish and Greek-Hellenistic Ideas in Origen's Interpretation of Redemption." Ph.D. diss., Drew University, 1962.

Clark, Elizabeth A. *The Origenist Controversy: The Cultural Construction of an Early Christian Debate*. Princeton, N.J.: Princeton University Press, 1992.

_____. "The Place of Jerome's Commentary on Ephesians in the Origenist Controversy: The Apokatastasis and Ascetic Ideals." *VC* 41, no. 2 (June 1987): 154-71.

Crouzel, Henri. "L'apocatastase chez Origène." In *Origeniana Quarta: Die Referate des 4. Internationalen Origeneskongresses, Innsbruck, 2-6 September 1985*, ed. Lothar Lies, 282-90. Innsbruck: Tyrolia, 1987.

————. "L'exégèse origénienne de I Cor 3,11-15 et la purification eschatologique." In *Epektasis: mélanges patristiques offerts au Cardinal Jean Daniélou*, ed. Jacques Fontaine and Charles Kannengiesser, 273-83. Paris: 1972.

————. "L'Hadès et la Géhenne selon Origène." *Greg* 59, no. 2 (1978): 291-331.

————. "A Letter from Origen 'To Friends in Alexandria.'" Translated by Joseph D. Gauthier. In *The Heritage of the Early Church: Essays in Honor of the Very Reverend Georges Vasilievich Florovsky*, ed. David Neiman and Margaret Schatkin, 135-50. OCA, no. 195. Rome: Pontificium Intstitutum Studiorum Orientalium, 1973.

————. "The Literature on Origen 1970-1988." *TS* 49, no. 3 (September 1988): 499-516.

————. *Origen*. Translated by A. S. Worrall. San Francisco: Harper & Row, 1989.

————. *Origène*. Paris, Éditions Lethielleux, 1985.

————. "Origenism." In *Encyclopedia of the Early Church*, ed. Angelo Di Berardino, trans. Adrian Walford, 2:623-24. New York: Oxford University Press, 1992.

————. "Die Patrologie und die Erneuerung der patristischen Studien." In *Bilanz der Theologie im 20. Jahrhundert: Perspektiven, Strömungen, Motive in der christlichen und nichtchristlichen Welt*, ed. Herbert Vorgrimler and Roland Vander Gucht, 3:504-29. Freiburg: Herder, 1970.

Crouzel, Henri, and Antonio Quacquarelli, eds. *Origeniana Secunda: Second colloque international des études origéniennes*. QVC, no. 15. Rome: Edizioni dell'Ateneo, 1980.

Crouzel, Henri, Gennaro Lomiento, and Josep Rius-Camps, eds. *Origeniana: Premier colloque international des études origéniennes*. QVC, no. 12. Bari: Istituto di Letteratura Cristiana Antica, 1975.

Daley, Brian E. "Apokatastasis and 'Honorable Silence' in the Eschatology of Maximus the Confessor." In *Maximus Confessor: Actes du Symposion sur Maxime le Confesseur*, ed. Felix Heinzer and Christoph Schönborn, 309-39. Paradosis, no. 27. Fribourg: Éditions Universitaires Fribourg Suisse, 1982.

————. *The Hope of the Early Church: A Handbook of Patristic Eschatology*. Cambridge: Cambridge University Press, 1991.

Daly, Robert J. "Translator's Epilogue." In Hans Urs von Balthasar, *Origen, Spirit and Fire: A Thematic Anthology of His Writings*, trans. Robert J. Daly, 371-73. Washington, D. C.: The Catholic University of America Press, 1984.

————, ed. *Origeniana Quinta: Papers of the 5th International Origen Congress*. BETL, vol. 105. Leuven: University Press, 1992.

Daniélou, Jean. "L'Adversus Arium et Sabellium de Grégoire de Nysse et l'origénisme cappadocien." *RSR* 54 (1966): 61-66.

_____. "L'apocatastase chez Saint Grégoire de Nysse." *RSR* 30 (1940): 328-47.

_____. "La chronologie des oeuvres de Grégoire de Nysse." In *StudPat*, vol. 7, ed. F. L. Cross, 346-72. Texte und Untersuchungen zur Geschichte der altchristlichen Literatur, no. 92. Berlin: Akademie-Verlag, 1966.

_____. "Le comble du mal et eschatologie chez Grégoire de Nysse." In *Festgabe Joseph Lortz*, ed. Erwin Iserloh and P. Mann, 27-45. Baden-Baden: Bruno Grimm, 1958.

_____. *L'Être et le temps chez Grégoire de Nysse*. Leiden: E. J. Brill, 1970.

_____. "Onction et baptême chez Grégoire de Nysse." *EL* 90 (1976): 440-45.

_____. *Origen*. Translated by Walter Mitchell. New York: Sheed & Ward, 1955.

_____. *Origène*. Paris: La Table Ronde, 1948.

_____. *Philon d'Alexandrie*. Paris: Librairie Arthème Fayard, 1958.

_____. "La résurrection des corps chez Grégoire de Nysse." *VC* 7, no. 3 (1953): 154-70.

de Lubac, Henri. *Histoire et Esprit: L'intelligence de l'Écriture d'après Origène*. Aubier: Éditions Montaigne, 1950.

de Margerie, Bertrand. *Introduction à l'histoire de l'exégèse*. Vol. 1. Paris: Éditions du Cerf, 1980.

de Faye, Eugène. *Origène, sa vie, son, oeuvre, sa penséee*. 3 vols. Paris: E. Leroux, 1923-28.

Dennis, T. J. "Gregory on the Resurrection of the Body." In *The Easter Sermons of Gregory of Nyssa, Translation and Commentary: Proceedings of the Fourth International Colloquium on Gregory of Nyssa*, ed. Andreas Spira and Christoph Klock, 55-80. PMS, no. 9. Philadelphia: Philadelphia Patristic Foundation, 1981.

Denniston, J. D. *The Greek Particles*. 2d ed. Oxford: Clarendon Press, 1954.

Diekamp, Franz. *Die origenistischen Streitigkeiten im sechsten Jahrhundert und das fünfte allgemeine Concil*. Münster: Verlag Aschendorff, 1899.

Diels, Hermann. *Die Fragmente der Vorsokratiker*. 3 vols. 10th ed. Edited by Walther Kranz. Berlin: Weidmannsche Verlagsbuchhandlung, 1960.

Dorival, Gilles, and Alain Le Boulluec, eds. *Origeniana Sexta: Origène et la Bible. Actes du Colloquium Origenianum Sextum, Chantilly, 30 Septembre 1993*. BETL, vol. 118. Leuven: Leuven University Press, 1995.

Dörrie, Heinrich. "Gregors Theologie auf dem Hintergrunde der neuplatonischen Metaphysik." In *Gregor von Nyssa und die Philosophie: Zweites internationales Kolloquium über Gregor von Nyssa*, ed. Heinrich Dörrie, Margarete Altenburger, and Uta Schramm, 21-42. Leiden: E. J. Brill, 1976.

Drobner, Hubertus R. *Bibelindex zu den Werken Gregors von Nyssa*. Paderborn: Self-published, 1988.

Dünzl, Franz. "Die Canticum-Exegese des Gregor von Nyssa und des Origenes im Vergleich." *JAC* 36 (1993): 94-109.

Dodd, C. H. *According to the Scriptures: The Sub-structure of New Testament Theology.* London: Nisbet & Co., 1952.

Ellis, E. Earle. *Christ and the Future in New Testament History.* NovTSup, vol. 97. Leiden: Brill, 2000.

Emerson, Stephen D. "The Work of Christ According to Gregory of Nyssa." Ph.D. diss., Vanderbilt University, 1998.

Escriban-Alberca, Ignacio. "Zum zyklischen Zeitbegriff der alexandrinischen und kappadokischen Theologie." In *StudPat*, vol. 11, pt. 2, ed. F. L. Cross, 42-51. TU, no. 108. Berlin: Akademie-Verlag, 1972.

Farkasfalvy, Denis. "Interpretation of the Bible." In *Encyclopedia of Early Christianity*, ed. Everett Ferguson, 466-69. GRLH, vol. 846. New York: Garland Publishing, 1990.

Floyd, W. E. G. *Clement of Alexandria's Treatment of the Problem of Evil.* Oxford: Oxford University Press, 1971.

Geerard, Maurice. *CPG.* 5 vols. Corpus Christianorum. Turnhout: Brepols, 1974-87.

Gnilka, Joachim. *Ist 1 Kor. 3,10-15 ein Schriftzeugnis für das Fegfeuer? Eine exegetisch-historische Untersuchung.* Düsseldorf: Michael Triltsch Verlag, 1955.

González, Justo L. *A History of Christian Thought.* Rev. ed. Vol. 1, *From the Beginnings to the Council of Chalcedon.* Nashville: Abingdon Press, 1970.

Gorday, Peter. *Principles of Patristic Exegesis: Romans 9-11 in Origen, John Chrysostom, and Augustine.* SBEC, vol. 4 .New York: Edwin Mellen Press, 1983.

Grant, Robert M., with David Tracy. *A Short History of the Interpretation of the Bible*, 2d rev. ed. Philadelphia: Fortress Press, 1984.

Gribomont, Jean. "Le *De instituto christiano* et le messalianisme de Grégoire de Nysse." In *Studia Patristica*, vol. 5, ed. F. L. Cross, 312-22. TU, no. 80. Berlin: Akademie-Verlag, 1962.

Guillaumont, Antoine. *Les "Kephalaia Gnostica" d'Evagre le Pontique et l'histoire de l'Origénisme chez les Grecs et chez les Syriens.* PatSor, no. 5. Paris: Éditions du Seuil, 1962.

Hammond, Charles P. "Notes on the Manuscripts and Editions of Origen's Commentary on the Epistle to the Romans in the Latin Translation by Rufinus." *JTS* n.s. 16 (1965): 338-57.

_____. "Some Textual Points in Origen's Commentary on Matthew." *JTS* n.s. 24 (1973): 380-404.

Hanson, Richard P. C. *Allegory and Event: A Study of the Sources and Significance of Origen's Interpretation of Scripture.* Richmond: John Knox Press, 1959.

Hanson, Richard P. C., and Henri Crouzel, eds. *Origeniana Tertia: The Third International Colloquium for Origen Studies.* Rome: Edizioni dell'Ateneo, 1985.

Harl, Marguerite. "La préexistence des âmes dans l'oeuvre d'Origène." In *Origeniana Quarta: Die Referate des 4. Internationalen Origeneskongress*, ed. Lothar Lies, 238-58. ITS, no. 19. Innsbruck: Tyrolia-Verlag, 1987.

Harmon, Steven R. "A Note on the Critical Use of *Instrumenta* for the Retrieval of Patristic Biblical Exegesis." *JECS* 11, no. 1 (Spring 2003): 95-107.

Harnack, Adolf von. *Geschichte der altchristlichen Litteratur bis Eusebius.* 2 pts. Leipzig: Hinrichs'sche Buchhandlung, 1893-1904.

_____. *Lehrbuch der Dogmengeschichte.* 5th rev. ed. 3 vols. Tübingen: J. C. B. Mohr (Paul Siebeck), 1909-10.

Harris, Rendel, and Vacher Burch. *Testimonies.* 2 pts. Cambridge: Cambridge University Press, 1916, 1920.

Heine, Ronald E. "Gregory of Nyssa's Apology for Allegory." *VC* 38, no. 4 (December 1984): 360-70.

Hennessey, Lawrence R. "The Place of Saints and Sinners after Death." In *Origen of Alexandria: His World and His Legacy,* ed. Kannengiesser and William L. Peterson, 295-312. CJAn, vol. 1. Notre Dame, Ind.: University of Notre Dame Press, 1988.

Hermaniuk, Maxime. *La Parabole Évangélique: enquête exégètique et critique.* ULD, ser. 2, vol. 38 Paris: Desclée de Brouwer, 1947.

Heussi, Carl. "Die Stromateis des Clemens Alexandrinus und ihr Verhältnis zum Protreptikos und Pädagogos." *ZWT* 45 (1902): 465-512.

Holl, Karl. "Über die Gregor von Nyssa zugeschriebene Schrift 'Adversus Arium et Sabellium.'" *ZKG* 25 (1904): 380-98.

Jaeger, Werner. *Two Rediscovered Works of Ancient Christian Literature: Gregory of Nyssa and Macarius.* Leiden: E. J. Brill, 1954.

Janowitz, Naomi. "The Rhetoric of Translation: Three Early Perspectives on Translating Torah." *HTR* 84, no. 2 (April 1991): 129-40.

Kelly, J[ohn] N[orman] D[avidson]. *Early Christian Doctrines.* Rev. ed. San Francisco: Harper & Row, 1978.

Kirk, G. S., and J. E. Raven. *The Presocratic Philosophers: A Critical History with a Selection of Texts.* Cambridge: Cambridge University Press, 1957.

Kittel, Gerhard, ed. *TDNT.* 10 vols. Translated by Geoffrey W. Bromiley. Grand Rapids: William B. Eerdmans Publishing Co., 1964-76.

Koch, Hal. *Pronoia und Paideusis: Studien über Origenes und sein Verhältnis zum Platonismus.* AKG, no. 22. Berlin: Walter de Gruyter, 1932.

Koch, Hugo. "War Klemens von Alexandrien Priester?" *ZNW* 20, nos. 1-2 (1921): 43-48.

Krause, Wilhelm. *Die Stellung der frühchristlichen Autoren zur heidnischen Literatur.* Vienna: Herder, 1958.

Lampe, G. W. H., ed. *A Patristic Greek Lexicon.* Oxford: Clarendon Press, 1961.

Lauterbach, J. Z. "The Ancient Jewish Allegorists in Talmud and Midrash" *JQR* n.s. 1 (1911): 525-26.

Leroy, Georges. "La présence du mal et de la mort dans la création." *Contacts* 38 (1986): 180-94.

Liddell, Henry George, and Robert Scott, eds. *Greek-English Lexicon.* Revised by Henry Stuart Jones and Roderick McKenzie. Oxford: Clarendon Press, 1968.

Lies, Lothar, ed. *Origeniana Quarta: Die Referate des 4. Internationalen Origeneskongress.* ITS, no. 19. Innsbruck: Tyrolia-Verlag, 1987.

Loofs, Friedrich. *Leitfaden zum Studium der Dogmengeschichte.* 6th rev. ed., ed. Kurt Aland. 2 pts. Tübingen: Max Niemeyer Verlag, 1959.

Lubac, Henri de. *Histoire et Esprit: L'intelligence de l'Écriture d'après Origène.* Théologie, no. 16. Paris: Aubier, 1950.

Ludlow, Morwenna. *Universal Salvation: Eschatology in the Thought of Gregory of Nyssa and Karl Rahner.* OTM. Oxford: Oxford University Press, 2000.

Lundberg, Peter. *La typologie baptismale dans l'ancienne église.* ASNU, no. 10. Leipzig: A. Lorentz, 1942.

Mann, Friedhelm, ed. *Lexicon Gregorianum: Wörterbuch zu den Schriften Gregors von Nyssa.* Leiden: Brill, 1991-.

Marriott, George Leicester. "The *De instituto Christiano* Attributed to Gregory of Nyssa." *JTS* 19 (1918): 328-30.

Mateo-Seco, Lucas Francisco. "La teologia de la muerte en la 'Oratio Catechetica Magna' de San Gregorio de Nissa." *ScrTh* 1 (1969): 453-73.

_____. "Kenosis, exaltación de Cristo y apocatástasis en la exégesis a Filipenses 2,5-11 de S. Gregorio de Nisa." *ScrTh* 3 (1971): 301-42.

Mees, Michael. *Die Zitate aus dem Neuen Testament bei Clemens von Alexandrien.* QVC, no. 2. Rome: Istituto di Letteratura Cristiana Antica, 1970.

Méhat, André. "Apocatastase: Origène, Clément d'Alexandrie, Act 3:21." *VC* 10 (1956): 196-214.

_____. "Clément d'Alexandrie et les sens de l'Écriture (Ier *Stromate*, 176,1 et 179,3)." In *Epektasis: Mélanges patristiques offers au Cardinal Jean Daniélou,* ed. Jacques Fontaine and Charles Kannengiesser, 356-57. Paris: Éditions Beauchesne, 1972.

Meredith, Anthony. "The Good and the Beautiful in Gregory of Nyssa." In *EPMHNEYMATA: Festschrift für Hadwig Hörner zum sechszigsten Geburtstag,* ed. Herbert Eisenberger, 133-45. BKAW, n.s., vol. 79. Heidelberg: Carl Winter Universitätsverlag, 1990.

_____. "Gregory of Nyssa and Plotinus." In *StudPat,* vol. 17, pt. 3, ed. Elizabeth A. Livingstone, 1120-26. Oxford: Pergamon Press, 1982.

Milbank, John, Catherine Pickstock, and Graham Ward, eds. *Radical Orthodoxy: A New Theology.* London: Routledge, 1999.

Moltmann, Jürgen. *The Coming of God: Christian Eschatology.* Translated by Margaret Kohl. Minneapolis: Fortress Press, 1996.

Mondésert, Claude. *Clément d'Alexandrie: Introduction à l'étude de sa pensée religieuse à partir de l'Écriture.* Théologie, no. 4. Paris: Aubier, 1944.

Mowinckel, Sigmund. *The Psalms in Israel's Worship.* Translated by D. R. Ap-Thomas. New York: Abingdon Press, 1962.

Müller, Gotthold A. *Ἀποκατάστασις πάντων: A Bibliography.* Basel: Garnier, 1969.

_____. "Origenes und die Apokatastasis." *TZ* 14, no. 3 (May-June 1958): 174-190.

_____. "Ungeheuerliche Ontologie: Erwägungen zur christlichen Lehre über Hölle und Allversöhnung." *EvT* 34, no. 3 (May-June 1974): 256-75.

Munck, Johannes. *Untersuchungen über Klemens von Alexandria.* FKGG, vol. 2. Stuttgart: W. Kohlhammer, 1933.

Nemeshegyi, Peter. *La paternité de Dieu chez Origène.* Bibliothèque de Théologie, ser. 4, HTh, vol. 2. Tournai: Desclée, 1960.

Norris, Frederick W. "Universal Salvation in Origen and Maximus." In *Universalism and the Doctrine of Hell: Papers Presented at the Fourth Edinburgh Conference in Christian Dogmatics, 1991,* ed. Nigel M. de S. Cameron, 35-72. Carlisle, U.K.: Paternoster Press, 1993; Grand Rapids: Baker Book House, 1993.

Oepke, Albrecht. "Ἀποκαθίστημι, ἀποκατάστασις." In *TDNT* 1:387-93. Translated by Geoffrey W. Bromiley. Grand Rapids: William B. Eerdmans Publishing Co., 1964-76.

Otis, Brooks. "Cappadocian Thought as a Coherent System." *DOP* 12 (1958): 95-124.

Outler, Albert C. "Origen and the *Regula Fidei.*" *SceCent* 4 (1984): 133-41.

Pagels, Elaine H. *The Gnostic Paul: Gnostic Exegesis of the Pauline Letters.* Philadelphia: Fortress Press, 1975.

_____. *The Johannine Gospel in Gnostic Exegesis* New York: Abingdon Press, 1973.

Painchaud, Louis. "The Use of Scripture in Gnostic Literature." *JECS* 4, no. 2 (Summer 1996): 129-46.

Patrick, John. *Clement of Alexandria.* Edinburgh: William Blackwood and Sons, 1914.

Pelikan, Jaroslav. *The Christian Tradition: A History of the Development of Doctrine.* Vol. 1, *The Emergence of the Catholic Tradition (100-600).* Chicago: University of Chicago Press, 1971.

_____. *Christianity and Classical Culture: The Metamorphosis of Natural Theology in the Christian Encounter with Hellenism.* New Haven: Yale University Press, 1993.

_____. *The Melody of Theology: A Philosophical Dictionary.* Cambridge: Harvard University Press, 1988.

Philippou, Angelos J. "The Doctrine of Evil in St. Gregory of Nyssa." In *StudPat,* vol. 9, ed. F. L. Cross, 251-56. TU, no. 94. Berlin: Akademie-Verlag, 1966.

_____. "The Eschatology of St. Gregory of Nyssa." D.Phil. diss., Oxford University, 1963.

Quasten, Johannes. *Patrology.* 3 vols. Utrecht: Spectrum, 1950; reprint, Westminster, Md.: Christian Classics, 1990.

Quatember, Friedrich. *Die christliche Lebenshaltung des Klemens von Alexandrien nach seinem Pädagogus.* Vienna: Herder, 1946.

Rabinowitz, Celia Ellen. "Apokatastasis and Sunteleia: Eschatological and Soteriological Speculation in Origen." Ph.D. diss., Fordham University, 1989.

Redepenning, Ernst Rudolf. *Origenes: eine Darstelling seines Lebens und seiner Lehre.* 2 vols. Bonn: Eduard Weber, 1841-46.

Reinhardt, Karl. "Heraklits Lehre vom Feuer." In *Vermächtnis der Antike: Gesammelte Essays zur Philosophie und Geschichtsschreibung*, ed. Carl Becker, 70-82. Göttingen: Vandenhoeck & Ruprecht, 1960.

Rondeau, Marie-Josèph. *Les Commentaires Patristiques du Psautier (IIIe-Ve siècles)*. 2 vols. OCA, no. 219. Rome: Pontificium Institutum Studiorum Orientalium, 1982-1985.

Runia, David T. *Philo in Early Christian Literature: A Survey*. CRINT, Section III, Jewish Traditions in Early Christian Literature, ed. Y. Aschkenasy and others, vol. 3. Assen, The Netherlands: Van Gorcum, 1993; Minneapolis: Fortress Press, 1993.

Ruwet, J. "Clément d'Alexandrie: Canon des Écritures et Apocryphes." *Bib* 29, nos. 1-2 (1948): 77-99, 240-68.

Sachs, John R. "Apocatastasis in Patristic Theology." *TS* 54, no. 4 (December 1993): 617-40.

Salmona, Bruno. "Origene e Gregorio di Nissa sulla resurrezione dei corpi e l'apocatastasi." *Aug* 18 (1978): 383-88.

Scouteris, Constantine. "*Malum Privatio Est*: St. Gregory of Nyssa and Pseudo-Dionysius on the Existence of Evil (Some Further Comments)." In *StuPat*, vol. 18, pt. 3, ed. Elizabeth A. Livingstone, 539-50. Kalamazoo, Mich.: Cistercian Publishers, 1989.

Sharp, Jeffrey R. "Philo's Method of Allegorical Interpretation." *EAJT* 2, no. 1 (April 1984): 94-102.

Simonetti, Manlio. *Biblical Interpretation in the Early Church: An Historical Introduction to Patristic Exegesis*. Translated by John A. Hughes. Edited by Anders Bergquist and Markus Bockmuehl. Edinburgh: T. & T. Clark, 1994.

Siniscalco, Paolo. "'Ἀποκατάστασις e ἀποκαθίστημι nella tradizione della Grande Chiesa fino ad Ireneo." In *StudPat*, vol. 3, ed. Frank Leslie Cross, 380-96. TU, vol. 78. Berlin: Akademie-Verlag, 1961.

Srawley, James Herbert. "Cappadocian Theology." In *Encyclopaedia of Religion and Ethics*, 2d ed., ed. James Hastings, 212-17. Edinburgh: T. & T. Clark, 1932.

Staats, Reinhart. *Makarios-Symeon Epistola Magna: Eine messalianische Mönchsregel und ihre Umschrift in Gregors von Nyssa "De instituto christiano."* AAWG.PH, no. 134. Göttingen: Vandenhoeck & Ruprecht, 1984.

_____. "Der Traktat des Gregor von Nyssa 'De instituto christiano': Beweis seiner Abhängigkeit vom Großen Brief des Symeon von Mesopotaien." D.Theol. diss., Universität Göttingen, 1964.

_____. "Der Traktat des Gregor von Nyssa 'De instituto christiano' und der Große Brief Symeons." *STL* 17 (1963): 120-28.

Stählin, Otto, ed. *Clemens Alexandrinus*. Vol. 4, *Register*. GCS, vol. 39. Leipzig: Hinrichs'sche Buchhandlung, 1936.

Steinmetz, David C. "The Superiority of Pre-Critical Exegesis." *ThTo* 37 (April 1980): 27-38.

Stiglmayr, Joseph. "Makarius der Große und Gregor von Nyssa." *ThGl* 2 (1910): 571.

Syme, Ronald. "Clemens, Flavius." In *The Oxford Classical Dictionary*, 2d. ed., ed. N. G. L. Hammond and H. H. Scullard, 249. Oxford: Clarendon Press, 1970.

Tate, Jonathan. "Allegory, Greek." In *The Oxford Classical Dictionary*, 2d. ed., ed. N. G. L. Hammond and H. H. Scullard, 45-46. Oxford: Clarendon Press, 1970.

_____. "The Beginnings of Greek Allegory," *ClassRev* 41 (1927): 211-29.

Tollinton, R. B. *Clement of Alexandria: A Study in Christian Liberalism.* 2 vols. London: Williams & Norgate, 1914.

Torjesen, Karen Jo. "'Body,' 'Soul,' and 'Spirit' in Origen's Theory of Exegesis." *AThR* 67, no. 1 (January 1985): 17-30.

_____. *Hermeneutical Procedure and Theological Method in Origen's Exegesis.* PTS, vol. 28. Berlin: Walter de Gruyter, 1986.

Trigg, Joseph W. "A Decade of Origen Studies." *RelSRev* 7, no. 1 (January 1981): 21-27.

_____. *Biblical Interpretation.* MFC, vol. 9. Wilmington, Del.: Michael Glazier, 1988.

Tsirpanlis, Constantine N. "The Concept of Universal Salvation in Saint Gregory of Nyssa." In *StudPat*, vol. 17, pt. 3, ed. Elizabeth A. Livingstone, 1131-44. Oxford: Pergamon Press, 1982.

Van den Hoek, Annewies. *Clement of Alexandria and His Use of Philo in the Stromateis: An Early Christian Reshaping of a Jewish Model.* SVC, vol. 3. Leiden: E. J. Brill, 1988.

_____. "Techniques of Quotation in Clement of Alexandria: A View of Ancient Literary Working Methods." *VC* 50, no. 3 (August 1996): 223-43.

Van Unnik, W. C. "The 'Wise Fire' in a Gnostic Eschatological Vision." In *Kyriakon: Festschrift Johannes Quasten*, ed. Patrick Granfield and Josef A. Jungmann, 277-88. Münster: Verlag Aschendorff, 1970.

Van Winden, J. C. M. "Quotations from Philo in Clement of Alexandria's Protrepticus." *VC* 32, no. 3 (September 1978): 208-13.

Volf, Miroslav. *Exclusion and Embrace: A Theological Exploration of Identity, Otherness, and Reconciliation.* Nashville: Abingdon Press, 1996.

Völker, Walther. *Das Vollkommenheitsideal des Origenes: eine Untersuchung zur Geschichte der Frömmigkeit und zu den Anfangen christlicher Mystik.* BHT, no. 7. Tübingen: J. C. B. Mohr, 1931.

Vollert, Wilhelm. *Die Lehre Gregors von Nyssa vom Guten und Bösen und von der schließlichen Überwindung des Bösen.* Leipzig: Deichert, 1897.

Wagner, Walter H. "Another Look at the Literary Problem in Clement of Alexandria's Major Writings." *CH* 37, no. 3 (September 1968): 251-60.

Wenger, A. "Grégoire de Nysse et le Pseudo-Macaire." *REByz* 13 (1955): 145-50.

Westlund, Virgil Ronald. "The Eschatology of Gregory of Nyssa." Th.D. diss., Union Theological Seminary, 1965.

Williams, Jacqueline. *Biblical Interpretation in the Gnostic Gospel of Truth from Nag Hammadi.* SBLDS, no. 79. Atlanta: Scholars Press, 1988.

Williamson, Ronald. *Jews in the Hellenistic World: Philo.* CCWJCW, vol. 1, pt. 2. Cambridge: Cambridge University Press, 1989.

Wilmart, André. "La tradition de l'hypotypose ou traité sur l'ascèse attribué à saint Grégoire de Nysse." *ROC* 21 (1919): 412-21.

Wilson, Robert McL. "The Gnostics and the Old Testament." In *Proceedings of the International Colloquium on Gnosticism*, ed. G. Widengren, 164-68. Stockholm: Almqvist & Wiskell, 1977.

Wilson-Kastner, Patricia. "Macrina: Virgin and Teacher," *AUSS* 17 (1979): 105-17.

Wintermute, Orval S. "A Study of Gnostic Exegesis of the Old Testament." In *The Use of the Old Testament in the New and Other Essays: Studies in Honor of William F. Stinespring*, ed. J. M. Efrid, 241-70. Durham, N.C.: Duke University Press, 1972.

Wolfson, Harry Austryn. *The Philosophy of the Church Fathers.* 2d rev. ed. SGPS, no. 3 Cambridge: Harvard University Press, 1964.

Young, Frances M. *Biblical Exegesis and the Formation of Christian Culture.* Cambridge: Cambridge University Press, 1997.

Zachhuber, Johannes. *Human Nature in Gregory of Nyssa: Philosophical Background and Theological Significance.* SVC, vol. 46. Leiden: Brill, 2000.

Zahn, Theodor. *Forschungen zur Geschichte des neutestamentlichen Kanons und der altkirchlichen Literatur.* Vol. 3, *Supplementum Clementinum.* Erlangen: Andreas Deichert, 1884.

_____. *Geschichte des neutestamentlichen Kanons.* 2 vols. Erlangen: Andreas Deichert, 1888.

Zöllig, August. *Die Inspirationslehre des Origenes.* StrThS, vol. 5, no. 1. Freiburg: Herder, 1902.

Index of Ancient and Modern Authors

About the Author

STEVEN R. HARMON (Ph.D., Southwestern Baptist Theological Seminary, Fort Worth, Texas; additional graduate study, The Catholic University of America, Washington, D.C., and the University of Dallas, Irving, Texas) is Assistant Professor of Christian Theology at Campbell University Divinity School in Buies Creek, North Carolina. The author of articles in *Journal of Early Christian Studies, Biblical Theology Bulletin, Perspectives in Religious Studies,* and *Review and Expositor,* he is currently working on an annotated English translation of Gregory of Nyssa's *Oratio catechetica magna.*